What a FINISH!

What a START!

THE MONTH JESUS MET MAN'S NEED

The Last Month on Earth of Jesus Christ and
the Synoptic Case for the Wednesday Crucifixion

FRED A KUYPERS

Preface

This work is accomplished to help anyone with a question about the most-discussed period of time in history. It is a month occurring at the center of time itself. No books, no films, and no documentaries have been written about any historical snapshot of time like the month of Nisan in the year of Christ's crucifixion. This month of Nisan is one of intense research, and there is no timeline taken from the Gospels about this important month in history that follows the synoptic account as undeniably true up to now, two thousand years after Jesus lived upon this earth. Sceptics have constantly ridiculed the Gospels as being non-synoptic. This book contends that there was no collaboration between the four writers and that each tells the exact truth of this period of time.

The King James Bible comes from a manuscript known as the Textus Receptus which was translated into English primarily by one man, William Tyndale. Tyndale's work of translation was instrumental in the publishing of the King James Bible which took place some eighty years later. In Tyndale's day a religious leader, who happened to be a Roman Catholic, and who blindly followed the false teachings of the religious leader known as the pope said to William Tyndale, "We were better to be without God's laws than the pope's." To this Mr. Tyndale replied, "I defy the pope and all his laws," and he added, "If God spare my life, ere many years I will cause a boy that driveth the plough to know more of the Scripture than thou dost."[1] So also is the title of this author who drives the plow. I personally want to thank William Tyndale some 500 years after he lived and made this quote taken from *Foxe's Book of Martyrs*.

"Plowboy" can be considered a derogatory term. It can be a name used to look down on someone who only knows enough to work with his hands and not with his mind. It comes from an old usage of a farmer's aid or perhaps even his own son that does not know much else but the basic work of tilling the ground behind a furrow plow being pulled by a servant animal. One of the best scenes in the movie *Men of Honor* is when Cuba Gooding was talking with Robert DeNiro and noticed his hands.

---

[1]   *Foxe's Book of Martyrs* by John Foxe, chapter 12

i

The scars of the leather straps that drove the animal that pulled the plow were evident and created a common bond between two farmers who both became military men.

As I write this book, I share this same sense of independence and freedom from a mother church that wants to control me and my way of thinking. For two thousand years, this traditional church has taught a Friday crucifixion. So in agreement with what Tyndale said five hundred years earlier, I say that "If God spares me and allows me to finish this work so that the average person can have the truth of the Word of God and if they will just open up and study the Scriptures and not follow men's fables, then God will be glorified." This is not an attempt to give a narration of the events for there are four solid accounts of that already. Matthew, Mark, Luke, and John are beautiful accounts as accurate as there will ever be for this month of time.

Matthew's Gospel will reveal to the reader key components that reflect Jesus as King of kings. The phrase "the kingdom of heaven" occurs thirty-two times in the Bible, and all thirty-two times occur in Matthew. He is the author of the Gospel to the Jews, teaching that Jesus Christ is the King that Israel should have looked for.

Mark will reflect on Jesus Christ as the servant. Most of His miracles appear in the Gospel of Mark as well as how He served mankind. Mark is the synoptic Gospel to the Gentiles.

The Gospel of Luke is about the humanity of Jesus Christ. Luke gives the best view of His birth, His death, and the fact that He sweats great drops of blood in the Holy Scriptures. His gospel also is to the Gentiles, in particular the Greco-Roman followers. And then there is John.

The Gospel of John is the last of the gospels and is not considered one of the synoptic gospels. John speaks of Jesus as the "Son of God." He speaks of a belief in this God to all who will listen as seen from the start of his Gospel:

John 1:12 But as many as received him, to them gave he power to become the sons of God, even to them that believe on his name:

To the end of his Gospel:

John 20:31 But these are written, that ye might believe that Jesus is the Christ, the Son of God; and that believing ye might have life through his name.

The term *Son of God* appears more in John's Gospel than any other book in the Bible. He includes Christ's most intimate moments with God the Father as seen in chapter 17. John also has most of the references toward "all" having a relationship with God.

Only scripture from that era can complement and confirm these four accounts, known as the Gospels, and not sources unaccepted as canon of scripture. It is right and correct to look to the quotes from scripture, as this quote taken from the second epistle (short letter) of Peter states:

2 Peter 1:20 Knowing this first, that no prophecy of the scripture is of any private interpretation.

That being said, I will rely on scripture as an accurate guide to the Gospels. Scripture itself will be used as the guide and not man's ideas or thoughts. The only way this can be done is if the Bible is taken by faith that every word of God is pure (Proverbs 30:5) and that all the words of God are pure (Psalm 12:6). God has spelled out this requirement of faith by stating:

Hebrews 11:6 But without faith *it is* impossible to please *him:* for he that cometh to God must believe that he is, and *that* he is a rewarder of them that diligently seek him.

The basis of a Christian's belief is that, by faith, they take the words of the Bible as the words of God. "But men wrote this book" some say. This is true. However in his second epistle Peter continues:

2 Peter 1:21 For the prophecy came not in old time by the will of man: but holy men of God spake *as they were* moved by the Holy Ghost.

By faith, it is understood that the Word of God (the Holy Scriptures, which are known as the Bible) was written by men as they were moved by God. Peter said they were moved by the Holy Ghost. Is the Holy Ghost God? Again the scripture is clear:

1 John 5:7 For there are three that bear record in heaven, the Father, the Word, and the Holy Ghost: and these three are one.

The Bible is a living book. It is also a powerful book:

Hebrews 4:12 For the word of God is quick, and powerful, and sharper than any two edged sword, piercing even to the dividing a sunder of soul and spirit, and of the joints and marrow, and *is* a discerner of the thoughts and intents of the heart.

When an important event takes place, it is good to have a history of the events as in a diary or a journal of sorts. Diaries are very interesting. Some give the story of a specific time and sometimes they give places and sometimes they give names. But the most important knowledge to acquire from a diary is fact. How can it be determined for sure that these things happened? Eyewitnesses (more than one) are the best factual account there is. This is biblical also:

Deuteronomy 19:15 One witness shall not rise up against a man for any iniquity, or for any sin, in any sin that he sinneth: at the mouth of two witnesses, or at the mouth of three witnesses, shall the matter be established.

And in the New Testament in 2 Corinthians, it says:

2 Corinthians 13:1 This *is* the third *time* I am coming to you. In the mouth of two or three witnesses shall every word be established.

What this does is lay out the premise that this study in scripture will follow. The writings of Matthew, Mark, Luke, and John, the four accounts of the life of Jesus Christ, will be used to chronicle this final month of the life of Jesus on this earth. There were plenty of eyewitnesses (over 500) to the resurrection of Jesus and as a passage is displayed, an attempt to explain any questionable phrase or word will be made:

1 Corinthians 15:3 For I delivered unto you first of all that which I also received, how that Christ died for our sins according to the scriptures;

What a Finish! What a Start! The Month Jesus Met Man's Need

Fred A Kuypers

1 Corinthians 15:4 And that he was buried, and that he rose again the third day according to the scriptures:

1 Corinthians 15:5 And that he was seen of Cephas, then of the twelve:

1 Corinthians 15:6 After that, he was seen of above five hundred brethren at once; of whom the greater part remain unto this present, but some are fallen asleep.

A name not understood in today's language may be *Cephas*, also known as Simon, which are names for Peter the apostle. The word *twelve* is often used as another title for the twelve apostles of which Peter is a member. The apostles had seen the risen Jesus Christ along with over five hundred eyewitnesses, other people alive on Planet Earth, who saw Jesus Christ in His glorified body after His resurrection.

As this chronology begins, I believe that at the mouth of four witnesses this matter of the life of Jesus Christ has been established. The need to establish this work by eyewitnesses has been met.

1. The need for more than one witness to the account of Christ's life has been met (Matthew, Mark, Luke, John).

2. The need for eyewitnesses, the apostles who were with Him during this eventful month, has been met.

3. The need for eyewitnesses to His resurrection has been met (1 Corinthians 15:6).

4. The only need now is that by faith, the Word of God is accepted by the reader and that Jesus Christ will be glorified. My desire is that each reader of this book realizes that Jesus Christ is real, and that He wants to be the Savior of your life.

This can only happen if you repent of your sins, realize you are a sinner and that your good deeds will never overcome even one bad deed. Realize, too, that the punishment for your bad deeds is eternity in hell, forever separated from God. However, God has a plan. This plan is completed by His Son, the Lord Jesus Christ. He went to the cross, died for the sins of the whole world (that includes you and me), and rose again to give eternal life to those who believe in Him. All a person has to do is repent of sin, believe (by faith), and ask Jesus Christ to save you. Ask Jesus Christ to save you? Yes:

Matthew 7:7 Ask, and it shall be given you; seek, and ye shall find; knock, and it shall be opened unto you:

Matthew 7:8 For every one that asketh receiveth; and he that seeketh findeth; and to him that knocketh it shall be opened.

Romans 10:9 That if thou shalt confess with thy mouth the Lord Jesus, and shalt believe in thine heart that God hath raised him from the dead, thou shalt be saved.

Romans 10:10 For with the heart man believeth unto righteousness; and with the mouth confession is made unto salvation.

John 3:16 For God so loved the world, that he gave his only begotten Son, that whosoever believeth in him should not perish, but have everlasting life.

John 3:17 For God sent not his Son into the world to condemn the world; but that the world through him might be saved.

John 3:18 He that believeth on him is not condemned: but he that believeth not is condemned already, because he hath not believed in the name of the only begotten Son of God.

The Month of Nisan in the Year of Our Lord's Death Was a Tumultuous Month.

It is extremely interesting to realize that the Lord kept the Jewish family tree down throughout history. There are so many traditions and memorials that have been used to hold the Jewish lineage together. One that this book will point out is the first month of the year known as *Abib*. Wait a minute—this book is all about The Month Nisan: *What a Finish! What a Start*! Which month is the first month of a Jewish new year? This book will attempt to answer the questions concerning this month. By the way, the first month of the Jewish New Year today is Nisan. In Moses' day it was *Abib* as it states in Exodus:

Exodus 13:4 This day came ye out in the month Abib.

This is the month that the Jews were told to have a memorial. Abib became the first month of the year due to God freeing the Jews from Egypt. This is when God allowed the Jews to escape from Pharaoh:

Deuteronomy 16:1 Observe the month of Abib, and keep the passover unto the LORD thy God: for in the month of Abib the LORD thy God brought thee forth out of Egypt by night.

So where did the name *Nisan* come from? During the years that the Jews were in captivity, that is, the Babylonian captivity, the name of the first month was changed, and the first mention of it is in the book of Nehemiah when Nehemiah writes:

Nehemiah 2:1 And it came to pass in the month Nisan, in the twentieth year of Artaxerxes the king, *that* wine *was* before him: and I took up the wine, and gave *it* unto the king. Now I had not been *beforetime* sad in his presence.

Soon the name *Nisan* became the accepted name of the first month of the Jewish calendar. As it is written in the book of Esther:

Esther 3:7 In the first month, that *is,* the month Nisan…

Understanding the Jewish day on the Jewish calendar which begins at 6:00 p.m. at sunset the night before, instead of at 12:00 midnight as the day begins within the Julian or the Gregorian calendar, is of utmost importance.[2] The Jews look to the

---

[2] Rabbi Nathan Bushwick. Understanding the Jewish Calendar. Moznaim Publishing Corporation. New York/Jerusalem.

What a Finish! What a Start! The Month Jesus Met Man's Need

Fred A Kuypers

scripture for the start of a day. In Genesis, it says the evening and the morning were the first day.

Genesis 1:5 And God called the light Day, and the darkness he called Night. And the evening and the morning were the first day.

The Jewish people would begin each day on the night before at 6:00 p.m. The first thing they would do in the night would be to eat, and then rest, then sleep, and then in the morning, they would wake up and be prepared for the day's work. The scriptures explained the day in Genesis and the Jews have always followed that example.

The Levitical law of when the day the Passover Lamb is slain has been described by God:

Leviticus 23:4 These *are* the feasts of the LORD, *even* holy convocations, which ye shall proclaim in their seasons.

Leviticus 23:5 In the fourteenth *day* of the first month at even *is* the LORD'S passover.

Leviticus 23:6 And on the fifteenth day of the same month *is* the feast of unleavened bread unto the LORD: seven days ye must eat unleavened bread.

Leviticus 23:7 In the first day ye shall have an holy convocation: ye shall do no servile work therein.

Notice the Passover occurs on the fourteenth of the month Abib or Nisan as it is called today. It is very important to note that the day after the fourteenth that is on the fifteenth of the month, the Feast of Unleavened Bread begins. This is the time that the Jews refer to as Pesach. Also note that the first day of unleavened bread is a special high day. No "servile work" is to be done therein. What does that mean? "No servile work" means no work of any kind. That means strict adherence to the laws on this high Sabbath was required by the Pharisees in addition to the usual Saturday Sabbath. God made it clear in Exodus 12:16 that no manner of work shall be done on this first day of unleavened bread, except that which every man must eat. That and that alone may be done by you.

It is interesting here to note a problem that many perceive with the King James Version (KJV) of the Bible. In the Acts of the Apostles, dealing with the days of unleavened bread, there is an account of the only time the word *Easter* appears in the KJV. This account is in Acts 12:1–5. The church was young, and King Herod was very much against the believers who claimed to be followers of this new organization called Christ's church. King Herod was seeking to vex or to hurt the people of the church. Herod had James, the brother of John, killed by the sword. Herod saw that this pleased the Jews, who were opposed to anyone who claimed Jesus Christ to be the true Messiah, so he ordered the capture of Peter. Now God spells it out very clearly that Peter was taken in the days of unleavened bread. The days of unleavened bread, remember, are after the Passover date of the fourteenth of Nisan. The KJV says

1989. P74

that Peter was captured and held by sixteen men who intended to try him after Easter. This is very possible as Easter was a pagan holiday of fertility that in many occasions will occur during or at the end of the days of unleavened bread.

In the year 2014, Passover was on April 14. The days of unleavened bread followed, beginning on April 15. Easter occurred on April 20 that year. The days of unleavened bread ended on the Monday, April 21. This explains that Peter could have been captured on Tuesday, the fifteenth of April, which was the first day of unleavened bread, or any day up to Saturday, the nineteenth of April. Herod could have ordered Peter to be held until after Easter Sunday, the twentieth of April (which would be the fifth day of unleavened bread, the pagan festival of Easter falling on a day of unleavened bread). Peter then could be tried Monday or Tuesday just a day or two later. This word *Easter* only occurs in the King James Version. Every other modern translation incorrectly changes the word to *Passover*.

Retelling this adventure since the word *Passover* is used in all modern versions is warranted at this point. Peter was captured in "the days of unleavened bread." This is after the Passover as Exodus, chapter 12, declares. Herod would have to hold Peter until after the Passover, which means that Peter would be in prison for a whole year or until the next Passover would arrive. Every modern version wrongly changes this word to Passover instead of Easter as the King James Version declares. It was William Tyndale who coined the term *Passover* in the English language. Since Tyndale invented this word, is it not logical that he would have used it here if that is what was meant in the original scriptures? However Tyndale used the word *Easter* because Easter is the correct translation at this point in scripture. The King James Version is the only Bible to get this right!

Acts 12:4 And when he had apprehended him, he put him in prison, and delivered him to four quaternions of soldiers to keep him; intending after Easter to bring him forth to the people.

What a Finish! What a Start! The Month Jesus Met Man's Need

Fred A Kuypers

Here for the reader is the full calendar of this Month of Nisan. Each day as shown includes the Jewish day beginning and ending at 6:00p.m. the previous night.

Month of Nisan: Year of Christ's Death.

1st day Yom Rishon Sunday	2nd day Yom Sheini Monday	3rd day Yom Shlishi Tuesday	4th day Yom R'vi'i Wednesday	5th day Yom Chamishi Thursday	6th day Yom Shishi Friday	Shabbat Yom Shabbat Saturday
Month Adar is the Month before Nisan	27th Adar 28th 6:00am to 6:00pm Each chapter beginning in the four gospels: Matthew 19 Mark 10 Luke 18 John 11	28th Adar 29th 6:00am to 6:00pm Travel from Galilee would be about 3 days to Judea where Bethabara is located.	29th Adar 1st 6:00am to 6:00pm The introduction of this book includes the twenty-ninth of Adar Jesus arrives in Bethabara, Lazarus is sick.	1st Nisan 2nd 6:00am to 6:00pm Sojourning at Bethabara This chapter begins at 6 p.m. the night before on the fourth day, Wednesday.	2nd Nisan 3rd 6:00am to 6:00pm Sojourning at Bethabara This is the second day Lazarus is sick. This day word is received that Lazarus dies.	3rd Nisan 4th 6:00am to 6:00pm Sojourning near the Jordan River the Sabbath day on the seventh day of the week. No work or travel on this Sabbath day.
4th Nisan 5th 6:00am to 6:00pm Travel to Jericho Luke alone records the visit to Zacchaeus on this first day of the week. Jesus will spend the night in Jericho.	5th Nisan 6th 6:00am to 6:00pm Travel to Jerusalem Jesus and his disciples spend a full day of travel to Jerusalem from Jericho about 20 miles.	6th Nisan 7th 6:00am to 6:00pm Travel to Bethany The short walk to Bethany and the resurrection of Lazarus witnessed by his sisters, Martha and Mary.	7th Nisan 8th 6:00am to 6:00pm Travel to Ephraim This day in the wilderness of Ephraim which lies to the north of Bethany and the Mount of Olives.	8th Nisan 9th 6:00am to 6:00pm Travel to Bethany This day Jesus presents Himself as the King of kings riding through the Golden Gate.	9th Nisan 10th 6:00am to 6:00pm Back to Bethany In the morning an interesting trip by the fig tree. In the Temple Jesus was angered by how His Father's house was being used.	10th Nisan 11th 6:00am to 6:00pm Jesus will again pass by the fig tree on His way to Jerusalem. Jesus delivers the Olivet Discourse. At the end of the day, He is selected as the Lamb to be killed.
11th Nisan 12th 6:00 a.m.to 6:00 pm. Jesus feet are anointed; Jesus prepares His disciples for the events of the crucifixion to take place in two days.	12th Nisan 13th 6:00am to 6:00pm Travel to Bethany to stay with Simon the leper Judas' betrayal of Jesus is arranged for 30 pieces of silver.	13th Nisan 14th 6:00am to 6:00pm Jesus and His disciples will go to Jerusalem and prepare for the Passover meal at 6:00 p.m.	14th Nisan 15th 6:00am to 6:00pm Jesus the Lamb of God is cut off and is placed in the grave before 6:00 p.m. when the high Sabbath begins. *1st day in tomb*	15th Nisan 16th 6:00am to 6:00pm Pesach, 1st day of unleavened bread, Holy convocation, high Sabbath	16th Nisan 17th 6:00am to 6:00pm 2nd day of unleavened bread This is only day spices could be prepared and Religious leaders could set a watch. *2nd day in tomb*	17th Nisan 18th 6:00am to 6:00pm 3rd day of unleavened bread Sabbath day of rest. Jesus could have risen at any time after 6:00 p.m. *3rd day in tomb*
18th Nisan 19th 6:00am to 6:00pm 4th day of unleavened bread Resurrection Sunday	19th Nisan 20th 6:00am to 6:00pm 5th day of unleavened bread First day of Travel to Galilee.	20th Nisan 21st 6:00am to 6:00pm 6th day of unleavened bread Second day of Travel to Galilee.	21st Nisan 22nd 6:00am to 6:00pm 7th day of unleavened bread high Sabbath, end of Feast of unleavened bread	22nd Nisan 23rd 6:00am to 6:00pm Leave Samaria Third day of travel to Galilee.	23rd Nisan 24th 6:00am to 6:00pm Travel to Galilee. Fourth day and final day of travel and arrival at Galilee.	24th Nisan 25th 6:00am to 6:00pm Sabbath day of rest at Sea of Galilee.
25th Nisan 26th 6:00am to 6:00pm Jesus meets the disciples at Galilee just as he promised not many days hence.	26th Nisan 27th 6:00am to 6:00pm After eight days Jesus showed Himself again to Thomas and His other disciples.	27th Nisan 28th 6:00am to 6:00pm Disciples at Galilee. Peter says he will go fishing.	28th Nisan 29th 6:00am to 6:00pm Disciples are out all night fishing. They catch nothing.	29th Nisan 30th 6:00am to 6:00pm Last passages of the Gospels. Tomorrow the month of Nisan will end.	30th Nisan 1st 6:00am to 6:00pm New Month of Iyar begins at 6:00pm this night.	Next Month Iyar

Each day will be discussed in detail and will have time divisions. These approximate time divisions are determined by the events described by each gospel. As certain things take place in daylight hours and others at dinner time, some in the morning, some at the sixth hour, that is, 12:00 noon, and so forth. Careful consideration will be given as to the time of occurrence each day. A sample day, the last day of the month, Adar 29, is given here in the introduction, to point out the divisions of each day and the difference in each day starting at 6:00 p.m. the night before:

Wednesday, the fourteenth of Nisan, is the day this book will center on. Nisan 14 began at 6:00 p.m. the night before, or Tuesday night. The Jewish "day" starts at sunset, rather than at midnight.[3] According to Exodus 12, the Passover lamb must be killed on the fourteenth. That evening at the end of Wednesday, Nisan 14 before Thursday begins at 6:00 p.m., when the day becomes Nisan 15, the holy convocation of Pesach begins.

According to the Talmud certain holy days could not coincide with the Saturday Sabbath. This first day of unleavened bread, a high Sabbath, can only occur on a Saturday, Sunday, Tuesday, or Thursday.[4] This is because Yom Kippur and Rosh Hashanah cannot fall on certain days:

> **The Jewish perpetual calendar was arranged in a manner that ensures that the first day of Rosh Hashanah will never fall on Sunday, Wednesday or Friday. This guarantees that Yom Kippur will not fall on a Friday or Sunday (i.e. Saturday night), which would produce two consecutive days when preparing food and burying the dead is prohibited, and that Hoshanah Rabbah will not occur on Shabbat, which would interfere with the custom of taking the willows on this day.[5]**

Remember that each day begins at 6:00 p.m. the night before. This is according to the calculations of the Jewish calendar.[6] Studying Jewish history, it has been determined that the first day of unleavened bread, a high Sabbath day, had not begun on a Monday (which would begin Sunday at 6:00 p.m.), a Wednesday (which would begin Tuesday at 6:00 p.m.), or a Friday (which would begin Thursday at 6:00 p.m.).

The fifteenth day is the first day of unleavened bread. The fifteenth is a "high Sabbath" in which no servile work is to be done. The Passover day, the fourteenth of Nisan, becomes the day of preparation for that following day, the high Sabbath day, the fifteenth of Nisan. This means that the crucifixion could not have been on a Sunday, Tuesday, or Thursday. Establishing this fact, the month of Nisan can be

---

3   http://www.jewfaq.org/calendr2.htm © Copyright 5756–5771 (1995–2011), Tracey R Rich. Viewed January 13, 2018
4   http://www.jewfaq.org/calendr2.htm Dechiyah 2: Lo A"DU Rosh). Tracey R Rich. Viewed January 4, 2019
5   https://www.chabad.org Why can't Yom Kippur ever begin on a Saturday night?. Malkie Janowski. Viewed January 4, 2019
6   http://www.jewfaq.org/calendar.htm © Copyright 5756–5771 (1995–2011), Tracey R Rich. Viewed February 28, 2018

calculated. By setting the fourteenth day, the Passover day beginning at 6:00 p.m. on Tuesday and going to 6:00 p.m. on Wednesday, the Lamb of God was slain on the fourteenth of Nisan, at 3:00 p.m. called the evening as John Gill explains:

Exodus 12:6
Ver. 6. And ye shall keep it up until the fourteenth day of the same month,....

1: and the whole assembly of the congregation shall kill it in the evening; that is, of the fourteenth of Nisan; not between the two suns, as the Targum of Jonathan, between the sun setting and the sun rising; nor between the setting of the sun, and the entire disappearance of its rays of light reflecting in the air and clouds after it, as Aben Ezra; so it is said in the Talmud {k}, after the sun is set, all the time that the face of the east is red; others say as long as a man can walk half a mile after sun setting; and others, the twinkling of an eye; but "between the two evening's" {l}, as it may be rendered; which respects that space of time after the sun begins to decline, and the entire setting of it; when the sun begins to decline, as it does after noon, that is the first evening, and when it is set, that is the second; and the middle space between the one and the other is about the nineth hour of the day, according to the Jewish computation, and, with us, about three o'clock in the afternoon, about which time the passover used to be killed; for they say {m},
"the daily sacrifice was slain at eight and a half, and offered at the nineth; but on the evening of the passover it was slain at seven and a half, and offered at eight and a half, whether on a common day, or on a sabbath; and if the evening of the passover happened to be on the evening of the sabbath, it was slain at six and a half, and offered up at seven and a half, and after that the passover;"
which was done, that there might be time before the last evening for the slaying of the passover lamb. Josephus {n} says, at the passover they slew the sacrifice from the nineth hour to the eleventh;
See Gill on "Mt 26:17", and it being at the nineth hour that our Lord was crucified, the agreement between him and the paschal lamb in this circumstance very manifestly appears, Mt 27:46 though it may also in general denote Christ's appearing in the last days, in the end of the world, to put away sin by the sacrifice of himself: the slaying of the paschal lamb is ascribed to the "whole assembly of the congregation", because it was to be slain by their order, and in their name, for their use, and they present;

and thus the crucifixion of Christ, his sufferings and death, are attributed to the men of Israel, and all the house of Israel, Ac 2:22.

{k} T. Bab. Sabbat, fol. 34. 2. {l} Mybreh Nyb "inter duas vesperas", Pagninus, Montanus, Junius & Tremellius, Piscator, Ainsworth. {m} Misn. Pesach. c. 5. sect. 1. {n} De Bello Jud. l. 6. c. 9. sect. 3.[7]

The first day of the month of Nisan can be established as seen in the previous calendar on a Thursday, which began at 6:00 p.m. Wednesday night. The fact that the resurrection took place on a Sunday establishes this fact. Jesus was in the grave for three days and three nights, ending at 6:00 p.m. on Saturday. The resurrection could then take place sometime after 6:00 p.m. Saturday and before Mary Magdalene visited the grave while it was still dark on the first day of the week, perhaps Sunday before 5:00 a.m. The chapter on the eighteenth of Nisan will have a detailed explanation of these events.

Each chapter will represent a new day and a calendar view of that day in its appropriate week. The day will begin at 6:00 p.m. the night before as it does in the Jewish calendar. Each statement this author makes will be backed up by scripture from one of the four Gospels to establish correct timing. May the Lord Jesus Christ bless you as you read the scriptures contained herein and realize that the power to save you lies in the Bible, the Word of God!

---

[7]   Gill, John. Gill's Commentary on the Entire Bible https://ia800207.us.archive.org/20/items/GillsCommentaryOnTheEntireBible/02%20-%20Exodus.txt. Viewed July 7 2018.

Introduction

Adar 29

Month of Nisan

1st day Yom Rishon Sunday	2nd day Yom Sheini Monday	3rd day Yom Shlishi Tuesday	4th day Yom R'vi'i Wednesday	5th day Yom Chamishi Thursday	6th day Yom Shishi Friday	Shabbat Yom Shabbat Saturday
Month Adar is the Month before Nisan	27th Adar 28th The month of Nisan begins with: Matthew chap19 Mark chap10 Luke chap18 John chap11	28th Adar 29th 6:00am to 6:00pm Wednesday 29th of Adar begins at 6:00pm.	29th Adar 1st 6:00am to 6:00pm The introduction of this book includes some time frame of the 29th of Adar. Jesus arrives in Bethabara; traveling from Galilee.	1st Nisan 2nd	2nd Nisan 3rd	3rd Nisan 4th

This chapter includes:

Matthew	Mark	Luke	John
19:1–19:12	10:1–10:9		10:40–11:6

What a Finish! What a Start! The Month Jesus Met Man's Need

Fred A Kuypers

Travel from Galilee to Bethabara beyond the Jordan River

6:00 p.m. on Tuesday, the Twenty-Ninth of Adar Jesus arrives in Judaea and is sent word that Lazarus is sick.

Many activities took place in the days before this month of Nisan began. Jesus had left Galilee in the North and traveled to a familiar place much closer to the temple in Jerusalem. The distance from the Sea of Galilee to the coasts of Judaea beyond Jordan is about seventy miles or 112 Kilometers. This is about a three- or four-day journey by foot over rough terrain, which describes the land of Israel.

Matthew 19:1 And it came to pass, *that* when Jesus had finished these sayings, he departed from Galilee, and came into the coasts of Judaea beyond Jordan;

Matthew 19:2 And great multitudes followed him; and he healed them there.

Mark records His arrival this way:

Mark 10:1 And he arose from thence, and cometh into the coasts of Judaea by the farther side of Jordan: and the people resort unto him again; and, as he was wont, he taught them again.

Matthew records that Jesus was healing people. Mark records that Jesus was teaching people. However, John records that Jesus was abiding beyond Jordan. Jesus is beyond Jordan in the place where John the Baptist first baptized. This is not a contradiction by each writer, but rather, it is pointing out that Jesus did each of these activities.

John 10:40 And went away again beyond Jordan into the place where John at first baptized; and there he abode.

Beyond Jordan means the opposite side of where Jerusalem is located. Since Jerusalem is in the West Bank of the Jordan River, Jesus would abide on the east side of the Jordan. In 1977 J. Carl Laney wrote his doctoral dissertation on "The Identification of Bethany Beyond the Jordan" and said:

"The identification of Bethany beyond the Jordan is without doubt a complicated geographical problem in the life of Christ."[8]

I would agree with this statement. However his dissertation concluding that this so-called Bethany may be misnamed as Bethabara and that it would be on the east side of the Jordan River I do not agree:

---

[8]   J. Carl Laney. The Identification of Bethany Beyond the Jordan. Dallas Theological Seminary. 1977. P 50

"It is possible that the ruins of Bethany beyond the Jordan will never be found, but an abundance of evidence indicates that cartographers should place it east of the Jordan River near the Hajlah ford in the vicinity of Wadi el-Kharrar."[9]

About thirty-five years after his dissertation, Laney would be surprised to note that the discovery of Bethabara would be opened as a baptismal site in 2011[10] exactly where he determined its location to be; however, his comment about the King James Version having "Origen's emendation"[11] meaning his making a revision to the text in naming the place Bethabara is in question and should be reviewed. At this writing I could find no proof of any archeological findings of either.

This place was called Bethabara. The scripture, according to the King James Version and only the KJV, declared this earlier.

John 1:28 These things were done in Bethabara beyond Jordan, where John was baptizing.

Jesus stayed beyond Jordan where John first baptized at a place called Bethabara. Bethabara is a location on the oldest known map of this region located on a mosaic wall in Modaba, Jordan.[12] Origen, Jerome, and Eusebius along with the Syriac Version use the term Beth Abara and The King James Version has not changed the name of this location. All the new versions changed it to Bethany. One reason is because a place called Bethabara was in doubt. Skeptics said it did not exist. But it existed. God has given more and more proof of existence, and in 2011 a public baptismal area was open to the public on the site where Bethabara was located.

Two thousand years ago, Jesus would retreat here many times to rest and get away from the press of the people who continually demanded His attention as seen earlier in Luke's Gospel:

Luke 12:1 In the mean time, when there were gathered together an innumerable multitude of people, insomuch that they trode one upon another, he began to say unto his disciples first of all, Beware ye of the leaven of the Pharisees, which is hypocrisy.

The press of the multitude was so severe that they even trampled each other. But Jesus remained focused on what He wanted to say. Jesus constantly declared Himself as one who came from God. He came not to condemn the world but to save the world (John 3:18). John the Baptist was not a miracle worker but declared that Jesus did perform them and the multitude was continually crowding around Jesus to see Him exercise some sort of miraculous event.

9   J. Carl Laney. The Identification of Bethany Beyond the Jordan. Dallas Theological Seminary. 1977. P 69
10   Leen Ritmeyer. https://www.ritmeyer.com/2011/01/08/jesus-baptismal-site-to-open-to-the-public/ Viewed January 29, 2019
11   J. Carl Laney. The Identification of Bethany Beyond the Jordan. Dallas Theological Seminary. 1977. P 53
12   Robin Ngo. https://www.biblicalarchaeology.org/daily/biblical-sites-places/biblical-archaeology-places/baptismal-site-bethany-beyond-the-jordan-added-to-unesco-world-heritage-list/. 2019. Viewed January 29, 2019

John 10:41 And many resorted unto him, and said, John did no miracle: but all things that John spake of this man were true. John 10:42 And many believed on him there.

He is concerned about the hypocrisy with His followers every day. The most quoted Bible verse by Christians used to be John 3:16. However today it is Matthew 7:1:
Matthew 7:1 Judge not, that ye be not judged.

This verse is falsely quoted regarding judging. Many use this verse to justify their sin condition. "Don't tell me I am sinning; you can't judge me!" Someone will quote this verse and continue to shack up with their lover or continue to drink alcohol or smoke weed or skim funds or material from their work or any sin that God knows all about. However, if they would read all of Matthew 7, they would see that God is not talking about judging but about being a hypocrite. As the chapter continues in verse 5, the command is given that we are to judge and take the mote or sliver out of our brother's eye! But first a Christian must not be a hypocrite. Our lives must be lined up with the Word of God.

8:00 a.m. on Wednesday, the Twenty-Ninth of Adar

As the night ends and this day began, Jesus hears for the first time that Lazarus is sick. Lazarus's sisters, Martha and Mary, get word to Jesus on this day. The time of day cannot be pinpointed, but the synoptic gospels will pick up from this point after the sickness of Lazarus is established.
John 11:1 Now a certain *man* was sick, *named* Lazarus, of Bethany, the town of Mary and her sister Martha.

Jesus has some really close friends that live in Bethany. It is about two miles east of Jerusalem on the southeastern slope of the Mount of Olives. The names of these close friends are Martha, Mary, and their brother Lazarus. John will now say that Mary anointed the Lord and wiped his feet with her hair. However, this has not happened yet. The anointing will not take place for five days from this point (John 12:3) in the town of Bethany, proving that the narrative of John's gospel was composed historically after the events of Christ's life took place.
John 11:2 (It was *that* Mary which anointed the Lord with ointment, and wiped his feet with her hair, whose brother Lazarus was sick.)
John 11:3 Therefore his sisters sent unto him, saying, Lord, behold, he whom thou lovest is sick.

But Jesus will not go and see him. He decides to wait for two days. Jesus knows all along that Lazarus's sickness and death will bring glory to God. Many will see this in six days when the raising of Lazarus takes place.

John 11:4 When Jesus heard *that,* he said, This sickness is not unto death, but for the glory of God, that the Son of God might be glorified thereby.

John 11:5 Now Jesus loved Martha, and her sister, and Lazarus.

Jesus had a special relationship with Martha and Mary and Lazarus. The word *love* here is the Greek word *agapaō*.[13] This is that love that God has for all of mankind as expressed in God's plan of salvation:

John 3:16 For God so loved the world, that he gave his only begotten Son, that whosoever believeth in him should not perish, but have everlasting life.

It must have been hard for Jesus to stay in Bethabara when Lazarus whom He loved was sick. He could have easily healed him. But Jesus was here not to do His will but the will of the Father, and that would be seen in six days as Jesus would enter Bethany and raise Lazarus from the grave. This will take place on the sixth of Nisan discussed later in chapter six.

John 11:6 When he had heard therefore that he was sick, he abode two days still in the same place where he was.

Jesus decides to stay two more days at Bethabara and try to rest. He knew a tumultuous two weeks were ahead of Him.

10:00 a.m. on Wednesday, the Twenty-Ninth of Adar

The crowds are still surrounding Jesus. At this point the religious leaders of the day, the Pharisees, come to Him trying to tempt Him and trap Him in His own words.

Matthew recorded:

Matthew 19:3 The Pharisees also came unto him, tempting him, and saying unto him, Is it lawful for a man to put away his wife for every cause?

Matthew 19:4 And he answered and said unto them, Have ye not read, that he which made *them* at the beginning made them male and female,

Matthew 19:5 And said, For this cause shall a man leave father and mother, and shall cleave to his wife: and they twain shall be one flesh?

Matthew 19:6 Wherefore they are no more twain, but one flesh. What therefore God hath joined together, let not man put asunder.

Mark recorded:

Mark 10:2 And the Pharisees came to him, and asked him, Is it lawful for a man to put away *his* wife? tempting him.

Mark 10:3 And he answered and said unto them, What did Moses command you?

Mark 10:4 And they said, Moses suffered to write a bill of divorcement, and to put *her* away.

---

[13]   Dr. James Strong, *Strongs Exhaustive Concordance of the Bible.* Dugan Publishers Inc. Gordonsville, TN. P. G25

Mark 10:5 And Jesus answered and said unto them, For the hardness of your heart he wrote you this precept.

Mark 10:6 But from the beginning of the creation God made them male and female.

Mark 10:7 For this cause shall a man leave his father and mother, and cleave to his wife;

Mark 10:8 And they twain shall be one flesh: so then they are no more twain, but one flesh.

Mark 10:9 What therefore God hath joined together, let not man put asunder.

This would become a statement that still rings true today. Male and female created He them, not male and male or female and female and not bisexual or transgender. And the male and the female would become one flesh.

This has always been God's plan for marriage.

12:00 noon on Wednesday, the Twenty-Ninth of Adar

The Pharisees were not satisfied, and throughout this day, they continually try to trap Jesus into saying something that they can use against Him:

Matthew 19:7 They say unto him, Why did Moses then command to give a writing of divorcement, and to put her away?

Matthew 19:8 He saith unto them, Moses because of the hardness of your hearts suffered you to put away your wives: but from the beginning it was not so.

Matthew 19:9 And I say unto you, Whosoever shall put away his wife, except *it be* for fornication, and shall marry another, committeth adultery: and whoso marrieth her which is put away doth commit adultery.

3:00 p.m. on Wednesday, the Twenty-Ninth of Adar

The questioning is constant throughout this day and toward evening. His disciples do not understand the statement by Jesus about putting away the wife. They now question Jesus if He is preaching against marriage altogether:

Matthew 19:10 His disciples say unto him, If the case of the man be so with *his* wife, it is not good to marry.

Matthew 19:11 But he said unto them, All *men* cannot receive this saying, save *they* to whom it is given.

Matthew 19:12 For there are some eunuchs, which were so born from *their* mother's womb: and there are some eunuchs, which were made eunuchs of men: and there be eunuchs, which have made themselves eunuchs for the kingdom of heaven's sake. He that is able to receive *it*, let him receive *it*.

As the month of Nisan began, Jesus was aware of all the activities that are going to consume His time and energy. He came down to this earth to accomplish the events that will take place in this next month of Nisan. All of history is centered and focused on this month's agenda as Jesus prepares to offer Himself for the sins of the whole world.

Galatians 1:3 Grace *be* to you and peace from God the Father, and *from* our Lord Jesus Christ,

Galatians 1:4 Who gave himself for our sins, that he might deliver us from this present evil world, according to the will of God and our Father:

Fred A Kuypers

1 John 2:1 My little children, these things write I unto you, that ye sin not. And if any man sin, we have an advocate with the Father, Jesus Christ the righteous:

1 John 2:2 And he is the propitiation for our sins: and not for ours only, but also for *the sins of* the whole world.

Have you been saved by the Lord Jesus Christ? If not will you receive Him today? First, admit you are a sinner. Everyone is a sinner (Romans 3:10). God says "for all have sinned and come short of His glory" (Romans 3:23).

Second, realize that you can do nothing to remove your sin from your account (Romans 4:3–5) and that the wages of sin is death (Romans 6:23)!

Third, repent of your sins by turning from them and admitting that your sin has kept you separate from Almighty God (Romans 6:16).

Fourth, believe with your heart the Gospel, and then ask Jesus with your mouth for Christ to save you from your sin (Romans 10:9–10).

Finally, realize now that you are saved by believing in the death, burial, and resurrection of Jesus Christ the Lord (1 Corinthians 15:1–4), start to serve the Lord with all that you do (Ephesians 2:8–10). When others see the change in your life (Matthew 7:20), you will begin to have assurance that you are a child of God (1 John 5:10–13).

May this book encourage you not to waste another day (2 Corinthians 6:2) but to ask Jesus into your heart. Hear how Isaiah the prophet expressed this:

Isaiah 35:4 Say to them *that are* of a fearful heart, Be strong, fear not: behold, your God will come *with* vengeance, *even* God *with* a recompence; he will come and save you.

Isaiah 35:5 Then the eyes of the blind shall be opened, and the ears of the deaf shall be unstopped.

Isaiah 35:6 Then shall the lame *man* leap as an hart, and the tongue of the dumb sing: for in the wilderness shall waters break out, and streams in the desert.

Chapter 1

Nisan 1

Month of Nisan

1st day Yom Rishon Sunday	2nd day Yom Sheini Monday	3rd day Yom Shlishi Tuesday	4th day Yom R'vi'i Wednesday	5th day Yom Chamishi Thursday	6th day Yom Shishi Friday	Shabbat Yom Shabbat Saturday
			29th $_{Adar}$ 1st 6:00pm **Thursday The 1st of Nisan begins at 6:00 p.m.**	1st $_{Nisan}$ 2nd 6:00am to 6:00pm Sojourning at Bethabara This chapter begins 12 hours before the first of Nisan at the 6pm time slot on the fourth day, Wednesday.		

This chapter includes:

Matthew	Mark	Luke	John
19:13–19:30	10:10–10:31	18:15–18:30	

What a Finish! What a Start! The Month Jesus Met Man's Need

Fred A Kuypers

Bethabara on the East Bank of the Jordan River

6:00 p.m. on Wednesday, the First of Nisan
First day after hearing that Lazarus is sick

Jesus is in Bethabara. This is the place where baptisms continually took place. It is where John the Baptist baptized followers. Little children are brought to Jesus, and He gives no command to baptize them. I claim here that baptism has no saving grace or power and does not "wash away your sin." Many religions teach this today. If this was true and baptism was required, would not Jesus be baptizing in Bethabara day and night? But Jesus would baptize no one.

Jesus will spend two nights in Bethabara according to John 11:6. This is the first night. Now the disciples along with Jesus retire to the house where they will dine and spend the night. And they are still questioning the response that Jesus gave to the Pharisees:

Mark 10:10 And in the house his disciples asked him again of the same *matter*.

Mark 10:11 And he saith unto them, Whosoever shall put away his wife, and marry another, committeth adultery against her.

Mark 10:12 And if a woman shall put away her husband, and be married to another, she committeth adultery.

That night, there was much discussion about marriage and adultery in the house mentioned here. Marriage is a very important commitment to God. Jesus will spend much of His time on earth discussing marriage and adultery. God's very first institution, marriage, is worthy of all the discussion taking place this night. God's word will speak to everyone on this topic.

7:00 a.m. on Thursday, the First of Nisan

After a night of rest, Jesus starts this day with His disciples at Bethabara in the house mentioned in Mark 10:10. Perhaps other questions were being asked about marriage and divorce and adultery. God gives much information in the scriptures about this topic because it affects everyone. Everyone must have a father and a mother, known as a husband and a wife. Two mothers will not make a family! Neither will a father and a father! Even in a society that refuses the instruction of God, there still must be a father and a mother.

9:00 a.m. on Thursday, the First of Nisan

As Jesus departs the house in the morning, multitudes follow Him. Some children are brought to Him, and He wishes to see the children. The disciples are not so happy. They have their own questions and would rebuke the parents of these children for bringing them all at once to Jesus. Here are three views of this gathering.

Matthew's view:

Matthew 19:13 Then were there brought unto him little children, that he should put *his* hands on them, and pray: and the disciples rebuked them.

Matthew 19:14 But Jesus said, Suffer little children, and forbid them not, to come unto me: for of such is the kingdom of heaven.

The phrase "kingdom of heaven" is unique to Matthew's Gospel. It appears thirty-two times and only in Matthew. Another phrase, "kingdom of God" also appears in Matthew five times. Is there a difference between the two sayings? Here is what scripture teaches. The kingdom of heaven is a spiritual place for when a person comes to Jesus as described in verse fourteen. It is being battled for in the heart of every man:

Matthew 11:12 And from the days of John the Baptist until now the kingdom of heaven suffereth violence, and the violent take it by force.

The kingdom of heaven is made up of believers but the "kingdom of God," must be within every believer:

Luke 17:20 And when he was demanded of the Pharisees, when the kingdom of God should come, he answered them and said, The kingdom of God cometh not with observation:

Luke 17:21 Neither shall they say, Lo here! or, lo there! for, behold, the kingdom of God is within you.

The kingdom of heaven is the spiritual place that man seeks. This place can only be achieved God's way through His Son, Jesus Christ. Any other way that man dreams up becomes a violent battle that takes place in every man's heart, who will not accept God's way. Spiritually speaking, the kingdom of God is in you when you become a born-again follower of Jesus Christ.

Matthew concludes with Jesus departing from the scene.

Matthew 19:15 And he laid *his* hands on them, and departed thence.

Mark's view:

Mark says the children were brought just to have Jesus touch them.

Mark 10:13 And they brought young children to him, that he should touch them: and *his* disciples rebuked those that brought *them*.

Fred A Kuypers

It is interesting to read that a major religious function was not performed here. Why was baptism not performed here? If baptism is essential to salvation, as many religions teach, then why didn't Jesus immediately baptize these children? Why didn't Jesus teach this here, especially as these little children were coming to Him? Jesus was at the place where baptisms were being performed and where John first baptized. If Jesus came to seek and to save those who were lost, why did He not immediately start to baptize all at this point? Perhaps because baptism is a work that has nothing to do with salvation! In fact, the scriptures state that Jesus baptized no one!

John 4:1 When therefore the Lord knew how the Pharisees had heard that Jesus made and baptized more disciples than John, John 4:2 (Though Jesus himself baptized not, but his disciples,)

When Paul was chosen to preach the gospel, he made it clear that his main work among men was not to baptize. His main work is to do what every Christian needs to do and that is to tell others the Gospel. The Gospel is God's plan for salvation of every man.

1 Corinthians 1:16 And I baptized also the household of Stephanas: besides, I know not whether I baptized any other.

1 Corinthians 1:17 For Christ sent me not to baptize, but to preach the gospel: not with wisdom of words, lest the cross of Christ should be made of none effect.

1 Corinthians 1:18 For the preaching of the cross is to them that perish foolishness; but unto us which are saved it is the power of God.

Jesus explains that He wanted the children to come and He would bless them.

Mark 10:14 But when Jesus saw *it,* he was much displeased, and said unto them, Suffer the little children to come unto me, and forbid them not: for of such is the kingdom of God.

Jesus describes how simple the plan of salvation truly is. Suffer or allow little children to come unto me. Even a little child can understand this truth. In fact, adults have to become like one of these little children as pertaining to faith. And so here is the first example in this month of Jesus speaking that all are to receive the kingdom of God as simply as a little child.

Mark 10:15 Verily I say unto you, Whosoever shall not receive the kingdom of God as a little child, he shall not enter therein.

Jesus states this single, narrow way of approaching God. Without the kingdom of God being in you, you are not saved! Remember earlier in His ministry Jesus' famous speech: the Sermon on the Mount:

Matthew 7:13 Enter ye in at the strait gate: for wide *is* the gate, and broad *is* the way, that leadeth to destruction, and many there be which go in thereat:

Matthew 7:14 Because strait *is* the gate, and narrow *is* the way, which leadeth unto life, and few there be that find it.

Mark concludes this meeting with a blessing:

Mark 10:16 And he took them up in his arms, put his hands upon them, and blessed them.

Luke's view:

Luke says that they (those looking for miracles to be performed by Jesus) brought Him infants. This was done just so Jesus would touch them. Whether this was for healing purposes or whether this was political, like today when people bring their children to the president or to the pope to have them touch them or even kiss them, the scripture says:

Luke 18:15 And they brought unto him also infants, that he would touch them: but when *his* disciples saw *it,* they rebuked them.

Luke 18:16 But Jesus called them *unto him,* and said, Suffer little children to come unto me, and forbid them not: for of such is the kingdom of God.

Luke concludes with an ultimatum, to receive the kingdom of God in order to enter into the kingdom of heaven.

Luke 18:17 Verily I say unto you, Whosoever shall not receive the kingdom of God as a little child shall in no wise enter therein.

Jesus will confirm the truth that John revealed earlier in his gospel but He does not baptize these infants:

John 3:16 For God so loved the world, that he gave his only begotten Son, that whosoever believeth in him should not perish, but have everlasting life.

John 3:17 For God sent not his Son into the world to condemn the world; but that the world through him might be saved.

John 3:18 He that believeth on him is not condemned: but he that believeth not is condemned already, because he hath not believed in the name of the only begotten Son of God.

1:00 p.m. on Thursday, the First of Nisan

Jesus is walking along the way from one spot to another in Bethabara when the rich young ruler approached Him. There are three accounts of this meeting, one each from Matthew, Mark, and Luke, and all three are noted.

Matthew's account

Matthew 19:16 And, behold, one came and said unto him, Good Master, what good thing shall I do, that I may have eternal life?

Matthew 19:17 And he said unto him, Why callest thou me good? there is none good but one, that is, God: but if thou wilt enter into life, keep the commandments.

Matthew 19:18 He saith unto him, Which? Jesus said, Thou shalt do no murder, Thou shalt not commit adultery, Thou shalt not steal, Thou shalt not bear false witness,

Fred A Kuypers

Matthew 19:19 Honour thy father and thy mother: and, Thou shalt love thy neighbour as thyself.

Matthew 19:20 The young man saith unto him, All these things have I kept from my youth up: what lack I yet?

Mark's account:

Mark 10:17 And when he was gone forth into the way, there came one running, and kneeled to him, and asked him, Good Master, what shall I do that I may inherit eternal life?

Mark 10:18 And Jesus said unto him, Why callest thou me good? there is none good but one, that is, God.

Mark 10:19 Thou knowest the commandments, Do not commit adultery, Do not kill, Do not steal, Do not bear false witness, Defraud not, Honour thy father and mother.

Mark 10:20 And he answered and said unto him, Master, all these have I observed from my youth.

Luke's account:

Luke 18:18 And a certain ruler asked him, saying, Good Master, what shall I do to inherit eternal life?

Luke 18:19 And Jesus said unto him, Why callest thou me good? none is good, save one, that is, God.

Luke 18:20 Thou knowest the commandments, Do not commit adultery, Do not kill, Do not steal, Do not bear false witness, Honour thy father and thy mother.

Luke 18:21 And he said, All these have I kept from my youth up.

Jesus took some time here to console this man. He loved him and wanted him to be saved. Mark explains that Jesus loved this ruler, but the man had a problem. He could not let go of his earthly possessions. This is a great lesson to be learned here. Do not put any trust in riches, as Jesus will explain. Again the very similar response of the three synoptic gospels speaks:

Matthew's account of "follow me":

Matthew 19:21 Jesus said unto him, If thou wilt be perfect, go and sell that thou hast, and give to the poor, and thou shalt have treasure in heaven: and come and follow me.

Matthew 19:22 But when the young man heard that saying, he went away sorrowful: for he had great possessions.

Mark's account of "follow me":

Mark 10:21 Then Jesus beholding him loved him, and said unto him, One thing thou lackest: go thy way, sell whatsoever thou hast, and give to the poor, and thou shalt have treasure in heaven: and come, take up the cross, and follow me.

Mark 10:22 And he was sad at that saying, and went away grieved: for he had great possessions.

Luke's account of "follow me":

Luke 18:22 Now when Jesus heard these things, he said unto him, Yet lackest thou one thing: sell all that thou hast, and distribute unto the poor, and thou shalt have treasure in heaven: and come, follow me.

Luke 18:23 And when he heard this, he was very sorrowful: for he was very rich.

Mark emphasizes this warning about riches that Jesus is about to give:

Mark 10:23 And Jesus looked round about, and saith unto his disciples, How hardly shall they that have riches enter into the kingdom of God!

Matthew, Mark, and Luke all add the same statement made by Jesus:

Matthew:

Matthew 19:23 Then said Jesus unto his disciples, Verily I say unto you, That a rich man shall hardly enter into the kingdom of heaven.

Matthew 19:24 And again I say unto you, It is easier for a camel to go through the eye of a needle, than for a rich man to enter into the kingdom of God.

Mark:

Mark 10:24 And the disciples were astonished at his words. But Jesus answereth again, and saith unto them, Children, how hard is it for them that trust in riches to enter into the kingdom of God!

Mark 10:25 It is easier for a camel to go through the eye of a needle, than for a rich man to enter into the kingdom of God.

Luke:

Luke 18:24 And when Jesus saw that he was very sorrowful, he said, How hardly shall they that have riches enter into the kingdom of God!

Luke 18:25 For it is easier for a camel to go through a needle's eye, than for a rich man to enter into the kingdom of God.

2:00 p.m. on Thursday, the First of Nisan

The synoptic gospels of Matthew, Mark, and Luke will now state the same message. However, this message will be stated in each man's own words, proving that there was no collusion between them. Jesus' disciples cannot believe what they have heard and are amazed. Jesus gives a truthful statement that will ring for all eternity. He states all things are possible with God:

Matthew:

Matthew 19:25 When his disciples heard *it,* they were exceedingly amazed, saying, Who then can be saved?

Matthew 19:26 But Jesus beheld *them,* and said unto them, With men this is impossible; but with God all things are possible.

Mark:

Mark 10:26 And they were astonished out of measure, saying among themselves, Who then can be saved?

Mark 10:27 And Jesus looking upon them saith, With men *it is* impossible, but not with God: for with God all things are possible.

Luke:

Luke 18:26 And they that heard *it* said, Who then can be saved?

Luke 18:27 And he said, The things which are impossible with men are possible with God.

3:00 p.m. on Thursday, the First of Nisan

Later in the afternoon, Peter speaks out and tells Jesus that he himself is a primary candidate for the kingdom of God. Peter is hard to control. Peter thinks that personal sacrifice is enough to become a child of God. But Peter's faith and belief were unsure. Jesus will get Peter under control. Jesus states that the first shall be last, and the last shall be first. Peter, like everyone, had to learn how to serve and put others first ahead of himself. The three synoptic gospels are in agreement again with these statements proving again no collusion.

Matthew:

Matthew 19:27 Then answered Peter and said unto him, Behold, we have forsaken all, and followed thee; what shall we have therefore?

Matthew 19:28 And Jesus said unto them, Verily I say unto you, That ye which have followed me, in the regeneration when the Son of man shall sit in the throne of his glory, ye also shall sit upon twelve thrones, judging the twelve tribes of Israel.

Matthew 19:29 And every one that hath forsaken houses, or brethren, or sisters, or father, or mother, or wife, or children, or lands, for my name's sake, shall receive an hundredfold, and shall inherit everlasting life.

Matthew 19:30 But many that are first shall be last; and the last shall be first.

Mark:

Mark 10:28 Then Peter began to say unto him, Lo, we have left all, and have followed thee.

Mark 10:29 And Jesus answered and said, Verily I say unto you, There is no man that hath left house, or brethren, or sisters, or father, or mother, or wife, or children, or lands, for my sake, and the gospel's,

Mark 10:30 But he shall receive an hundredfold now in this time, houses, and brethren, and sisters, and mothers, and children, and lands, with persecutions; and in the world to come eternal life.

Mark 10:31 But many that are first shall be last; and the last first.

Luke:

Luke 18:28 Then Peter said, Lo, we have left all, and followed thee.

Luke 18:29 And he said unto them, Verily I say unto you, There is no man that hath left house, or parents, or brethren, or wife, or children, for the kingdom of God's sake,

Luke 18:30 Who shall not receive manifold more in this present time, and in the world to come life everlasting.

5:00 p.m. on Thursday, the First of Nisan

As this first day of Nisan comes to an end, it has been one day since Jesus heard that Lazarus was sick. This is important for establishing the day and time that this narrative is following. Today Jesus has notified His disciples that unless you are willing to forsake every possession you have in this world for His sake, you are not worthy to be a child of God and to enter the kingdom of God. There is a fallacy that is spoken many times in this world, and it says: "We are all God's children." However, not everyone is a child of God's. All mankind is God's creation. But no one becomes a child of God unless he or she is born again.

John 3:3 Jesus answered and said unto him, Verily, verily, I say unto thee, Except a man be born again, he cannot see the kingdom of God.

John 3:4 Nicodemus saith unto him, How can a man be born when he is old? can he enter the second time into his mother's womb, and be born?

John 3:5 Jesus answered, Verily, verily, I say unto thee, Except a man be born of water and *of* the Spirit, he cannot enter into the kingdom of God.

John 3:6 That which is born of the flesh is flesh; and that which is born of the Spirit is spirit. John 3:7 Marvel not that I said unto thee, Ye must be born again.

Jesus then explains to Nicodemus how to be born again. Notice the King James Version has two different words describing who Jesus is talking to in verse 7 above. This makes the verse extremely clear. Jesus was speaking to Nicodemus and used the singular form of "thee." All other versions of course change this to "you". Here Jesus is speaking to one man, Nicodemus. However, the command to be born again is plural: "Ye." All other versions translate "you" at this point. The assumption with the modern versions can be made that Jesus commands Nicodemus, and Nicodemus only, to be born again!

Jesus is clear on being born again. Just as certain as there was a moment in time that a person was born physically by water from a mother; so too there is a moment in time when a person is born again, this time of the Spirit. It is not by personal sacrifice as Jesus has just explained to Peter and the apostles. It is not by baptism as was pointed out at the beginning of this chapter. It is not by possessions. A bumper sticker I had observed while driving read, "The one who dies with the most toys wins!" Job made it clear that this statement is wrong when he said:

Job 1:20 Then Job arose, and rent his mantle, and shaved his head, and fell down upon the ground, and worshipped,

Job 1:21 And said, Naked came I out of my mother's womb, and naked shall I return thither: the LORD gave, and the LORD hath taken away; blessed be the name of the LORD.

What a Finish! What a Start! The Month Jesus Met Man's Need

Fred A Kuypers

Remember that Jesus said that the kingdom of God must be within you (Luke 17:21). Is the kingdom of God within you? How can you know this? It is very simple. Just take God at His Word. His Word cannot fail. Read it and believe it!

Acts 8:37 And Philip said, If thou believest with all thine heart, thou mayest. And he answered and said, I believe that Jesus Christ is the Son of God.

Chapter 2

Nisan 2

Month of Nisan

1st day Yom Rishon Sunday	2nd day Yom Sheini Monday	3rd day Yom Shlishi Tuesday	4th day Yom R'vi'i Wednesday	5th day Yom Chamishi Thursday	6th day Yom Shishi Friday	Shabbat Yom Shabbat Saturday
				Nisan 2nd 6:00pm Friday begins	2nd Nisan 3rd 6:00am to 6:00pm Sojourning at Bethabara This is the second day Lazarus is sick. This day the hour will come when word is received that Lazarus dies.	

This chapter includes:

Matthew	Mark	Luke	John
20:1–20:16			11:7–11:16

What a Finish! What a Start! The Month Jesus Met Man's Need

Fred A Kuypers

Bethabara on the East Bank of the Jordan River

Jesus remains in Bethabara and hears that Lazarus dies. He will wait four days before going to see Martha and Mary after Lazarus' death.

6:00 p.m. on Thursday, the Second of Nisan

Jesus stays tonight again in Bethabara. This is the second "evening and morning" after hearing of Lazarus' sickness according to John 11:6. Remember what John recorded that Jesus would abide two days after hearing that Lazarus was sick and that he would be dead four days in the grave at Bethany.

9:00 a.m. on Friday, the Second of Nisan

Jesus is still in Bethabara where John first baptized in the Jordan River. He knows this is the second day since Lazarus was mentioned as being sick. However Jesus continues to teach His disciples what the kingdom of heaven is like. This passage in Matthew not only teaches us a principle of God in that He can reward whom and when He desires, but it also gives us a thorough idea of how time was marked during a twelve-hour period. The first hour of the day would be 6:00 a.m. to 7:00 a.m. This would be early in the morning:

Matthew 20:1 For the kingdom of heaven is like unto a man *that is* an householder, which went out early in the morning to hire labourers into his vineyard.

Matthew 20:2 And when he had agreed with the labourers for a penny a day, he sent them into his vineyard.

The third hour mentioned here would be three hours after the sunrise or 9:00 a.m.

Matthew 20:3 And he went out about the third hour, and saw others standing idle in the marketplace,

Matthew 20:4 And said unto them; Go ye also into the vineyard, and whatsoever is right I will give you. And they went their way.

The following verses in Matthew instruct us about how daytime is marked in scripture. The third hour mentioned above would be three hours after the sunrise or 9:00 a.m. The sixth hour would be 12:00 noon or six hours after the rising of the sun. The ninth hour would then be 3:00 p.m. in the afternoon. By just following these examples, there will be no problem with the times Matthew used in this timeline. The passage continues:

Matthew 20:5 Again he went out about the sixth and ninth hour, and did likewise.

Matthew 20:6 And about the eleventh hour he went out, and found others standing idle, and saith unto them, Why stand ye here all the day idle?

Matthew 20:7 They say unto him, Because no man hath hired us. He saith unto them, Go ye also into the vineyard; and whatsoever is right, *that* shall ye receive.

Matthew 20:8 So when even was come, the lord of the vineyard saith unto his steward, Call the labourers, and give them *their* hire, beginning from the last unto the first.

Matthew 20:9 And when they came that *were hired* about the eleventh hour, they received every man a penny.

Matthew 20:10 But when the first came, they supposed that they should have received more; and they likewise received every man a penny.

In this passage from Matthew, Jesus instructs as to the mercy of God. When reading this scripture of the laborers in the field, this is how it is to be interpreted:

Romans 9:14 What shall we say then? *Is there* unrighteousness with God? God forbid.

Romans 9:15 For he saith to Moses, I will have mercy on whom I will have mercy, and I will have compassion on whom I will have compassion.

Romans 9:16 So then *it is* not of him that willeth, nor of him that runneth, but of God that sheweth mercy.

It was Moses who asked God to show him His glory while at the cleft of the rock. Then God declared this truth to Moses and said:

Exodus 33:19 And he said, I will make all my goodness pass before thee, and I will proclaim the name of the LORD before thee; and will be gracious to whom I will be gracious, and will shew mercy on whom I will shew mercy.

Matthew continues:

Matthew 20:11 And when they had received *it*, they murmured against the goodman of the house,

Matthew 20:12 Saying, These last have wrought *but* one hour, and thou hast made them equal unto us, which have borne the burden and heat of the day.

Matthew 20:13 But he answered one of them, and said, Friend, I do thee no wrong: didst not thou agree with me for a penny?

Matthew 20:14 Take *that* thine *is,* and go thy way: I will give unto this last, even as unto thee.

Matthew 20:15 Is it not lawful for me to do what I will with mine own? Is thine eye evil, because I am good?

Matthew 20:16 So the last shall be first, and the first last: for many be called, but few chosen.

What is Jesus saying with this teaching? He instructs that when a person turns to God and becomes saved, it does not matter how old you are or how much time you have left on this earth. God will give the same reward to all, and that reward is eternal life with God in heaven forever and ever. Saved early in life or at the end of your life, eternal life is the same for all. The problem however, is that no one

What a Finish! What a Start! The Month Jesus Met Man's Need

Fred A Kuypers

knows when their life will be over, and many who think they will turn to Christ at the eleventh hour often die at ten-thirty. A traffic accident or sickness can end a life suddenly. Jesus is always reiterating that today is the day to accept Him as Savior.

2Corinthians 6:2 (For he saith, I have heard thee in a time accepted, and in the day of salvation have I succoured thee: behold, now *is* the accepted time; behold, now *is* the day of salvation.)

12:00 noon on Friday, the Second of Nisan

Jesus and His disciples originally heard that Lazarus had been sick two days earlier. However, on this day, He will be notified that Lazarus is dead. This day of notification will allow four days to pass before Jesus goes to Bethany for the purpose of raising Lazarus. The scriptures say at that time he will be in the grave for four days. But Jesus has a divine appointment waiting for Him in Jericho prior to His going to Bethany to raise Lazarus as the scriptures will point out.

John recorded two days earlier in verse six that Jesus heard that Lazarus had been sick. However, He abides two additional days in Bethabara. After the two days He makes a decision to head back again to the Judaea area.

John 11:7 Then after that saith he to his disciples, Let us go into Judaea again.

Judaea is the area west of the Jordan River, around Jerusalem that includes Mount Moriah and the Mount of Olives to the east of Jerusalem and Mount Zion to the south and west along with the towns around Jerusalem. The disciples are very concerned about this travel, knowing that Jesus is becoming a hunted man. The disciples are wondering why Jesus wants to go up to Judaea. From where He is abiding, it is about thirty kilometers, or twenty miles, a full day's walk.

John 11:8 *His* disciples say unto him, Master, the Jews of late sought to stone thee; and goest thou thither again?

He knows they will need a full twelve hours of daylight to accomplish this. Jesus established that a day consists of twelve hours of day light with this statement:

John 11:9 Jesus answered, Are there not twelve hours in the day? If any man walk in the day, he stumbleth not, because he seeth the light of this world.

John 11:10 But if a man walk in the night, he stumbleth, because there is no light in him.

Jesus spoke of traveling through the daylight hours but also spiritually refers to the daylight as His disciples having Christ in their heart because Jesus is the light of the world.

John 8:12 Then spake Jesus again unto them, saying, I am the light of the world: he that followeth me shall not walk in darkness, but shall have the light of life.

Jesus Christ says that if you do not have Him in your heart, you stumble just as sure as walking in the night and stumbling in darkness. Earlier in the Gospel of John, Jesus declared to be the light of the world:

John 9:5 As long as I am in the world, I am the light of the world.

The apostles also would have that designation as the "light of the world." Anyone who proclaims Jesus Christ as Lord is a light to the world. It would be carried down generation to generation to all who believe:

Matthew 5:14 Ye are the light of the world. A city that is set on an hill cannot be hid.

Matthew 5:15 Neither do men light a candle, and put it under a bushel, but on a candlestick; and it giveth light unto all that are in the house.

Matthew 5:16 Let your light so shine before men, that they may see your good works, and glorify your Father which is in heaven.

2:00 p.m. on Friday, the Second of Nisan
Word comes that Lazarus is dead

Sometime this day, after his disciples were trying to understand what Jesus meant when He says our friend Lazarus sleeps, Jesus now says plainly that Lazarus is dead. From this time, four days will have to pass so that Lazarus' body can lie in the grave for four full days. Lazarus will have to be placed in the grave this day before 6:00 p.m. as the Sabbath will begin. One of the four days, tomorrow, will be the weekly Saturday Sabbath.

John 11:11 These things said he: and after that he saith unto them, Our friend Lazarus sleepeth; but I go, that I may awake him out of sleep.

John 11:12 Then said his disciples, Lord, if he sleep, he shall do well.

John 11:13 Howbeit Jesus spake of his death: but they thought that he had spoken of taking of rest in sleep.

John 11:14 Then said Jesus unto them plainly, Lazarus is dead.

Jesus will wait four days before going to see Martha and Mary, Lazarus's sisters. From Friday until Tuesday, Jesus will not be in Bethany. On Tuesday, it is recorded that Jesus raised Lazarus. That will accomplish the four days. Besides that, the chief priests and the Pharisees are constantly badgering Him with question after question. But Jesus wants to make this point very clear. He is going to show His disciples the resurrection of Lazarus as an example of His resurrection.

John 11:15 And I am glad for your sakes that I was not there, to the intent ye may believe; nevertheless let us go unto him.

John 11:16 Then said Thomas, which is called Didymus, unto his fellowdisciples, Let us also go, that we may die with him.

What a Finish! What a Start! The Month Jesus Met Man's Need

Fred A Kuypers

His disciples will decide to go with Jesus to be with Lazarus. They do not understand why Jesus decides to go to Lazarus if he is already dead. They think they will die also. Thomas is again in doubt of what Jesus is doing, but that is typical of him. Thomas thinks that Mary and Martha and friends of Lazarus must be extremely upset with Jesus. He is among those who think they will all die. But Jesus has decided to wait four days, which will allow corruption, or decomposition, to take place. Jesus knew that Thomas and all others need to see this powerful miracle that would take place.

Today salvation must be accepted by faith. Faith is the only merit of man that will please God. Faith pleases God because with faith, a man places the control of his destiny squarely on God Himself, just as Noah did in preparing the ark for something that he had never seen before—rain!

Hebrews 11:6 But without faith it is impossible to please him: for he that cometh to God must believe that he is, and that he is a rewarder of them that diligently seek him.

Hebrews 11:7 By faith Noah, being warned of God of things not seen as yet, moved with fear, prepared an ark to the saving of his house; by the which he condemned the world, and became heir of the righteousness which is by faith.

Chapter 3

Nisan 3

Month of Nisan

1st day Yom Rishon Sunday	2nd day Yom Sheini Monday	3rd day Yom Shlishi Tuesday	4th day Yom R'vi'i Wednesday	5th day Yom Chamishi Thursday	6th day Yom Shishi Friday	Shabbat Yom Shabbat Saturday
					Nisan 3rd 6:00pm **Saturday begins**	3rd Nisan 4th 6:00am to 6:00pm Sojourning near Jordan, Jesus does not travel. This Sabbath day is the first full day that Lazarus is in the grave.

This chapter includes:

Matthew	Mark	Luke	John
		18:31–18:34	

What a Finish! What a Start! The Month Jesus Met Man's Need

Fred A Kuypers

The West Bank of Jordan River

Saturday Sabbath at the Jordan River near Bethabara First day after hearing of Lazarus death

6:00 p.m. on Friday, the Third of Nisan
The Saturday Sabbath Begins

Jesus will not travel this day. He stays near the Jordan river to allow for the four-day interval to transpire in order to raise Lazarus. Jesus shows how to act on the Sabbath and every day. He just followed the commands of God:

Isaiah 58:13 If thou turn away thy foot from the sabbath, from doing thy pleasure on my holy day; and call the sabbath a delight, the holy of the LORD, honourable; and shalt honour him, not doing thine own ways, nor finding thine own pleasure, nor speaking thine own words:

Isaiah 58:14 Then shalt thou delight thyself in the LORD; and I will cause thee to ride upon the high places of the earth, and feed thee with the heritage of Jacob thy father: for the mouth of the LORD hath spoken it.

The Sabbath was to be a day in delighting in the Lord. It was a day to honor Him and not follow our own pleasure. This scripture is not being followed today! Even on Sunday, the Lord's Day, football and other sports, boating, golfing, travel, and vacations do the opposite of what this and other scripture say. No wonder this country is having so many terrible calamities. The United States is no longer riding on high places of the earth. The need is to get back to honoring Him every day, which begins with the Lord's Day! Understanding what Sabbath commands say concerning travel:

Exodus 16:29 See, for that the LORD hath given you the sabbath, therefore he giveth you on the sixth day the bread of two days; abide ye every man in his place, let no man go out of his place on the seventh day.

Exodus 16:30 So the people rested on the seventh day.

A Sabbath day's journey is a measurement designed by man. This measurement was two thousand cubits. Remember, this is not found in the original command. This was based on a passage in Joshua:

Joshua 3:4 Yet there shall be a space between you and it, about two thousand cubits by measure: come not near unto it, that ye may know the way by which ye must go: for ye have not passed this way heretofore.

Joshua 3:5 And Joshua said unto the people, Sanctify yourselves: for to morrow the LORD will do wonders among you.

Over the centuries, this measurement changed and soon included the distance from Jerusalem to the Mount of Olives.

Acts 1:12 Then returned they unto Jerusalem from the mount called Olivet, which is from Jerusalem a sabbath day's journey.

Remember on the Sabbath Jesus did many other deeds that infuriated the religious leaders of the day.

Mark 2:23 And it came to pass, that he went through the corn fields on the sabbath day; and his disciples began, as they went, to pluck the ears of corn.

Mark 2:24 And the Pharisees said unto him, Behold, why do they on the sabbath day that which is not lawful?

Jesus used this Sabbath day to rest. He had two very busy weeks ahead of Him. Nothing is described to have happened on this Sabbath. Martha and Mary are not sure why Jesus did not come and heal their brother Lazarus. But He does not go on this day, for it is the Sabbath day. Many people are here at the Jordan River near Bethabara to watch and see Jesus and to hear what He has to say. But the Sabbath day goes by uneventfully.

12:00 noon on Saturday, the Third of Nisan
The Sabbath Continues First day
that Lazarus is in the grave

Jesus continued to be sought after. Many were there for the entertainment. Many came to see Jesus perform His miracles. In comparison, John the Baptist was not known for any miracles.

John 10:41 And many resorted unto him, and said, John did no miracle: but all things that John spake of this man were true.

But what John had to say about Jesus was true enough. Bethabara is where John the Baptist' ministry to Jesus started as told by John's Gospel:

John 1:28 These things were done in Bethabara beyond Jordan, where John was baptizing.

Though John worked no miracle, he would be born by a miracle:

Luke 1:13 But the angel said unto him, Fear not, Zacharias: for thy prayer is heard; and thy wife Elisabeth shall bear thee a son, and thou shalt call his name John.

John was known for heralding the coming of the Lord. It is understood that John the Baptist came in the spirit and the power of Elijah.

Luke 1:17 And he shall go before him in the spirit and power of Elias, to turn the hearts of the fathers to the children, and the disobedient to the wisdom of the just; to make ready a people prepared for the Lord.

And Jesus said that there was no greater man on earth:

Luke 7:28 For I say unto you, Among those that are born of women there is not a greater prophet than John the Baptist: but he that is least in the kingdom of God is greater than he.

3:00 p.m. on Saturday, the Third of Nisan
The Sabbath Continues

Many other events were about to happen. Jesus is thinking of Lazarus after yesterday hearing of Lazarus's death before heading to Judaea and arriving at his grave in Bethany, according to John's Gospel. This Sabbath day is the first of the four days that Lazarus is in the grave. Jesus is also thinking of the upcoming Passover and will try to explain this to His twelve disciples:

Luke 18:31 Then he took *unto him* the twelve, and said unto them, Behold, we go up to Jerusalem, and all things that are written by the prophets concerning the Son of man shall be accomplished.

Jesus decides to depart the next morning on the first day of the week, and He and His disciples will go up to Jerusalem. Luke records Jesus unveiling a far more detailed account of what was to happen to Him as was written by the prophets:

Luke 18:32 For he shall be delivered unto the Gentiles, and shall be mocked, and spitefully entreated, and spitted on:

Luke 18:33 And they shall scourge *him,* and put him to death: and the third day he shall rise again.

The disciples did not understand anything that Jesus was saying to them.

Luke 18:34 And they understood none of these things: and this saying was hid from them, neither knew they the things which were spoken.

The disciples did not understand because without the Holy Spirit being poured out on all men, no one was able to comprehend the price Jesus paid. But God explained in the Acts of the Apostles that in the last days during this church age that began at Pentecost, it would be just like Joel the prophet said:

Acts 2:16 But this is that which was spoken by the prophet Joel;

Acts 2:17 And it shall come to pass in the last days, saith God, I will pour out of my Spirit upon all flesh: and your sons and your daughters shall prophesy, and your young men shall see visions, and your old men shall dream dreams:

Joel the prophet said it like this:

Joel 2:28 And it shall come to pass afterward, that I will pour out my spirit upon all flesh; and your sons and your daughters shall prophesy, your old men shall dream dreams, your young men shall see visions:

Joel 2:29 And also upon the servants and upon the handmaids in those days will I pour out my spirit.

Joel 2:30 And I will shew wonders in the heavens and in the earth, blood, and fire, and pillars of smoke.

Joel 2:31 The sun shall be turned into darkness, and the moon into blood, before the great and the terrible day of the LORD come.

Joel 2:32 And it shall come to pass, that whosoever shall call on the name of the LORD shall be delivered: for in mount Zion and in Jerusalem shall be deliverance, as the LORD hath said, and in the remnant whom the LORD shall call.

What makes a man call on the name of the Lord? What brings a man to the point of trusting in a Savior that he has never seen? How does faith come about? Repentance is what Jesus, John the Baptist, and Paul preached over and over again.

Jesus explained this:

Luke 13:2 And Jesus answering said unto them, Suppose ye that these Galilaeans were sinners above all the Galilaeans, because they suffered such things?

Luke 13:3 I tell you, Nay: but, except ye repent, ye shall all likewise perish.

Luke 13:4 Or those eighteen, upon whom the tower in Siloam fell, and slew them, think ye that they were sinners above all men that dwelt in Jerusalem?

Luke 13:5 I tell you, Nay: but, except ye repent, ye shall all likewise perish.

In the Acts of the Apostles, the historical account of the beginning of the church, Luke tells us that God demands repentance:

Acts 17:30 And the times of this ignorance God winked at; but now commandeth all men every where to repent:

Paul states that all the Gentiles need to repent (turn from sin) and in faith turn to God:

Acts 26:20 But shewed first unto them of Damascus, and at Jerusalem, and throughout all the coasts of Judaea, and then to the Gentiles, that they should repent and turn to God, and do works meet for repentance.

It is amazing that God declares in the Old Testament how a man can be saved. It is the exact same way that Joel the prophet and the apostle Paul stated. All one must do is "call upon the name of the Lord," and you shall be delivered. This calling takes place only when a man has given up on his attempt to do good and has repented of that type of thinking. This is the step of faith one needs to have in order to please God. God established this plan as His plan on how He would save a man. That plan is through His Son the Lord Jesus Christ. What a person must do to have eternal life is follow Jesus Christ. Jesus cried for us to repent, to believe God, and to call on His name in order to be saved.

Here is where Jesus Christ stated this:

Matthew 4:17 From that time Jesus began to preach, and to say, Repent: for the kingdom of heaven is at hand.

Here is where Peter stated this:

Acts 3:19 Repent ye therefore, and be converted, that your sins may be blotted out, when the times of refreshing shall come from the presence of the Lord;

And here is where Paul stated this:

Act 20:21 Testifying both to the Jews, and also to the Greeks, repentance toward God, and faith toward our Lord Jesus Christ.

How important is repentance? The following verses will give an idea of what Jesus wants to express about true repentance. Heaven takes notice not when a person gets saved through faith but when a person repents. Understand that repentance will not save you. I know many people who have repented of a sinful lifestyle and have never turned to Jesus Christ to save them by faith. Grace from God is what saves you through faith not repentance. However this faith cannot come without repentance. When someone changes their mind about the sin or wrong direction they are heading toward and turn from it, then God can direct you by grace to His Son and by faith one can believe in the death burial and resurrection of the Lord Jesus Christ.

Luke 15:7 I say unto you, that likewise joy shall be in heaven over one sinner that repenteth, more than over ninety and nine just persons, which need no repentance.

Luke 15:8 Either what woman having ten pieces of silver, if she lose one piece, doth not light a candle, and sweep the house, and seek diligently till she find it?

Luke 15:9 And when she hath found it, she calleth her friends and her neighbours together, saying, Rejoice with me; for I have found the piece which I had lost.

Luke 15:10 Likewise, I say unto you, there is joy in the presence of the angels of God over one sinner that repenteth.

God works repentance through certain things one of which is sorrow. When sorrow comes into a person's life God can use that to bring that one to salvation. But after a tragedy it happens much that a man will say I am going to live a good life from now on. He changes his mind about how he used to live. But if by faith he does not come to the Savior, Jesus Christ, soon he will go back to his old ways and repent of his repentance. God explains it best to the church at Corinth:

2Corinthians 7:10 For godly sorrow worketh repentance to salvation not to be repented of: but the sorrow of the world worketh death.

Repentance will not save a person but it is a continual requirement to come to God and escape the sorrow of this world. Are you living a life that you know is wrong? Repent of that life! Turn to Jesus Christ and by faith accept Him as your Lord and Savior.

Chapter 4

❧❧❧

Nisan 4

Month of Nisan

1st day Yom Rishon Sunday	2nd day Yom Sheini Monday	3rd day Yom Shlishi Tuesday	4th day Yom R'vi'i Wednesday	5th day Yom Chamishi Thursday	6th day Yom Shishi Friday	Shabbat Yom Shabbat Saturday
						Nisan 4th 6:00pm Sunday begins
4th Nisan 5th 6:00am to 6:00pm Travel to Jericho Luke alone records the visit to Zacchaeus on this first day of the week. Jesus will spend the night in Jericho.						

This chapter includes:

Matthew	Mark	Luke	John
20:17-20:28	10:32-10:45	18:35–19:27	

What a Finish! What a Start! The Month Jesus Met Man's Need

Fred A Kuypers

Trip from Jordan River to Jericho (about Five Kilometers)

Jesus and Zacchaeus in Jericho

6:00 p.m. on Saturday, the Fourth of Nisan
The First Day of the week, Sunday Begins

The Sabbath day ends, and the first day of the week begins. Jesus has announced His plans to go up to Jerusalem. But now the night is upon them, and they must sleep. Jesus has told His disciples that everything the prophets have ever prophesied about the Messiah suffering is about to be accomplished. He surely needed this night of rest. They are intending to walk from near the Jordan River all the way to Jerusalem, about thirty-five kilometers, which would be a long walk. So a night's rest is in order. This day, an unexpected stop for the disciples is about to take place in Jericho.

6:00 a.m. on Sunday, the Fourth of Nisan

Jesus awakens early to go to Jerusalem. It is a full day's walk, and they will be leaving Bethabara as the pressure of the upcoming Passion Week begins to mount. Jesus lays out exactly what is going to happen to Him. He is as clear as He can be to His disciples about the torture and death He is about to face.

Matthew records:

Matthew 20:17 And Jesus going up to Jerusalem took the twelve disciples apart in the way, and said unto them,

Matthew 20:18 Behold, we go up to Jerusalem; and the Son of man shall be betrayed unto the chief priests and unto the scribes, and they shall condemn him to death,

Matthew 20:19 And shall deliver him to the Gentiles to mock, and to scourge, and to crucify *him:* and the third day he shall rise again.

Mark records:

Mark 10:32 And they were in the way going up to Jerusalem; and Jesus went before them: and they were amazed; and as they followed, they were afraid. And he took again the twelve, and began to tell them what things should happen unto him,

Mark 10:33 *Saying,* Behold, we go up to Jerusalem; and the Son of man shall be delivered unto the chief priests, and unto the scribes; and they shall condemn him to death, and shall deliver him to the Gentiles:

Mark 10:34 And they shall mock him, and shall scourge him, and shall spit upon him, and shall kill him: and the third day he shall rise again.

The Bible always says that Jerusalem is up. No matter where someone was coming from, it was always "up to Jerusalem." Jesus describes this all the time. This is because Jerusalem is God's city. The religions of the world all have their main cities. For the Catholics, it is Rome. For the Muslims, it is Mecca. For the Mormons, it is Salt Lake City, Utah. But the place mentioned in the Bible more than 600 times is Jerusalem. This is God's city, and Jesus speaks of going *up* to Jerusalem.

8:00 a.m. on Sunday, the Fourth of Nisan

As this day's journey begins with Jesus going up to Jerusalem from Bethabara, many questions are put to Him. The first question comes from the mother of James and John:

Matthew 20:20 Then came to him the mother of Zebedee's children with her sons, worshipping *him*, and desiring a certain thing of him.

Matthew 20:21 And he said unto her, What wilt thou? She saith unto him, Grant that these my two sons may sit, the one on thy right hand, and the other on the left, in thy kingdom.

The questions continue, and now James and John themselves approach Jesus. They must have been discussing this all morning if even their mother gets into the conversation.

Mark 10:35 And James and John, the sons of Zebedee, come unto him, saying, Master, we would that thou shouldest do for us whatsoever we shall desire.

Mark 10:36 And he said unto them, What would ye that I should do for you?

Mark 10:37 They said unto him, Grant unto us that we may sit, one on thy right hand, and the other on thy left hand, in thy glory.

Matthew says Jesus responds to James and John's request:

Matthew 20:22 But Jesus answered and said, Ye know not what ye ask. Are ye able to drink of the cup that I shall drink of, and to be baptized with the baptism that I am baptized with? They say unto him, We are able.

Matthew 20:23 And he saith unto them, Ye shall drink indeed of my cup, and be baptized with the baptism that I am baptized with: but to sit on my right hand, and on my left, is not mine to give, but *it shall be given to them* for whom it is prepared of my Father.

Mark says the same:

Mark 10:38 But Jesus said unto them, Ye know not what ye ask: can ye drink of the cup that I drink of? and be baptized with the baptism that I am baptized with?

Mark 10:39 And they said unto him, We can. And Jesus said unto them, Ye shall indeed drink of the cup that I drink of; and with the baptism that I am baptized withal shall ye be baptized:

Mark 10:40 But to sit on my right hand and on my left hand is not mine to give; but *it shall be given to them* for whom it is prepared.

Jesus is clear that what you are asking for is not His to give. Not sure they would want it anyway. Later, on day ten, Jesus will explain why this is not a good question as He talks about the sheep and the goats of this world. The ten other apostles respond to James and John's request:

Matthew:

Matthew 20:24 And when the ten heard *it,* they were moved with indignation against the two brethren.

Matthew 20:25 But Jesus called them *unto him,* and said, Ye know that the princes of the Gentiles exercise dominion over them, and they that are great exercise authority upon them.

Matthew 20:26 But it shall not be so among you: but whosoever will be great among you, let him be your minister;

Matthew 20:27 And whosoever will be chief among you, let him be your servant:

Matthew 20:28 Even as the Son of man came not to be ministered unto, but to minister, and to give his life a ransom for many.

Mark:

Mark 10:41 And when the ten heard *it,* they began to be much displeased with James and John.

Mark 10:42 But Jesus called them *to him,* and saith unto them, Ye know that they which are accounted to rule over the Gentiles exercise lordship over them; and their great ones exercise authority upon them.

Mark 10:43 But so shall it not be among you: but whosoever will be great among you, shall be your minister:

Mark 10:44 And whosoever of you will be the chiefest, shall be servant of all.

Mark 10:45 For even the Son of man came not to be ministered unto, but to minister, and to give his life a ransom for many.

9:00 a.m. on Sunday, the Fourth of Nisan

The travel began from the Jordan River, and after a short walk, Jericho comes into sight. Many are seeking to see and touch Jesus. Jesus commands that a blind man be brought to Him. This will increase the swell of the crowds to see if Jesus performs another miracle:

Luke 18:35 And it came to pass, that as he was come nigh unto Jericho, a certain blind man sat by the way side begging:

Luke 18:36 And hearing the multitude pass by, he asked what it meant.

Luke 18:37 And they told him, that Jesus of Nazareth passeth by.

Luke 18:38 And he cried, saying, Jesus, *thou* Son of David, have mercy on me.

Luke 18:39 And they which went before rebuked him, that he should hold his peace: but he cried so much the more, *Thou* Son of David, have mercy on me.

Luke 18:40 And Jesus stood, and commanded him to be brought unto him: and when he was come near, he asked him,

Luke 18:41 Saying, What wilt thou that I shall do unto thee? And he said, Lord, that I may receive my sight.

Luke 18:42 And Jesus said unto him, Receive thy sight: thy faith hath saved thee.

Luke 18:43 And immediately he received his sight, and followed him, glorifying God: and all the people, when they saw *it*, gave praise unto God.

As another miracle is performed by Jesus, the crowd reacts accordingly. Some praise God and begin to follow Him into Jericho. Others in the crowd, as it continues to grow, become excited at the fact Jesus just performed another miracle. They are there for the show and entertainment.

10:00 a.m. on Sunday, the Fourth of Nisan

The meeting of Jesus and Zacchaeus is very important to establish when Jesus was in Jericho. Jericho is just a short distance from Bathabara and the Jordan River. About five kilometers from the Jordan River, Jericho was a good walk already on this Sunday, leaving about thirty kilometers to Jerusalem. When Jesus decides to walk to Jerusalem from Jericho tomorrow morning, it will be an all-day journey. This would have to take place the following day because it will take a full ten to twelve hours to accomplish this. Jesus would decide to spend this day with Zacchaeus. There is only one gospel that gives the narrative of the meeting with Zacchaeus. It is in the Gospel of Luke:

Luke 19:1 And *Jesus* entered and passed through Jericho.

Luke 19:2 And, behold, *there was* a man named Zacchaeus, which was the chief among the publicans, and he was rich.

Zacchaeus will have to climb a tree to see Him.

Luke 19:3 And he sought to see Jesus who he was; and could not for the press, because he was little of stature.

Luke 19:4 And he ran before, and climbed up into a sycomore tree to see him: for he was to pass that *way*.

Jesus decides to stay with Zacchaeus. Perhaps this is so He can get an early start for Jerusalem the next morning. Or perhaps the stop is made to accomplish the four days needed for Lazarus to be in the grave. He considers Jericho to be close enough to Jerusalem to be reachable in one day of travel.

Luke 19:5 And when Jesus came to the place, he looked up, and saw him, and said unto him, Zacchaeus, make haste, and come down; for to day I must abide at thy house.

What a Finish! What a Start! The Month Jesus Met Man's Need

Fred A Kuypers

12:00 noon on Sunday, the Fourth of Nisan

Second day Lazarus is in the grave

To abide at the home of Zacchaeus would be an all-day affair. Jesus stays with Zacchaeus, and many questions are raised about this since Zacchaeus was a hated publican, that is, a principle tax collector.

Luke 19:6 And he made haste, and came down, and received him joyfully.

Luke 19:7 And when they saw *it,* they all murmured, saying, That he was gone to be guest with a man that is a sinner.

Zacchaeus discusses the good deeds he has done and states that he has given money to the poor. Jesus declares He has the message of salvation and that Zacchaeus, who is depending on his good deeds as an honest and generous man, is lost and was sought by Jesus to save him as salvation had come to his house.

Luke 19:8 And Zacchaeus stood, and said unto the Lord; Behold, Lord, the half of my goods I give to the poor; and if I have taken any thing from any man by false accusation, I restore him fourfold.

Luke 19:9 And Jesus said unto him, This day is salvation come to this house, forsomuch as he also is a son of Abraham.

Luke 19:10 For the Son of man is come to seek and to save that which was lost.

Jesus now speaks a parable for all who will listen:

Luke 19:11 And as they heard these things, he added and spake a parable, because he was nigh to Jerusalem, and because they thought that the kingdom of God should immediately appear.

Luke 19:12 He said therefore, A certain nobleman went into a far country to receive for himself a kingdom, and to return.

Luke 19:13 And he called his ten servants, and delivered them ten pounds, and said unto them, Occupy till I come.

Luke 19:14 But his citizens hated him, and sent a message after him, saying, We will not have this *man* to reign over us.

Luke 19:15 And it came to pass, that when he was returned, having received the kingdom, then he commanded these servants to be called unto him, to whom he had given the money, that he might know how much every man had gained by trading.

Luke 19:16 Then came the first, saying, Lord, thy pound hath gained ten pounds.

Luke 19:17 And he said unto him, Well, thou good servant: because thou hast been faithful in a very little, have thou authority over ten cities.

Luke 19:18 And the second came, saying, Lord, thy pound hath gained five pounds.

Luke 19:19 And he said likewise to him, Be thou also over five cities.

Luke 19:20 And another came, saying, Lord, behold, *here is* thy pound, which I have kept laid up in a napkin:

Luke 19:21 For I feared thee, because thou art an austere man: thou takest up that thou layedst not down, and reapest that thou didst not sow.

Luke 19:22 And he saith unto him, Out of thine own mouth will I judge thee, *thou* wicked servant. Thou knewest that I was an austere man, taking up that I laid not down, and reaping that I did not sow:

Luke 19:23 Wherefore then gavest not thou my money into the bank, that at my coming I might have required mine own with usury?

Luke 19:24 And he said unto them that stood by, Take from him the pound, and give *it* to him that hath ten pounds.

Luke 19:25 (And they said unto him, Lord, he hath ten pounds.)

Luke 19:26 For I say unto you, That unto every one which hath shall be given; and from him that hath not, even that he hath shall be taken away from him.

Luke 19:27 But those mine enemies, which would not that I should reign over them, bring hither, and slay *them* before me.

Jesus sets forth a principal doctrine that will follow throughout the new age about to start. The church age, or as some call it the age of grace, is this new and current dispensation. It began on the day of Pentecost:

Acts 2:1 And when the day of Pentecost was fully come, they were all with one accord in one place.

Acts 2:2 And suddenly there came a sound from heaven as of a rushing mighty wind, and it filled all the house where they were sitting.

Acts 2:3 And there appeared unto them cloven tongues like as of fire, and it sat upon each of them.

Acts 2:4 And they were all filled with the Holy Ghost, and began to speak with other tongues, as the Spirit gave them utterance.

This current dispensation will end on the day when Christians are "caught up" (raptured) to meet the Lord in the air, that is, the air we breathe. At the rapture Jesus never touches the earth, so it is not His second coming:

1Thesalonians 4:16 For the Lord himself shall descend from heaven with a shout, with the voice of the archangel, and with the trump of God: and the dead in Christ shall rise first:

1Thesalonians 4:17 Then we which are alive and remain shall be caught up together with them in the clouds, to meet the Lord in the air: and so shall we ever be with the Lord.

1Thesalonians 4:18 Wherefore comfort one another with these words.

God laid down the principle doctrine that from those who have been given much; much will be required:

Luke 12:48 But he that knew not, and did commit things worthy of stripes, shall be beaten with few stripes. For unto whomsoever much is given, of him shall be much required: and to whom men have committed much, of him they will ask the more.

Those who have been born in this glorious land of the United States of America have already been given much. Our freedoms here in America should encourage you and me to use every ounce of our being to tell others of this great gift of God, His only begotten Son (John 3:16) and to spread this truth throughout the world. However, understand this that reaching out to the rest of the world should be secondary to getting your own house, family, and neighborhood to hear the gospel message. Many

What a Finish! What a Start! The Month Jesus Met Man's Need

Fred A Kuypers

want to spread the gospel overseas and to other parts while our own neighbors die and go to hell because they were neglected and not given the message of the cross.

Joshua 24:15 And if it seem evil unto you to serve the LORD, choose you this day whom ye will serve; whether the gods which your fathers served that were on the other side of the flood, or the gods of the Amorites, in whose land ye dwell: but as for me and my house, we will serve the LORD.

The Great Commission is given to all, and that begins with those closest to us.

Acts 1:8 But ye shall receive power, after that the Holy Ghost is come upon you: and ye shall be witnesses unto me both in Jerusalem, and in all Judaea, and in Samaria, and unto the uttermost part of the earth.

To follow the parable given on this day, the value of witnessing and winning souls to Christ is explained. It would be a wise thing to take the one precious pound of the gospel that God has given and produce ten new souls for Him. This is a very wise act in the eyes of God.

Proverbs 11:30 The fruit of the righteous is a tree of life; and he that winneth souls is wise.

Chapter 5

Nisan 5

Month of Nisan

1st day Yom Rishon Sunday	2nd day Yom Sheini Monday	3rd day Yom Shlishi Tuesday	4th day Yom R'vi'i Wednesday	5th day Yom Chamishi Thursday	6th day Yom Shishi Friday	Shabbat Yom Shabbat Saturday
Nisan 5th 6:00pm Monday begins	5th Nisan 6th 6:00am to 6:00pm Travel to Jerusalem Jesus and his disciples spend a full day of travel to Jerusalem from Jericho about 20 miles					

This chapter includes:

Matthew	Mark	Luke	John
20:29–20:34	10:46–10:52	19:28	

What a Finish! What a Start! The Month Jesus Met Man's Need

Fred A Kuypers

Trip from Jericho to Jerusalem about Thirty Kilometers

Jesus Travels to Jerusalem

6:00 p.m. on Sunday, the Fifth of Nisan
The Second Day of the week, Monday Begins

This night begins with the disciples not understanding some statements Jesus said. They did not understand why He stayed with Zacchaeus. But they did know one thing. After this night of sleep on the fifth of Nisan, Jesus said they would be going up to Jerusalem.

6:00 a.m. on Monday, the Fifth of Nisan

This morning, Jesus will continue the walk up to Jerusalem. Time has moved on and today will be the third day that Lazarus is in the grave. Jesus must rise and eat and start His travel early. He will leave a new friend, Zacchaeus, who was seeking Him and now has a new understanding of salvation as Jesus spent this past night at his house.

8:00 a.m. on Monday, the Fifth of Nisan

On the way out of Jericho, Jesus passes by two blind men and He stops. This will increase the swell of the crowds to see Him as it did yesterday.

Matthew describes it here:

Matthew 20:29 And as they departed from Jericho, a great multitude followed him.

Matthew 20:30 And, behold, two blind men sitting by the way side, when they heard that Jesus passed by, cried out, saying, Have mercy on us, O Lord, thou Son of David.

Mark moves his narrative right along by not explaining anything that happened in Jericho. Mark writes that Jesus is about to meet one of the blind men. Mark is the only Gospel that mentions his name. His name is Bartimaeus:

Mark 10:46 And they came to Jericho: and as he went out of Jericho with his disciples and a great number of people, blind Bartimaeus, the son of Timaeus, sat by the highway side begging.

Fred A Kuypers

Mark 10:47 And when he heard that it was Jesus of Nazareth, he began to cry out, and say, Jesus, thou Son of David, have mercy on me.

Matthew mentions two blind men at this point. Matthew is always precise in his numbers. Remember he was a tax collector and numbers are his business. In just two days Matthew will be the only Gospel writer to talk about two animals on Palm Day. He quotes from the Old Testament as Zachariah and Matthew are the only writers who mention the two animals that Jesus orders His disciples to find. Mark, Luke, and John speak only of one animal that Jesus comes riding into Jerusalem on. Matthew, writing to the Jews, is precise with his numbers and says there are two blind men on the way out of Jericho.

Mark focused solely on Bartimaeus. Mark is the only writer that quotes Jesus saying "thy faith hath made thee whole" But Matthew and Mark still say the same thing. This again points to no collusion between the two writers.

Matthew speaks in plural about two men who are blind that the crowd is rebuking:

Matthew 20:31 And the multitude rebuked them, because they should hold their peace: but they cried the more, saying, Have mercy on us, O Lord, thou Son of David.

Mark speaks to hold your peace and is in singular about one man, Bartimaeus, who is blind:

Mark 10:48 And many charged him that he should hold his peace: but he cried the more a great deal, Thou Son of David, have mercy on me.

Jesus saw their importunity. Earlier in Luke's Gospel, God used this word to describe someone who would not stop asking his neighbor for some bread in Luke 11:8. The blind men would not stop asking for Jesus to heal them. That is importunity!

Matthew says Jesus asks and then answers the blind men:

Matthew 20:32 And Jesus stood still, and called them, and said, What will ye that I shall do unto you?

Matthew 20:33 They say unto him, Lord, that our eyes may be opened.

Matthew 20:34 So Jesus had compassion on them, and touched their eyes: and immediately their eyes received sight, and they followed him.

Mark says Jesus asks Bartimaeus what He can do for him, and Bartimaeus is quick to respond to Jesus:

Mark 10:49 And Jesus stood still, and commanded him to be called. And they call the blind man, saying unto him, Be of good comfort, rise; he calleth thee.

Mark 10:50 And he, casting away his garment, rose, and came to Jesus.

Mark 10:51 And Jesus answered and said unto him, What wilt thou that I should do unto thee? The blind man said unto him, Lord, that I might receive my sight.

Mark says his faith hath made him whole just as Luke said a day earlier.

Mark 10:52 And Jesus said unto him, Go thy way; thy faith hath made thee whole. And immediately he received his sight, and followed Jesus in the way.

12:00 noon on Monday, the Fifth of Nisan
Third Day that Lazarus is in the Grave

The full day's walk from Jericho to Jerusalem continues. It takes Jesus the rest of the day to walk along the way with His disciples. Luke says Jesus ascended up to Jerusalem. This walk is heading southwesterly. North is always up on a map so most would say that walking south, you go down. Again, it is said that Jerusalem is always up.

Luke 19:28 And when he had thus spoken, he went before, ascending up to Jerusalem.

5:00 p.m. on Monday, the Fifth of Nisan
Third Day that Lazarus is in the Grave

As the walk from Jericho to Jerusalem comes to an end and the temple wall is in sight just beyond the Mount of Olives, Jesus and His followers are tired. A long day's journey has come to an end. Jesus is going to need this night of rest somewhere in or near Jerusalem as tomorrow a great event will be taking place. The raising of Lazarus from the grave will be witnessed by many including the chief priests and Pharisees. Even Caiaphas would prophesy that Jesus should die for the whole nation of Israel.

Chapter 6

Nisan 6

Month of Nisan

1st day Yom Rishon Sunday	2nd day Yom Sheini Monday	3rd day Yom Shlishi Tuesday	4th day Yom R'vi'i Wednesday	5th day Yom Chamishi Thursday	6th day Yom Shishi Friday	Shabbat Yom Shabbat Saturday
	Nisan 6th 6:00pm Tuesday begins	6th Nisan 7th 6:00am to 6:00pm Travel to Bethany. The short walk to Bethany and the resurrection of Lazarus witnessed by his sisters, Martha and Mary.				

This chapter includes:

Matthew	Mark	Luke	John
			11:17–11:53

What a Finish! What a Start! The Month Jesus Met Man's Need

Fred A Kuypers

From Jerusalem to Bethany— Less Than Two miles

6:00 p.m. on Monday, the Sixth of Nisan
The Third Day of the week, Tuesday Begins

Jesus and His disciples arrive in Jerusalem this night. They are somewhere in Jerusalem and will spend this night there. Tomorrow morning, they will walk from Jerusalem to Bethany, about two miles.

6:00 a.m. on Tuesday, the Sixth of Nisan

Upon rising this morning Jesus prepares to go to Bethany to see Martha and Mary. He knows that Lazarus, their brother, has been dead for four days. It has been six days since Martha and Mary sent word to Him that Lazarus was sick. Two days later, Lazarus died, and he was buried, and now he has been in the grave for four days.

9:00 a.m. on Tuesday, the Sixth of Nisan

Flesh begins to corrupt or decay shortly after death. After an hour or so, the tissue hardens, which is called *rigor mortis*.[14] Soon after this, the flesh will begin to decay. After three days, flesh will begin to stink and decay. Everyone knew this, and so by the fourth day of being dead in the grave, Lazarus's body should have begun to really stink. Jesus purposely waited for this day. The body of Lazarus would have four days to corrupt by now. Jesus wanted to reveal that He truly was God, and He was able to bring someone back to life after decomposition had been occurring for more than three days. Jesus will prove this once again at His own death and burial. He would be dead for more than three days even though this Holy One's body saw no corruption that is decomposition. This is why it is so important to know that He was in the grave longer than three days, or more than seventy-two hours.

Matthew 12:40 For as Jonas was three days and three nights in the whale's belly; so shall the Son of man be three days and three nights in the heart of the earth.

---

[14] https://medical-dictionary.thefreedictionary.com/rigor+mortis viewed January 5, 2017

Jesus arrived at Bethany where Lazarus, Martha, and Mary lived. Lazarus was dead and in the grave.

John 11:17 Then when Jesus came, he found that he had lain in the grave four days already.

Jesus walked to Bethany from Jerusalem. This is about a forty minute walk. Fifteen furlongs are a little less than two miles. A brisk walk is about three miles per hour. One furlong is an eighth of a mile.

John 11:18 Now Bethany was nigh unto Jerusalem, about fifteen furlongs off:

10:00 a.m. on Tuesday, the Sixth of Nisan

Many people came to comfort Mary and Martha, Lazarus's sisters. The three have become well known because of Jesus, and they have been real friends to Jesus throughout His public ministry.

John 11:19 And many of the Jews came to Martha and Mary, to comfort them concerning their brother.

Martha's emotions are running high. She does not know exactly how to approach Jesus and begins to question His arrival.

John 11:20 Then Martha, as soon as she heard that Jesus was coming, went and met him: but Mary sat still in the house.

John 11:21 Then said Martha unto Jesus, Lord, if thou hadst been here, my brother had not died.

Suddenly she understands who she is talking to. She realizes that Jesus had done so many miracles, and this would be another miracle He could perform.

John 11:22 But I know, that even now, whatsoever thou wilt ask of God, God will give it thee.

Jesus reassures Martha:

John 11:23 Jesus saith unto her, Thy brother shall rise again.

Martha misses the implication of Lazarus being raised from the dead; right here, right now! Instead she is thinking spiritually of the future resurrection. Jesus said six days earlier that the Son of God would be glorified by this meeting with Martha and Mary, and soon Lazarus. Jesus said back in John 11:4 that this sickness of Lazarus was not unto death but for the glory of God. Martha is a believer in the resurrection. But the resurrection she believes in is at the last day. She truly believes in a resurrection to come.

John 11:24 Martha saith unto him, I know that he shall rise again in the resurrection at the last day.

What a Finish! What a Start! The Month Jesus Met Man's Need

Fred A Kuypers

The resurrection was taught by many, even the Pharisees. The Pharisees believed in a resurrection, but the Sadducees did not:

Acts 23:8 For the Sadducees say that there is no resurrection, neither angel, nor spirit: but the Pharisees confess both.

Jesus was to reveal a special resurrection for the believer. Jesus said believers shall never die. He is referring to the second death—a spiritual death. Even though the body goes to the grave, it will be resurrected. This is why 1 Thessalonians 4:16 says "the dead shall rise first." Jesus explains that the resurrection is all about Him. The resurrection Jesus is referring to will occur on the last day of this church age. It is called the rapture of the saints.

John 11:25 Jesus said unto her, I am the resurrection, and the life: he that believeth in me, though he were dead, yet shall he live:

John 11:26 And whosoever liveth and believeth in me shall never die. Believest thou this?

The Gospel of John has seven "I am" verses that distinguish Jesus as the "I AM" This is the name taken by God at the burning bush with Moses. In the Gospel of John seven times Jesus refers to Himself as I AM; in other words, He takes the name of God:

1. Jesus says "I am" the bread of Life in John 6:35. This is something the Jews would know from their history. Bread coming down from heaven was called manna, which meant what is this? Exodus 16 is the first mention of manna, which God supplied as food to the Israelites for forty years when they wandered in the desert. In Numbers 11 tells us how the Jews really felt about God supplying this life-giving miracle. They hated it!

2. Jesus says "I am" the Light of the World. In John 8:12, Jesus says that you do not have to walk in darkness. If you have Jesus in your heart, you will always be in the light.

3. In John 8:58, Jesus says "before Abraham was, I AM."

4. John 10:7 quotes Jesus as saying "I am the door of the sheep."

5. Jesus says in John 10:11, "I am the good shepherd."

6. Jesus says in John 11:25 that "I am the resurrection and the life."

7. And finally Jesus says, "I am the way, the truth, and the life. No man comes to the Father but by me" in John 14:6.

In the KJV, Jesus declares that He is the great I AM many times. The translators added the word "he" for proper English. A review of these verses will declare that Jesus continually called Himself I AM:

- John 4:26 Jesus saith unto her, I that speak unto thee am *he.*
- John 8:24 I said therefore unto you, that ye shall die in your sins: for if ye believe not that I am *he,* ye shall die in your sins.
- John 8:28 Then said Jesus unto them, When ye have lifted up the Son of man, then shall ye know that I am *he,* and *that* I do nothing of myself; but as my Father hath taught me, I speak these things.
- John 9:9 Some said, This is he: others *said,* He is like him: *but* he said, I am *he.*
- John 13:19 Now I tell you before it come, that, when it is come to pass, ye may believe that I am *he.*
- John 18:5 They answered him, Jesus of Nazareth. Jesus saith unto them, I am *he.* And Judas also, which betrayed him, stood with them.
- John 18:6 As soon then as he had said unto them, I am *he,* they went backward, and fell to the ground.
- John 18:8 Jesus answered, I have told you that I am *he:* if therefore ye seek me, let these go their way:

11:00 a.m. on Tuesday, the Sixth of Nisan

At this point in the gospel of John, Martha contends that she is a believer:

John 11:27 She saith unto him, Yea, Lord: I believe that thou art the Christ, the Son of God, which should come into the world.

John 11:28 And when she had so said, she went her way, and called Mary her sister secretly, saying, The Master is come, and calleth for thee.

Her sister Mary comes to Jesus and expresses her faith in Him:

John 11:29 As soon as she heard that, she arose quickly, and came unto him.

John 11:30 Now Jesus was not yet come into the town, but was in that place where Martha met him.

John 11:31 The Jews then which were with her in the house, and comforted her, when they saw Mary, that she rose up hastily and went out, followed her, saying, She goeth unto the grave to weep there.

John 11:32 Then when Mary was come where Jesus was, and saw him, she fell down at his feet, saying unto him, Lord, if thou hadst been here, my brother had not died.

Jesus knows that Mary is hurting. He had such a close, family-like relationship with Mary and Martha and Lazarus.

John 11:33 When Jesus therefore saw her weeping, and the Jews also weeping which came with her, he groaned in the spirit, and was troubled,

Jesus groaned in the spirit? Could Jesus be weak here? Some skeptics say Jesus was very weak here and showed frailty. I disagree. He certainly showed compassion. This is what the scriptures say:

Hebrews 4:15 For we have not an high priest which cannot be touched with the feeling of our infirmities; but was in all points tempted like as we are, yet without sin.

Jesus was able to groan here without sin. It is important to know that God will not tempt anyone above what they are able to bear:

1 Corinthians 10:13 There hath no temptation taken you but such as is common to man: but God is faithful, who will not suffer you to be tempted above that ye are able; but will with the temptation also make a way to escape, that ye may be able to bear it.

Jesus shows His compassion and love for Lazarus with emotion:

John 11:34 And said, Where have ye laid him? They said unto him, Lord, come and see.

12:00 noon on Tuesday, the Sixth of Nisan
Fourth Day Lazarus is in the Grave

The shortest verse in the Bible is:

John 11:35 Jesus wept.

Jesus wept with compassion and love.

John 11:36 Then said the Jews, Behold how he loved him!

As always, there are skeptics in the crowd, and Jesus must deal with them.

John 11:37 And some of them said, Could not this man, which opened the eyes of the blind, have caused that even this man should not have died?

John 11:38 Jesus therefore again groaning in himself cometh to the grave. It was a cave, and a stone lay upon it.

Jesus again groans, but I believe this was a righteously indignant kind of a groan. Notice that the words "in the spirit" are not here. Jesus was going to show the skeptics His power over death:

John 11:39 Jesus said, Take ye away the stone. Martha, the sister of him that was dead, saith unto him, Lord, by this time he stinketh: for he hath been dead four days.

John 11:40 Jesus saith unto her, Said I not unto thee, that, if thou wouldest believe, thou shouldest see the glory of God?

Jesus begins to pray. He says He knows that God has heard Him and again declares His submission to the Father by stating that it was the Father who sent Him.

John 11:41 Then they took away the stone from the place where the dead was laid. And Jesus lifted up his eyes, and said, Father, I thank thee that thou hast heard me.

John 11:42 And I knew that thou hearest me always: but because of the people which stand by I said it, that they may believe that thou hast sent me.

John 11:43 And when he thus had spoken, he cried with a loud voice, Lazarus, come forth.

Jesus raises Lazarus from the dead.

John 11:44 And he that was dead came forth, bound hand and foot with graveclothes: and his face was bound about with a napkin. Jesus saith unto them, Loose him, and let him go.

Some were astonished to see this, but many were saved from this point as they believed on Him:

John 11:45 Then many of the Jews which came to Mary, and had seen the things which Jesus did, believed on him.

12:30 p.m. on Tuesday, the Sixth of Nisan
Lazarus is Raised from the Grave

Others were not as believing, so they went to the chief priests and Pharisees who received this information and had to decide what to do about this Jesus.

John 11:46 But some of them went their ways to the Pharisees, and told them what things Jesus had done.

The chief priests and the Pharisees called a quick council and gathered together:

John 11:47 Then gathered the chief priests and the Pharisees a council, and said, What do we? for this man doeth many miracles.

John 11:48 If we let him thus alone, all men will believe on him: and the Romans shall come and take away both our place and nation.

Caiaphas steps up to speak. He speaks with an attitude:

John 11:49 And one of them, named Caiaphas, being the high priest that same year, said unto them, Ye know nothing at all,

John 11:50 Nor consider that it is expedient for us, that one man should die for the people, and that the whole nation perish not.

At this time Caiaphas was the high priest. He was taking over for Annas the high priest who was Caiaphas's father-in-law. Annas was grooming his son-in-law to be the upcoming high priest.

John 18:13 And led him away to Annas first; for he was father in law to Caiaphas, which was the high priest that same year.

Annas had others who were related to him, but only Caiaphas is listed as a high priest:

Acts 4:6 And Annas the high priest, and Caiaphas, and John, and Alexander, and as many as were of the kindred of the high priest, were gathered together at Jerusalem.

Caiaphas now prophesies about Jesus:

John 11:51 And this spake he not of himself: but being high priest that year, he prophesied that Jesus should die for that nation;

John 11:52 And not for that nation only, but that also he should gather together in one the children of God that were scattered abroad.

1:00 p.m. on Tuesday, the Sixth of Nisan

The pressure to apprehend Jesus was going to increase from this time on. The chief priests and Pharisees now seek a way to trap Jesus and kill Him.

John 11:53 Then from that day forth they took counsel together for to put him to death.

Here it is said that they "took counsel" to put Him to death. Later on the tenth of Nisan, Matthew's narrative will declare that Jesus is finally chosen to be put to death. This coincides with the Passover lamb that was selected on the tenth of Nisan to prepare for the Passover to take place on the fourteenth of Nisan. On the tenth of Nisan, in just four days, Caiaphas the high priest will select Jesus to be the sacrificial Lamb. But this night Jesus decided to go into the wild country of Ephraim to get away from the Pharisees who are hunting for Him.

Have you trusted in the sacrifice of the Lord Jesus Christ? By faith, do you believe that He could pay for your sins? Do you believe that Jesus Christ was killed on the cross and was buried and after three full days rose again? That is the Gospel message for all to believe!

Chapter 7

Nisan 7

Month of Nisan

1st day Yom Rishon Sunday	2nd day Yom Sheini Monday	3rd day Yom Shlishi Tuesday	4th day Yom R'vi'i Wednesday	5th day Yom Chamishi Thursday	6th day Yom Shishi Friday	Shabbat Yom Shabbat Saturday
		Nisan 7th 6:00pm Wednesday begins	7th Nisan 8th 6:00am to 6:00pm Travel to Ephraim The time in the wilderness of Ephraim which lies to the north of Bethany and the Mount of Olives.			

This chapter includes:

Matthew	Mark	Luke	John
			11:54–11:57

What a Finish! What a Start! The Month Jesus Met Man's Need

Fred A Kuypers

From Bethany to Ephraim

Jesus goes to Ephraim

6:00 p.m. on Tuesday, the Seventh of Nisan

The Fourth Day of the Week, Wednesday Begins

Ephraim is a wilderness land in which our Lord retired this night with his disciples. After He had raised Lazarus, and when the priests were conspiring against him, He needed to go where many would not want to go. Ephraim was in the wild, uncultivated hill country to the north of Jerusalem[15] and the Mount of Olives, with Jericho to the east and Bethel to the west. This country would be near the road Jesus would take from Zacchaeus's home in Jericho on the walk to Jerusalem. Bethany is on the south side of the Mount of Olives, and Ephraim is the land to the north. The city called Ephraim where He would spend this night was north of Jerusalem. This was a tough walk over hilly terrain. Not much else could be accomplished this day.

John 11:54 Jesus therefore walked no more openly among the Jews; but went thence unto a country near to the wilderness, into a city called Ephraim, and there continued with his disciples.

During this night in Ephraim, the feast of Passover was drawing near. It was just one week before the night when the Passover meal could first be eaten.

John 11:55 And the Jews' passover was nigh at hand: and many went out of the country up to Jerusalem before the passover, to purify themselves.

Ephraim was the brother of Manasseh, and both were the children of Joseph. Joseph received a double portion of land and it was given to his two sons to keep the total land portions at twelve, The Levites, being the priests of Israel, could own no land. This was done because of Joseph's faithfulness to God when he was sold into slavery. God blessed Joseph so much because of his faithfulness. Not only was he Pharaoh's right-hand man with riches and power, but God gave him a double portion of the land with his two sons each receiving a portion.

The land of Ephraim, however, united with the northern tribes of Israel, and God removed his blessing from all ten tribes of the north. Remember only two tribes remained faithful to God and against Jeroboam's false god set up in the cities of

---

[15] http://bibleatlas.org/ephraim.htm viewed January 31, 2017

Bethel and in Dan as stated in 1 Kings 12. The two faithful tribes were Judah and Benjamin. The city of Bethel is in this land of Ephraim where Deborah judged Israel:

Judges 4:5 And she dwelt under the palm tree of Deborah between Ramah and Bethel in mount Ephraim: and the children of Israel came up to her for judgment.

8:00 a.m. on Wednesday, the Seventh of Nisan

The time Jesus spent in Ephraim is not mentioned much in the scriptures. Ephraim was a wilderness area a long walk from Jerusalem and a good place to avoid the religious leaders who were trying to trap Him. In going to Ephraim, Jesus would avoid those who were looking for Him.

John 11:56 Then sought they for Jesus, and spake among themselves, as they stood in the temple, What think ye, that he will not come to the feast?

The prophets would speak about Ephraim. They did not have much good to say about Ephraim, as it was said the people had pride and stoutness of heart:

Isaiah 9:9 And all the people shall know, even Ephraim and the inhabitant of Samaria, that say in the pride and stoutness of heart,

Isaiah was particularly vocal about the sins of Ephraim in chapters 7, 9, and 28.

12:00 noon on Wednesday, the Seventh of Nisan

As Passover approached, many would need to be cleansed and to purify themselves. Numbers 9 has the laws for the purifying before the Passover feast and for the days of unleavened bread.

Numbers 9:1 And the LORD spake unto Moses in the wilderness of Sinai, in the first month of the second year after they were come out of the land of Egypt, saying,

Numbers 9:2 Let the children of Israel also keep the passover at his appointed season.

Numbers 9:3 In the fourteenth day of this month, at even, ye shall keep it in his appointed season: according to all the rites of it, and according to all the ceremonies thereof, shall ye keep it.

Numbers 9:4 And Moses spake unto the children of Israel, that they should keep the passover.

Numbers 9:5 And they kept the passover on the fourteenth day of the first month at even in the wilderness of Sinai: according to all that the LORD commanded Moses, so did the children of Israel.

3:00 p.m. on Wednesday, the Seventh of Nisan

Jesus was well hidden this day after walking in the wilderness of Ephraim. He decided to return and spend the upcoming night with His friends Martha, Mary, and Lazarus. They lived just over the other side of the Mount of Olives. This is a long journey again; very dangerous and always with the chance of running into more religious leaders who would want to capture Him.

John 11:57 Now both the chief priests and the Pharisees had given a commandment, that, if any man knew where he were, he should shew it, that they might take him.

The thought of how and when they might take Him was haunting the chief priests. They were conspiring with anyone who was close to Jesus. Soon, in days to follow, Judas would become the focal point as the biggest traitor in history. Judas was one who walked with Jesus and knew Him for the three years of Christ's public ministry. But he never had a new birth experience with the Christ he was following. What about you? Have you known Jesus Christ for a long time? If so, have you ever had this new-birth experience that Jesus spoke of?

John 3:3 Jesus answered and said unto him, Verily, verily, I say unto thee, Except a man be born again, he cannot see the kingdom of God.

If you read this book and do not see the evidence of a born-again believer and a love for Jesus Christ and His Word in your life, then read on! This should be enough to motivate anyone to understand this life of Jesus Christ and His desire (and the desire of those who are saved) to do the will of the Father.

Chapter 8

Nisan 8

Month of Nisan

1st day Yom Rishon Sunday	2nd day Yom Sheini Monday	3rd day Yom Shlishi Tuesday	4th day Yom R'vi'i Wednesday	5th day Yom Chamishi Thursday	6th day Yom Shishi Friday	Shabbat Yom Shabbat Saturday
			Nisan 8th 6:00pm Thursday begins	8th Nisan 9th 6:00am to 6:00pm Travel back to Bethany. Supper at Martha and Mary's house. Jesus presents Himself as the King of kings riding on a colt through the Golden Gate.		

This chapter includes:

Matthew	Mark	Luke	John
21:1–21:11	11:1–11:11	19:29–19:44	12:1–12:19

What a Finish! What a Start! The Month Jesus Met Man's Need

Fred A Kuypers

From Ephraim to Bethany at Night and Bethphage in the Morning

Six days before Passover; Palm Thursday

6:00 p.m. on Wednesday, the Eighth of Nisan

The Fifth Day of the Week, Thursday Begins Palm Day (known erroneously as Palm Sunday)

This night Jesus will have supper with Lazarus in Bethany. The timing of this night is important to understand when all the events that are about to take place will transpire. Six days before the Passover can be easily understood if the Passover is Tuesday night, the fourteenth of Nisan, at 6:00 p.m. With Lazarus already raised, Jesus will spend some time with His friends here in Bethany at the home of Mary, Martha, and Lazarus.

John 12:1 Then Jesus six days before the Passover came to Bethany, where Lazarus was which had been dead, whom he raised from the dead.

Jesus had supper with Mary, Martha, and Lazarus at their house in Bethany. Supper is the meal served at 6:00 p.m. usually the last meal before it is time to retire. Again, Martha is a take-action type of person. Here she serves the supper to all. But Mary, her sister, is not assisting with any of the serving:

John 12:2 There they made him a supper; and Martha served: but Lazarus was one of them that sat at the table with him.

7:00 p.m. on Wednesday, the Eighth of Nisan Palm Day

After supper, Jesus' feet are anointed. This was a custom in those days, and Mary, who was a different kind of person than her sister Martha, gets a pound of some very expensive ointment (Song of Solomon1:3) and anoints the feet of Jesus. This ointment of spikenard was extremely fragrant and expensive. This ointment was a type of the sweet savor of Christ, in the administration of what will become the Gospel to the whole world. This anointing is not like that which would take place a few days from this time when Jesus will be at Simon the leper's house in Bethany as recorded in Mark chapter 14 when at that time Christ's head is anointed.

John 12:3 Then took Mary a pound of ointment of spikenard, very costly, and anointed the feet of Jesus, and wiped his feet with her hair: and the house was filled with the odour of the ointment.

In verse two above, those who sat at the table refers to the disciples of Jesus who were at the meal with Martha and Mary and Lazarus. If not during the meal, the disciples were there after the meal. Scripture declares that Judas argued about the cost of the ointment used to anoint the feet of Jesus:

John 12:4 Then saith one of his disciples, Judas Iscariot, Simon's *son*, which should betray him,

John 12:5 Why was not this ointment sold for three hundred pence, and given to the poor?

John 12:6 This he said, not that he cared for the poor; but because he was a thief, and had the bag, and bare what was put therein.

John 12:7 Then said Jesus, Let her alone: against the day of my burying hath she kept this.

John 12:8 For the poor always ye have with you; but me ye have not always.

8:00 p.m. on Wednesday, the Eighth of Nisan

Palm Day

Again the crowds are circulating around Jesus. Remember they are not coming because they want to be with Jesus or because they love the Savior, but they want to see the miracles or the result of the miracles. In this case it is Lazarus being raised from the dead whom they wanted to see.

John 12:9 Much people of the Jews therefore knew that he was there: and they came not for Jesus' sake only, but that they might see Lazarus also, whom he had raised from the dead.

The crowds have discouraged the religious leaders so much that they are talking about killing Lazarus. They want to keep the Jews from believing in Jesus. The religious leaders keep trying to entrap Him.

John 12:10 But the chief priests consulted that they might put Lazarus also to death;

John 12:11 Because that by reason of him many of the Jews went away, and believed on Jesus.

This night, many Jews would go to sleep with a different view of Jesus. They would believe on Jesus, but don't forget that in a few days, every one of them would turn on Him and shout "Crucify Him."

6:00 a.m. on Thursday, the Eighth of Nisan
Palm Day

As seen in the following verse, the next day after Jesus came to Bethany will be the morning of the eighth of Nisan. Last night, when the eighth of Nisan began, He had supper with Mary, Martha, and Lazarus as recorded earlier. Today Jesus will fulfill a prophecy in scripture by the prophet Zechariah as He enters Jerusalem. Again, Bethany is on the Mount of Olives which is a Sabbath's day journey to Jerusalem according to Acts 1:12.

John 12:12 On the next day much people that were come to the feast, when they heard that Jesus was coming to Jerusalem,

8:00 a.m. on Thursday, the Eighth of Nisan
Palm Day

Early this morning, many things begin to happen. It is going to be a fulfilling prophetic day. Jesus Christ will present Himself as the King of kings to all at the temple. Bethphage is a town on the northeast slope of the Mount of Olives. It is a Sabbath's day journey from Jerusalem, which is about two thousand cubits or three thousand feet. He probably traveled through Bethphage on the same road that connects Jericho and Jerusalem a few days earlier. Departing from Bethany and heading north to the road from Jericho to Jerusalem, He arrived at Bethphage, which is less than a thirty minute walk to Jerusalem. Jesus instructs two of His disciples to go and locate two animals, an ass (donkey) and a colt:

Matthew 21:1 And when they drew nigh unto Jerusalem, and were come to Bethphage, unto the mount of Olives, then sent Jesus two disciples,

Matthew 21:2 Saying unto them, Go into the village over against you, and straightway ye shall find an ass tied, and a colt with her: loose them, and bring them unto me.

Why did Matthew describe Jesus wanting two animals? The terrain around the Mount of Olives is hilly with many steep ups and downs. Jesus would need the strength of the donkey to carry Him up and down and through the Kidron Valley that separates the Mount of Olives from the temple mount. However, there is an alternative reason for the two animals. Jesus is about to switch from using the Jews to express God's plan to using the Gentiles. As Jesus approaches the Eastern Gate, Matthew describes the need for two animals. However, Mark and Luke talk only of the colt.

Matthew describes the event:

Matthew 21:3 And if any man say ought unto you, ye shall say, The Lord hath need of them; and straightway he will send them.

Matthew 21:4 All this was done, that it might be fulfilled which was spoken by the prophet, saying,

Matthew 21:5 Tell ye the daughter of Sion, Behold, thy King cometh unto thee, meek, and sitting upon an ass, and a colt the foal of an ass.

As He approaches the Eastern Gate, He dismounts the donkey and mounts the colt so that the prophecy in Zechariah will be fulfilled. The donkey symbolizes the Old Testament and the burden of the law where God gave the people what they asked for when they asked to be put under the law (Exodus 19:8) symbolized by this beast of burden, the ass. However, to enter through the Beautiful Gate, Jesus switches to the young colt that was not yet broke. This unbroken colt symbolized God's switch to the Gentiles to bear the good news of the Gospel, the wild olive tree of Romans chapter 11, which describes the Gentiles about to be grafted in with Jesus and the beginning of the church age. Matthew, who primarily has a Jewish audience, describes this switch mentioning both, the ass and the untamed colt that the Jews should have known already from the prophet Zechariah. But Mark and Luke who primarily write to the Gentiles in more detail and explain only the unbroken colt with the Lord riding on this colt, symbolizing the switch from Israel to the church which is to come about in a little over fifty days on the day of Pentecost.

Mark describes this event:

Mark 11:1 And when they came nigh to Jerusalem, unto Bethphage and Bethany, at the mount of Olives, he sendeth forth two of his disciples,

Mark 11:2 And saith unto them, Go your way into the village over against you: and as soon as ye be entered into it, ye shall find a colt tied, whereon never man sat; loose him, and bring him.

Mark 11:3 And if any man say unto you, Why do ye this? say ye that the Lord hath need of him; and straightway he will send him hither.

Luke describes this event:

Luke 19:29 And it came to pass, when he was come nigh to Bethphage and Bethany, at the mount called the mount of Olives, he sent two of his disciples,

Luke 19:30 Saying, Go ye into the village over against you; in the which at your entering ye shall find a colt tied, whereon yet never man sat: loose him, and bring him hither.

Luke 19:31 And if any man ask you, Why do ye loose him? thus shall ye say unto him, Because the Lord hath need of him.

What a Finish! What a Start! The Month Jesus Met Man's Need

Fred A Kuypers

9:00 a.m. on Thursday, the Eighth of Nisan
Palm Day

The disciples obey Jesus' command and go to find the donkey and the colt. This fulfills the prophecy of scripture in the book of Zechariah:

Zechariah 9:9 Rejoice greatly, O daughter of Zion; shout, O daughter of Jerusalem: behold, thy King cometh unto thee: he is just, and having salvation; lowly, and riding upon an ass, and upon a colt the foal of an ass.

Matthew records:

Matthew 21:6 And the disciples went, and did as Jesus commanded them,

Matthew 21:7 And brought the ass, and the colt, and put on them their clothes, and they set him thereon.

Mark records:

Mark 11:4 And they went their way, and found the colt tied by the door without in a place where two ways met; and they loose him.

Mark 11:5 And certain of them that stood there said unto them, What do ye, loosing the colt?

Mark 11:6 And they said unto them even as Jesus had commanded: and they let them go.

Mark 11:7 And they brought the colt to Jesus, and cast their garments on him; and he sat upon him.

Luke records:

Luke 19:32 And they that were sent went their way, and found even as he had said unto them.

Luke 19:33 And as they were loosing the colt, the owners thereof said unto them, Why loose ye the colt?

Luke 19:34 And they said, The Lord hath need of him.

Luke 19:35 And they brought him to Jesus: and they cast their garments upon the colt, and they set Jesus thereon.

The retrieving of the donkey and the colt takes some time since they must locate them, corral them, halter them, and then walk them back to Bethphage where Jesus was located which would take several hours. John also will have something to say about the palm branches on this day and about the colt but not the ass or donkey as prophesied in Zechariah.

12:00 noon on Thursday, the Eighth of Nisan

Palm Day

Palm Sunday is really Palm Thursday. Erroneously, many have followed the false teaching that this day must be on the tenth of Nisan, the day the lamb is chosen according to Exodus 12. However, on this day Jesus presents Himself, but He is not chosen by the high priest. He will be selected on the tenth of Nisan as explained at the end of chapter ten of this book. The lamb then will be sacrificed on the fourteenth of Nisan. The timetable developed here has the day of triumphal entry into Jerusalem as Thursday, the eighth of Nisan. The contention now is that the selection to kill Jesus was not made until after the Olivet Discourse on the tenth of Nisan as presented in Matthew 26:3-4, two days after this eighth day of Nisan.

I contend that the Lord Jesus Christ offered Himself as the Lamb of God and the King of kings and the Lord of lords without spot or blemish on the eighth of Nisan, a Thursday, and He was selected by the high priest on the tenth of Nisan, a Saturday, to be the lamb that was to be slain.

Here is what took place as the scriptures reveal. This day that the whole world calls Palm Sunday is in reality Palm Thursday, or the fifth day of the week.

Matthew has the scripture:

Matthew 21:8 And a very great multitude spread their garments in the way; others cut down branches from the trees, and strawed them in the way.

Matthew 21:9 And the multitudes that went before, and that followed, cried, saying, Hosanna to the Son of David: Blessed is he that cometh in the name of the Lord; Hosanna in the highest.

Matthew 21:10 And when he was come into Jerusalem, all the city was moved, saying, Who is this?

Matthew 21:11 And the multitude said, This is Jesus the prophet of Nazareth of Galilee.

Mark has the scripture:

Mark 11:8 And many spread their garments in the way: and others cut down branches off the trees, and strawed them in the way.

Mark 11:9 And they that went before, and they that followed, cried, saying, Hosanna; Blessed is he that cometh in the name of the Lord:

Mark 11:10 Blessed be the kingdom of our father David, that cometh in the name of the Lord: Hosanna in the highest.

Luke has the scripture:

Luke 19:36 And as he went, they spread their clothes in the way.

Luke 19:37 And when he was come nigh, even now at the descent of the mount of Olives, the whole multitude of the disciples began to rejoice and praise God with a loud voice for all the mighty works that they had seen;

Luke 19:38 Saying, Blessed be the King that cometh in the name of the Lord: peace in heaven, and glory in the highest.

Finally describing the branches coming from Palm trees, John has the scripture:

John 12:13 Took branches of palm trees, and went forth to meet him, and cried, Hosanna: Blessed is the King of Israel that cometh in the name of the Lord.

The Pharisees were not happy to hear the people crying "Hosanna: Blessed is the King of Israel." They requested that Jesus silence the multitude:

Luke 19:39 And some of the Pharisees from among the multitude said unto him, Master, rebuke thy disciples.

However, in another part of scripture, the Word of God declares that all creation groans and travails for the return of the Creator. Jesus knew that those who believed in Him could not hold their peace:

Romans 8:21 Because the creature itself also shall be delivered from the bondage of corruption into the glorious liberty of the children of God.

Romans 8:22 For we know that the whole creation groaneth and travaileth in pain together until now.

So Jesus explains His creation by saying even the rocks may cry out:

Luke 19:40 And he answered and said unto them, I tell you that, if these should hold their peace, the stones would immediately cry out.

John has more to add to this glorious moment:

John 12:14 And Jesus, when he had found a young ass, sat thereon; as it is written,

John 12:15 Fear not, daughter of Sion: behold, thy King cometh, sitting on an ass's colt.

John 12:16 These things understood not his disciples at the first: but when Jesus was glorified, then remembered they that these things were written of him, and that they had done these things unto him.

John 12:17 The people therefore that was with him when he called Lazarus out of his grave, and raised him from the dead, bare record.

John 12:18 For this cause the people also met him, for that they heard that he had done this miracle.

John 12:19 The Pharisees therefore said among themselves, Perceive ye how ye prevail nothing? behold, the world is gone after him.

4:00 p.m. on Thursday, the Eighth of Nisan
Palm Day

Luke the physician again shows the humanity of Christ as He now weeps over the city but more so, He weeps over His own people, the Jews, who lived in the city. By switching to the colt that no man had ridden, Jesus knows what is about to happen to the Jewish race over the next two thousand years. He weeps knowing they will be hunted down and tortured and killed by the ruling religious leaders of the day for what they did to Jesus at Calvary.

Luke 19:41 And when he was come near, he beheld the city, and wept over it,

Luke 19:42 Saying, If thou hadst known, even thou, at least in this thy day, the things which belong unto thy peace! but now they are hid from thine eyes.

Luke 19:43 For the days shall come upon thee, that thine enemies shall cast a trench about thee, and compass thee round, and keep thee in on every side,

Luke 19:44 And shall lay thee even with the ground, and thy children within thee; and they shall not leave in thee one stone upon another; because thou knewest not the time of thy visitation.

5:00 p.m. on Thursday, the Eighth of Nisan
Palm Day

Notice that Mark's Gospel is very concise about this afternoon that Jesus spends in Jerusalem's temple. Jesus is seeing all the corruption and all the wheeling and dealings for filthy lucre's sake. He looks around the temple and leaves but not without righteous anger. Earlier in Mark 3:5, the scriptures say that Jesus could become angry with men doubting Him. Jesus is angry with how the temple is being used. He will show His displeasure when He comes back tomorrow.

Mark 11:11 And Jesus entered into Jerusalem, and into the temple: and when he had looked round about upon all things, and now the eventide was come, he went out unto Bethany with the twelve.

Remember it is about a forty-five minute walk from Jerusalem to Bethany, or about fifteen furlongs. Enough time to think about who Jesus really is. Is He the King of kings in your life? Is He your Lord?

Chapter 9

Nisan 9

Month of Nisan

1st day Yom Rishon Sunday	2nd day Yom Sheini Monday	3rd day Yom Shlishi Tuesday	4th day Yom R'vi'i Wednesday	5th day Yom Chamishi Thursday	6th day Yom Shishi Friday	Shabbat Yom Shabbat Saturday
				Nisan 9th 6:00pm Friday begins	9th Nisan 10th 6:00am to 6:00pm Travel back to Bethany. An interesting trip to the fig tree. Time in the Temple similar to the time when Jesus was angered by how His Father's house was being used.	

This chapter includes:

Matthew	Mark	Luke	John
21:12–21:17	11:12–11:18	19:45–19:48	

What a Finish! What a Start! The Month Jesus Met Man's Need

Fred A Kuypers

Bethany to the Temple Mount in Jerusalem

Five days before Passover; Jesus Overthrows the Tables and the High Priest Seeks to Destroy Him.

6:00 p.m. on Thursday, the Ninth of Nisan

The Sixth Day of the Week, Friday Begins

Following the time frame established in the last chapter when John stated that there was six days before the Passover, the countdown has begun. Now five days before Passover, Jesus had several places where He would stay in Bethany. Simon the leper had a home there. So did Lazarus and his sisters. It was where Jesus spent many a night when He was in Jerusalem. There were many nights He just slept on the Mount of Olives also. But this night He lodged in Bethany.

7:00 a.m. on Friday, the Ninth of Nisan

This morning, Mark states that Jesus, returning to Jerusalem from Bethany, has come to the fig tree, the emblem of the people of Israel. No fruit indicates that there will be no more Jews who, as the chosen nation, no longer needed to proclaim the Messiah; God would no longer be dealing exclusively with the Jews. Since Matthew is the Gospel to the Jew and Mark to the Gentiles, Mark will give more insight as to the relationship of the fig tree and the Jew. Matthew will not, as the Jews already know of this relationship as taught by Jeremiah.

Mark 11:12 And on the morrow, when they were come from Bethany, he was hungry:

Mark 11:13 And seeing a fig tree afar off having leaves, he came, if haply he might find any thing thereon: and when he came to it, he found nothing but leaves; for the time of figs was not yet.

Mark 11:14 And Jesus answered and said unto it, No man eat fruit of thee hereafter for ever. And his disciples heard it.

The humanity and deity of Christ are revealed here. His humanity showing He was hungry and His deity showing that He can control nature. The time of the figs was not yet. This means that the Jews were not ready to accept Jesus as their Messiah.

The fig tree in scripture represents the nation of Israel centered in Jerusalem. The figs are the Jewish people themselves. Jesus was showing that no more prophets, no more man of God, and no more King of kings would come from Israel. Jesus had fulfilled all, and the nation of Israel centered in Jerusalem would not have any prophet come out of her again. The oracles of God would be completed with this last generation of Jews who had been alive when Jesus would walk the earth. The eight Jewish men to pen the final twenty-seven books of the New Testament would be the last. Jeremiah tells about the figs:

Jeremiah 24:1 The LORD shewed me, and, behold, two baskets of figs were set before the temple of the LORD, after that Nebuchadrezzar king of Babylon had carried away captive Jeconiah the son of Jehoiakim king of Judah, and the princes of Judah, with the carpenters and smiths, from Jerusalem, and had brought them to Babylon.

Jeremiah 24:2 One basket had very good figs, even like the figs that are first ripe: and the other basket had very naughty figs, which could not be eaten, they were so bad.

Jeremiah 24:3 Then said the LORD unto me, What seest thou, Jeremiah? And I said, Figs; the good figs, very good; and the evil, very evil, that cannot be eaten, they are so evil.

Jeremiah 24:4 Again the word of the LORD came unto me, saying,

Jeremiah 24:5 Thus saith the LORD, the God of Israel; Like these good figs, so will I acknowledge them that are carried away captive of Judah, whom I have sent out of this place into the land of the Chaldeans for their good.

Jeremiah 24:6 For I will set mine eyes upon them for good, and I will bring them again to this land: and I will build them, and not pull them down; and I will plant them, and not pluck them up.

Jeremiah 24:7 And I will give them an heart to know me, that I am the LORD: and they shall be my people, and I will be their God: for they shall return unto me with their whole heart.

Jeremiah 24:8 And as the evil figs, which cannot be eaten, they are so evil; surely thus saith the LORD, So will I give Zedekiah the king of Judah, and his princes, and the residue of Jerusalem, that remain in this land, and them that dwell in the land of Egypt:

Jeremiah 24:9 And I will deliver them to be removed into all the kingdoms of the earth for their hurt, to be a reproach and a proverb, a taunt and a curse, in all places whither I shall drive them.

Jeremiah 24:10 And I will send the sword, the famine, *and the* pestilence, among them, till they be consumed from off the land that I gave unto them and to their fathers.

Jeremiah describes the figs as representing the Jews. The laws of the Old Testament were written primarily to the Jews for instruction and sacrifice. Matthew, writing primarily to the Jews, says over and over that the message of Jesus as the Christ or the Messiah was to go to the Jews because they should have been able to recognize Him:

Matthew 10:5 These twelve Jesus sent forth, and commanded them, saying, Go not into the way of the Gentiles, and into any city of the Samaritans enter ye not:

Matthew 10:6 But go rather to the lost sheep of the house of Israel.

Matthew also stated:

Matthew 15:24 But he answered and said, I am not sent but unto the lost sheep of the house of Israel.

9:00 a.m. on Friday, the Ninth of Nisan

Many times during His life on earth, Jesus went to the temple. Even though He was hunted and badgered by the chief priests, the Pharisees, the Sadducees, and the scribes, Jesus was not afraid to minister to the people. There is no need to be afraid to present the Gospel to anyone. This is following in Jesus' footsteps.

Mark tells of two encounters with the fig tree. To know that is very important. Mark does much more explaining of Jewish tradition. Since Matthew's audience was Jewish and they already observed the Torah, many things did not have to be repeated. The fig tree symbolizes that God will soon turn to the Gentiles instead of the Jews to call out a people for His name. This will be seen tomorrow in the morning on the tenth of Nisan.

10:00 a.m. on Friday, the Ninth of Nisan

Jesus presented Himself as the King yesterday, but He did not like what He had encountered in the temple. Tomorrow would be the Sabbath so the merchants were selling what they could today for tomorrow's sacrifices. People were buying and selling within His house, when the temple should have been a house of prayer. So, this day He decides to do something about it!

Matthew:

Matthew 21:12 And Jesus went into the temple of God, and cast out all them that sold and bought in the temple, and overthrew the tables of the moneychangers, and the seats of them that sold doves,

Matthew 21:13 And said unto them, It is written, My house shall be called the house of prayer; but ye have made it a den of thieves.

Mark:

Mark 11:15 And they come to Jerusalem: and Jesus went into the temple, and began to cast out them that sold and bought in the temple, and overthrew the tables of the moneychangers, and the seats of them that sold doves;

Mark 11:16 And would not suffer that any man should carry any vessel through the temple.

Mark 11:17 And he taught, saying unto them, Is it not written, My house shall be called of all nations the house of prayer? but ye have made it a den of thieves.

Luke:

Luke 19:45 And he went into the temple, and began to cast out them that sold therein, and them that bought;

Luke 19:46 Saying unto them, It is written, My house is the house of prayer: but ye have made it a den of thieves.

Jesus for the second time casts out of the temple those who would use His Father's house as a money-making scheme. This happened once before. In the beginning of Jesus public ministry, recorded in John 2:13–23. He overthrew tables and drove out the money changers. From the start of His ministry, Jesus declared Himself to be the one and only Son of the Father (John 3:16). Jesus was equal to His Father, and the religious leaders knew exactly what Jesus was saying. In John 5:17-18, Jesus declared that He was related to the Father in a unique way. He was using the term Father as His real Father[16]. The Jews knew exactly what Jesus was saying. They would seek to kill Jesus because of His healing on the Sabbath. At this point their hatred for Him peaked. In John's Gospel He revealed Himself to be equal to God by declaring God to be His Father.

John 5:17 But Jesus answered them, My Father worketh hitherto, and I work.

John 5:18 Therefore the Jews sought the more to kill him, because he not only had broken the sabbath, but said also that God was his Father, making himself equal with God.

11:00 a.m. on Friday, the Ninth of Nisan

Jesus would teach continually to all who would listen no matter how dangerous it was for Him to remain in the temple:

Luke 19:47 And he taught daily in the temple. But the chief priests and the scribes and the chief of the people sought to destroy him,

12:00 noon on Friday, the Ninth of Nisan

The enemies of God relentlessly sought how to destroy Jesus. However, people would continue to listen to His doctrine and were astonished by it. His enemies were still there. James would later say in his epistle that the enemies of God were anyone that is a friend to this world:

James 4:4 Ye adulterers and adulteresses, know ye not that the friendship of the world is enmity with God? whosoever therefore will be a friend of the world is the enemy of God.

Mark points out how His enemies sought Jesus to destroy Him:

Mark 11:18 And the scribes and chief priests heard it, and sought how they might destroy him: for they feared him, because all the people was astonished at his doctrine.

Luke describes what stopped the scribes. They were stopped by the words of Jesus as He spoke to the people:

Luke 19:48 And could not find what they might do: for all the people were very attentive to hear him.

---

[16]   Dr. James Strong, Strongs Exhaustive Concordance of the Bible. Dugan Publishers Inc. Gordonsville, TN.P337

What a Finish! What a Start! The Month Jesus Met Man's Need

Fred A Kuypers

4:00 p.m. on Friday, the Ninth of Nisan

Many people sought and believed Jesus. The blind and the lame would be healed just like He told John the Baptist earlier in Luke's gospel:

Luke 7:22 Then Jesus answering said unto them, Go your way, and tell John what things ye have seen and heard; how that the blind see, the lame walk, the lepers are cleansed, the deaf hear, the dead are raised, to the poor the gospel is preached.

Most importantly, He preached Messiah's coming to everyone that would listen. Most everyone focuses on the miracles Jesus performed. Luke's gospel commentary in the passage above reveals how important it is that the good news is to be preached to everyone. Jesus continues to heal, and the chief priests are very displeased with what Jesus is doing, as well as the favorable reaction toward Him.

Matthew 21:14 And the blind and the lame came to him in the temple; and he healed them.

Matthew 21:15 And when the chief priests and scribes saw the wonderful things that he did, and the children crying in the temple, and saying, Hosanna to the Son of David; they were sore displeased,

Matthew 21:16 And said unto him, Hearest thou what these say? And Jesus saith unto them, Yea; have ye never read, Out of the mouth of babes and sucklings thou hast perfected praise?

Jesus quotes here from the book of Psalms, chapter 8. Notice the perfect praise:

Psalm 8:1 A Psalm of David. O LORD our Lord, how excellent is thy name in all the earth! who hast set thy glory above the heavens

And the mouths of where this praise would come from:

Psalm 8:2 Out of the mouth of babes and sucklings hast thou ordained strength because of thine enemies, that thou mightest still the enemy and the avenger.

5:00 p.m. on Friday, the Ninth of Nisan

Jesus finishes this day teaching and quoting from the scriptures. He departs again for Bethany to spend the night:

Matthew 21:17 And he left them, and went out of the city into Bethany; and he lodged there.

Chapter 10

❧⟡❧

Nisan 10

Month of Nisan

1st day Yom Rishon Sunday	2nd day Yom Sheini Monday	3rd day Yom Shlishi Tuesday	4th day Yom R'vi'i Wednesday	5th day Yom Chamishi Thursday	6th day Yom Shishi Friday	Shabbat Yom Shabbat Saturday
					Nisan 10th 6:00pm Saturday the Sabbath begins	10th Nisan 11th 6:00am to 6:00 pm Jesus will again pass by the fig tree on His way to Jerusalem. He will go to the Mount of Olives. He delivers His Olivet Discourse. At the end of the day, He will be selected as the Lamb to be killed at Passover.

This chapter includes:

Matthew	Mark	Luke	John
21:18–26:5	11:19–14:2	20:1–21:36	

What a Finish! What a Start! The Month Jesus Met Man's Need

Fred A Kuypers

Jerusalem to Mount of Olives; Sermon on the Mount of Olives

Four days before Passover; Olivet Discourse and a Busy Day for Jesus.

6:00 p.m. on Friday, the Tenth of Nisan

The Seventh Day of the Week, Sabbath Begins

As the tenth of Nisan begins, it is just four days before the Passover. Jesus retires this night outside of Jerusalem at Bethany, as Matthew's account revealed. Mark confirms this by saying He went out of the city of Jerusalem;

Mark 11:19 And when even was come, he went out of the city.

Jesus would spend this night before this upcoming, challenging day in Bethany. The only day more challenging than this upcoming day is the crucifixion day of Nissan 14. He spent this night perhaps at a friend's house in Bethany, but surely somewhere outside of Jerusalem.

7:00 a.m. on Saturday, the Tenth of Nisan

Jesus and his disciples leave Bethany and go to the temple on the Sabbath day. For the second time, they pass by the fig tree. Matthew reviews what took place yesterday when Jesus said no man would eat thereof and notices that the fig tree on the second day is withered away:

Matthew 21:18 <u>Now</u> in the morning as he returned into the city, he hungered.

Matthew 21:19 And when he saw a fig tree in the way, he came to it, and found nothing thereon, but leaves only, and said unto it, Let no fruit grow on thee henceforward for ever. And presently the fig tree withered away.

Matthew 21:20 And when the disciples saw it, they marvelled, saying, How soon is the fig tree withered away!

Mark confirms this. Yesterday, Mark noted Jesus saying no man would eat figs from the tree. Early this morning Jesus and His disciples walked by the fig tree again that Jesus said no man would eat thereof yesterday. However, today Jesus says no fruit would grow forever on that tree. Peter confirms that the Lord had cursed the tree yesterday.

Mark 11:20 And in the morning, as they passed by, they saw the fig tree dried up from the roots.

Mark 11:21 And Peter calling to remembrance saith unto him, Master, behold, the fig tree which thou cursedst is withered away.

Some say that an error occurs here. Matthew has the fig tree dying and the statement of faith by Jesus occurring on this day. Mark has the disciples walking by the tree on two successive days. Both are correct! In Matthew's gospel, there is nothing recorded about the fig tree on the first day. Since Matthew is the gospel primarily to the Jews, they already know from Jeremiah 24 who the figs represent. Mark on the previous day, says the fig tree was cursed to have no man eat thereof and the next day the tree was dried up from the roots. This was done to explain more clearly to a Gentile audience. But Matthew has no comment about the tree on the first day. He goes right to the statement on the second day when the tree withered away. This is an indication of how quickly the Jewish nation was to be of no effect, no longer a nation centered in Jerusalem, as the tree withers and dies. As expressed two days ago by Jesus riding on two animals into Jerusalem, God would now turn from the Jew to the Gentile and away from the Jewish nation because of their rejection of Christ. Jesus knew the Jewish nation would be forced out of Jerusalem and be dispersed as Ezekiel and the other prophets declared. However, later this day, Jesus would record in His Olivet Discourse that God is not quite done with the Jew. There is still the matter of the seventieth week of Daniel's prophecy to deal with.

8:00 a.m. on Saturday, the Tenth of Nisan

Jesus has some special comments about a man's relationship to God and his faith. Jesus instructs His disciples about faith on the second day of coming into contact with the fig tree recorded by Matthew and Mark:

Matthew talks about faith:

Matthew 21:21 Jesus answered and said unto them, Verily I say unto you, If ye have faith, and doubt not, ye shall not only do this which is done to the fig tree, but also if ye shall say unto this mountain, Be thou removed, and be thou cast into the sea; it shall be done.

Mark talks about faith:

Mark 11:22 And Jesus answering saith unto them, Have faith in God.

Mark 11:23 For verily I say unto you, That whosoever shall say unto this mountain, Be thou removed, and be thou cast into the sea; and shall not doubt in his heart, but shall believe that those things which he saith shall come to pass; he shall have whatsoever he saith.

Notice that Jesus does not say "great faith." He also does not speak of large quantities or amounts of faith. He is only concerned with the quality of one's faith. Earlier Jesus compared faith to a mustard seed, the smallest of seeds:

Matthew 17:20 And Jesus said unto them, Because of your unbelief: for verily I say unto you, If ye have faith as a grain of mustard seed, ye shall say unto this mountain, Remove hence to yonder place; and it shall remove; and nothing shall be impossible unto you.

It is quality, not quantity. If quantity was the requirement for faith, then the terrorists that flew the planes into the World Trade Center towers are surely in heaven for it took great, great amounts of faith to do something this evil. But it was the wrong faith—no quality! The best way to show your faith is by trusting and believing God will provide:

Matthew:

Matthew 21:22 And all things, whatsoever ye shall ask in prayer, believing, shall receive.

Mark:

Mark 11:24 Therefore I say unto you, What things soever ye desire, when ye pray, believe that ye receive *them*, and ye shall have *them*.

Mark 11:25 And when ye stand praying, forgive, if ye have ought against any: that your Father also which is in heaven may forgive you your trespasses.

Mark 11:26 But if ye do not forgive, neither will your Father which is in heaven forgive your trespasses.

8:15 a.m. on Saturday, the Tenth of Nisan

Jesus and his disciples headed to the temple on the Sabbath day. For the second time, they stopped by the fig tree. Jesus had a lesson here for his disciples as they see the withered tree. No longer will the house and or lineage of the Jewish race have exclusive favor with God. Remember Jesus always told His disciples to go to the house of Israel, and not to the Gentiles:

Matthew 10:5 These twelve Jesus sent forth, and commanded them, saying, Go not into the way of the Gentiles, and into any city of the Samaritans enter ye not:

Matthew 10:6 But go rather to the lost sheep of the house of Israel.

Jesus declared that He was sent to the Jews and would declare the good news of the kingdom of heaven to the lost sheep of Israel:

Matthew 15:24 But he answered and said, I am not sent but unto the lost sheep of the house of Israel.

But now with just four days until the Passover sacrifice, Jesus has the fig tree wither and die. Jesus endorsed the plan for all Gentile people and ages to come to Him by faith. Faith always will be the determining factor in God's grace to save anyone. It has always been by faith, however God has His chosen race in Israel. God extends the invitation in this new church age, called the age of grace, to both Jew and Gentile.

Ephesians 2:8 For by grace are ye saved through faith; and that not of yourselves: it is the gift of God:

Ephesians 2:9 Not of works, lest any man should boast.

Ephesians 2:10 For we are his workmanship, created in Christ Jesus unto good works, which God hath before ordained that we should walk in them.

The word for "faith" in the Greek language is *pistis*[17]. It has a root word meaning of "ascending" or "moving up." Putting faith in Christ will automatically raise a person to a life that God has ordained as explained above. In fact, the Bible actually declares that one becomes a new creature:

2Corinthians 5:17 Therefore if any man *be* in Christ, *he is* a new creature: old things are passed away; behold, all things are become new.

When a person humbles himself to the point that he realizes there is no hope in keeping the law to earn eternal life and then admits their sin to God and calls upon Jesus to save them, this can only be done entirely by an act of faith.

Romans 10:13 For whosoever shall call upon the name of the Lord shall be saved.

The only way to receive this faith is by hearing the Word of God. This must come from another Christian, using the Bible, who will witness to the lost.

Romans 10:14 How then shall they call on him in whom they have not believed? and how shall they believe in him of whom they have not heard? and how shall they hear without a preacher?

Romans 10:15 And how shall they preach, except they be sent? as it is written, How beautiful are the feet of them that preach the gospel of peace, and bring glad tidings of good things!

Romans 10:16 But they have not all obeyed the gospel. For Esaias saith, Lord, who hath believed our report?

Romans 10:17 So then faith cometh by hearing, and hearing by the word of God.

God chooses this method, the foolishness of preaching, to win and establish disciples:

1 Corinthians 1:17 For Christ sent me not to baptize, but to preach the gospel: not with wisdom of words, lest the cross of Christ should be made of none effect.

1 Corinthians 1:18 For the preaching of the cross is to them that perish foolishness; but unto us which are saved it is the power of God.

This is the faith that Elijah had when he stood up to King Ahab. Remember it was at the word of Elijah that it did not rain for three and a half years!

1Kings 17:1 And Elijah the Tishbite, who was of the inhabitants of Gilead, said unto Ahab, As the LORD God of Israel liveth, before whom I stand, there shall not be dew nor rain these years, but according to my word.

---

[17]   Dr. James Strong, *Strongs Exhaustive Concordance of the Bible*. Dugan Publishers Inc. Gordonsville, TN.

What a Finish! What a Start! The Month Jesus Met Man's Need

Fred A Kuypers

8:30 a.m. on Saturday, the Tenth of Nisan

On this Sabbath day, many things happened at the temple. The people are coming to worship. They are bringing their tithes and the chief priests and religious leaders were there also. The first thing the chief priests did was to question the authority of Jesus as the three synoptic gospels declare:

Matthew:

Matthew 21:23 And when he was come into the temple, the chief priests and the elders of the people came unto him as he was teaching, and said, By what authority doest thou these things? and who gave thee this authority?

Matthew 21:24 And Jesus answered and said unto them, I also will ask you one thing, which if ye tell me, I in like wise will tell you by what authority I do these things.

Matthew 21:25 The baptism of John, whence was it? from heaven, or of men? And they reasoned with themselves, saying, If we shall say, From heaven; he will say unto us, Why did ye not then believe him?

Matthew 21:26 But if we shall say, Of men; we fear the people; for all hold John as a prophet.

Matthew 21:27 And they answered Jesus, and said, We cannot tell. And he said unto them, Neither tell I you by what authority I do these things.

Mark:

Mark 11:27 And they come again to Jerusalem: and as he was walking in the temple, there come to him the chief priests, and the scribes, and the elders,

Mark 11:28 And say unto him, By what authority doest thou these things? and who gave thee this authority to do these things?

Mark 11:29 And Jesus answered and said unto them, I will also ask of you one question, and answer me, and I will tell you by what authority I do these things.

Mark 11:30 The baptism of John, was *it* from heaven, or of men? answer me.

Mark 11:31 And they reasoned with themselves, saying, If we shall say, From heaven; he will say, Why then did ye not believe him?

Mark 11:32 But if we shall say, Of men; they feared the people: for all *men* counted John, that he was a prophet indeed.

Mark 11:33 And they answered and said unto Jesus, We cannot tell. And Jesus answering saith unto them, Neither do I tell you by what authority I do these things.

Luke:

Luke 20:1 And it came to pass, *that* on one of those days, as he taught the people in the temple, and preached the gospel, the chief priests and the scribes came upon *him* with the elders,

Luke 20:2 And spake unto him, saying, Tell us, by what authority doest thou these things? or who is he that gave thee this authority?

Luke 20:3 And he answered and said unto them, I will also ask you one thing; and answer me:

Luke 20:4 The baptism of John, was it from heaven, or of men?

Luke 20:5 And they reasoned with themselves, saying, If we shall say, From heaven; he will say, Why then believed ye him not?

Luke 20:6 But and if we say, Of men; all the people will stone us: for they be persuaded that John was a prophet.

Luke 20:7 And they answered, that they could not tell whence *it was.*

Luke 20:8 And Jesus said unto them, Neither tell I you by what authority I do these things.

Jesus said that the scribes and the elders are going to be held accountable for what they know of the scriptures. Every man is going to be held accountable to God for the scriptures. The moral law of God is written in the hearts of man:

Romans 2:13 (For not the hearers of the law are just before God, but the doers of the law shall be justified.

Romans 2:14 For when the Gentiles, which have not the law, do by nature the things contained in the law, these, having not the law, are a law unto themselves:

Romans 2:15 Which shew the work of the law written in their hearts, their conscience also bearing witness, and their thoughts the mean while accusing or else excusing one another;)

Every man knows that when he disobeys even the simplest commands, (the Ten Commandments for example), he is guilty:

Romans 3:23 For all have sinned, and come short of the glory of God;

All means all! It means everyone! Matthew has some more for the chief priests and scribes to digest:

Matthew 21:28 But what think ye? A *certain* man had two sons; and he came to the first, and said, Son, go work to day in my vineyard.

Matthew 21:29 He answered and said, I will not: but afterward he repented, and went.

Matthew 21:30 And he came to the second, and said likewise. And he answered and said, I *go*, sir: and went not.

Matthew 21:31 Whether of them twain did the will of *his* father? They say unto him, The first. Jesus saith unto them, Verily I say unto you, That the publicans and the harlots go into the kingdom of God before you.

Matthew 21:32 For John came unto you in the way of righteousness, and ye believed him not: but the publicans and the harlots believed him: and ye, when ye had seen *it*, repented not afterward, that ye might believe him.

Again, Jesus refers to repentance. It seems He always comes back to this word. Is repentance that important in the overall plan to save man? Remember the first words of Jesus when He began his public ministry:

Matthew 4:17 From that time Jesus began to preach, and to say, Repent: for the kingdom of heaven is at hand.

9:00 a.m. on Saturday, the Tenth of Nisan

As the morning develops, Jesus gives the parable of the vineyard. He goes back to the Old Testament to show the religious leaders that they should have known this already. Isaiah records this message about the vineyard and who it represents (the nation of Israel):

Isaiah 5:1 Now will I sing to my wellbeloved a song of my beloved touching his vineyard. My wellbeloved hath a vineyard in a very fruitful hill:

Fred A Kuypers

Isaiah 5:2 And he fenced it, and gathered out the stones thereof, and planted it with the choicest vine, and built a tower in the midst of it, and also made a winepress therein: and he looked that it should bring forth grapes, and it brought forth wild grapes.

Isaiah 5:3 And now, O inhabitants of Jerusalem, and men of Judah, judge, I pray you, betwixt me and my vineyard.

Isaiah 5:4 What could have been done more to my vineyard, that I have not done in it? wherefore, when I looked that it should bring forth grapes, brought it forth wild grapes?

Isaiah 5:5 And now go to; I will tell you what I will do to my vineyard: I will take away the hedge thereof, *and* it shall be eaten up; and break down the wall thereof, and it shall be trodden down:

Isaiah 5:6 And I will lay it waste: it shall not be pruned, nor digged; but there shall come up briers and thorns: I will also command the clouds that they rain no rain upon it.

Isaiah 5:7 For the vineyard of the LORD of hosts is the house of Israel, and the men of Judah his pleasant plant: and he looked for judgment, but behold oppression; for righteousness, but behold a cry.

Isaiah has laid out several definitions that need to be pointed out here. The One who sings here sings of the beloved as the beloved of God's only Son, the Lord Jesus Christ. Jesus calls the vineyard "My vineyard" and in verse 7 describes the men of Judah as His pleasant plant. Jesus notes that all that come His way are oppression and cries from the men of Judah. This is one of the few parables that all three synoptic gospels comment on:

Matthew:

Matthew 21:33 Hear another parable: There was a certain householder, which planted a vineyard, and hedged it round about, and digged a winepress in it, and built a tower, and let it out to husbandmen, and went into a far country:

Matthew 21:34 And when the time of the fruit drew near, he sent his servants to the husbandmen, that they might receive the fruits of it.

Matthew 21:35 And the husbandmen took his servants, and beat one, and killed another, and stoned another.

Matthew 21:36 Again, he sent other servants more than the first: and they did unto them likewise.

Matthew 21:37 But last of all he sent unto them his son, saying, They will reverence my son.

Matthew 21:38 But when the husbandmen saw the son, they said among themselves, This is the heir; come, let us kill him, and let us seize on his inheritance.

Matthew 21:39 And they caught him, and cast *him* out of the vineyard, and slew *him*.

Matthew 21:40 When the lord therefore of the vineyard cometh, what will he do unto those husbandmen?

Matthew 21:41 They say unto him, He will miserably destroy those wicked men, and will let out *his* vineyard unto other husbandmen, which shall render him the fruits in their seasons.

Matthew 21:42 Jesus saith unto them, Did ye never read in the scriptures, The stone which the builders rejected, the same is become the head of the corner: this is the Lord's doing, and it is marvellous in our eyes?

Mark:

Mark 12:1 And he began to speak unto them by parables. A *certain* man planted a vineyard, and set an hedge about *it*, and digged *a place for* the winefat, and built a tower, and let it out to husbandmen, and went into a far country.

Mark 12:2 And at the season he sent to the husbandmen a servant, that he might receive from the husbandmen of the fruit of the vineyard.

Mark 12:3 And they caught *him*, and beat him, and sent *him* away empty.

Mark 12:4 And again he sent unto them another servant; and at him they cast stones, and wounded *him* in the head, and sent *him* away shamefully handled.

Mark 12:5 And again he sent another; and him they killed, and many others; beating some, and killing some.

Mark 12:6 Having yet therefore one son, his wellbeloved, he sent him also last unto them, saying, They will reverence my son.

Mark 12:7 But those husbandmen said among themselves, This is the heir; come, let us kill him, and the inheritance shall be ours.

Mark 12:8 And they took him, and killed *him*, and cast *him* out of the vineyard.

Mark 12:9 What shall therefore the lord of the vineyard do? he will come and destroy the husbandmen, and will give the vineyard unto others.

Mark 12:10 And have ye not read this scripture; The stone which the builders rejected is become the head of the corner:

Mark 12:11 This was the Lord's doing, and it is marvellous in our eyes?

Luke:

Luke 20:9 Then began he to speak to the people this parable; A certain man planted a vineyard, and let it forth to husbandmen, and went into a far country for a long time.

Luke 20:10 And at the season he sent a servant to the husbandmen, that they should give him of the fruit of the vineyard: but the husbandmen beat him, and sent *him* away empty.

Luke 20:11 And again he sent another servant: and they beat him also, and entreated *him* shamefully, and sent *him* away empty.

Luke 20:12 And again he sent a third: and they wounded him also, and cast *him* out.

Luke 20:13 Then said the lord of the vineyard, What shall I do? I will send my beloved son: it may be they will reverence *him* when they see him.

Luke 20:14 But when the husbandmen saw him, they reasoned among themselves, saying, This is the heir: come, let us kill him, that the inheritance may be ours.

Luke 20:15 So they cast him out of the vineyard, and killed him. What therefore shall the lord of the vineyard do unto them?

Luke 20:16 He shall come and destroy these husbandmen, and shall give the vineyard to others. And when they heard *it*, they said, God forbid.

Luke 20:17 And he beheld them, and said, What is this then that is written, The stone which the builders rejected, the same is become the head of the corner?

Matthew and Luke add this incredible statement:

Matthew 21:43 Therefore say I unto you, The kingdom of God shall be taken from you, and given to a nation bringing forth the fruits thereof.

Matthew 21:44 And whosoever shall fall on this stone shall be broken: but on whomsoever it shall fall, it will grind him to powder.

Luke 20:18 Whosoever shall fall upon that stone shall be broken; but on whomsoever it shall fall, it will grind him to powder.

Notice the "stone." This stone is Jesus, the rock! Daniel calls Him the stone made without hands in Daniel 2:44–45. He is that "head of the corner" stone referred to here and taken from Psalm 118:22. What does this passage in Matthew mean? That there are two ways to approach Christ: the first is to turn to Him and fall on Him with a broken heart and a contrite spirit (Psalm 34:18). If a man learns the truth and truly believes that Christ's death, burial, and resurrection is the answer to life's eternal question that man will fall on the stone and be broken in heart and in spirit. But, if during this life that man does not fall on the stone, the stone will fall on him, and it will grind him to powder or destroy him in hell forever.

Christ the stone is revealed in three parts:

1. To Israel, as Christ came as a servant to man, which is a stumbling stone to the Jew. This is brought out in both the Old Testament located in Isaiah 8:14–15 and in the New Testament in Romans 9:32–33, 1 Corinthians 1:23, and 1 Peter 2:8.

2. To the church as Christ is the foundation stone and the head of the corner, which is found in 1 Corinthians 3:11, Ephesians 2:20–22, and 1 Peter 2:4.

3. To the Gentile world: Daniel spoke of the nations for whom Christ is to be the smiting stone that will come down and destroy the world governments and start the 1000-year millennial reign of Jesus Christ. See Daniel 2.

This parable about the vineyard really hit the chief priests and the Pharisees hard. They were very upset with Jesus, thinking that they were the ones He was talking about. After all, the chief priests, the Pharisees, the Sadducees, and the scribes knew all that the scriptures had to say, did they not? And they were still planning to take Jesus and kill Him.

Matthew:

Matthew 21:45 And when the chief priests and Pharisees had heard his parables, they perceived that he spake of them.

Matthew 21:46 But when they sought to lay hands on him, they feared the multitude, because they took him for a prophet.

Mark:

Mark 12:12 And they sought to lay hold on him, but feared the people: for they knew that he had spoken the parable against them: and they left him, and went their way.

Luke:

Luke 20:19 And the chief priests and the scribes the same hour sought to lay hands on him; and they feared the people: for they perceived that he had spoken this parable against them.

The religious leaders sought to take Jesus again. This day the tenth of Nisan, according to Exodus 12, is an important day. It will be on the tenth day that the lamb is selected to be killed. Here the religious leaders are contemplating to select Jesus and lay hands on Him to kill Him, but the leaders fear the people and back away. If the Passover comes as seen in Exodus 12, then the Lamb of God, selected by the leaders on this day, will need to be slain on the fourteenth. However here in the morning of the tenth of Nisan, they back down.

Jesus added another parable, according to Matthew. This one is about the marriage feast and is similar to Luke chapter 14 about the man who made a great feast. However, Jesus will be using it to explain that one man is not esteemed better than another.

Matthew:

Matthew 22:1 And Jesus answered and spake unto them again by parables, and said,

Matthew 22:2 The kingdom of heaven is like unto a certain king, which made a marriage for his son,

Matthew 22:3 And sent forth his servants to call them that were bidden to the wedding: and they would not come.

Matthew 22:4 Again, he sent forth other servants, saying, Tell them which are bidden, Behold, I have prepared my dinner: my oxen and *my* fatlings *are* killed, and all things *are* ready: come unto the marriage.

Matthew 22:5 But they made light of *it*, and went their ways, one to his farm, another to his merchandise:

Matthew 22:6 And the remnant took his servants, and entreated *them* spitefully, and slew *them*.

Matthew 22:7 But when the king heard *thereof*, he was wroth: and he sent forth his armies, and destroyed those murderers, and burned up their city.

Matthew 22:8 Then saith he to his servants, The wedding is ready, but they which were bidden were not worthy.

Matthew 22:9 Go ye therefore into the highways, and as many as ye shall find, bid to the marriage.

Matthew 22:10 So those servants went out into the highways, and gathered together all as many as they found, both bad and good: and the wedding was furnished with guests.

Matthew 22:11 And when the king came in to see the guests, he saw there a man which had not on a wedding garment:

Matthew 22:12 And he saith unto him, Friend, how camest thou in hither not having a wedding garment? And he was speechless.

Matthew 22:13 Then said the king to the servants, Bind him hand and foot, and take him away, and cast him into outer darkness; there shall be weeping and gnashing of teeth.

Matthew 22:14 For many are called, but few *are* chosen.

The chief priests sent certain trained religious leaders and teachers to catch Jesus in a lie if they could. Matthew:

Matthew 22:15 Then went the Pharisees, and took counsel how they might entangle him in his talk.

What a Finish! What a Start! The Month Jesus Met Man's Need

Fred A Kuypers

Mark:

Mark 12:13 And they send unto him certain of the Pharisees and of the Herodians, to catch him in *his* words.

They even use spies to try to trap Jesus:

Luke:

Luke 20:20 And they watched him, and sent forth spies, which should feign themselves just men, that they might take hold of his words, that so they might deliver him unto the power and authority of the governor.

9:30 a.m. on Saturday, the Tenth of Nisan

A group of men called the Herodians come on the scene. They try to catch Jesus in a lie. The Herodians thought the trap was set. Remember the Herodians were a government group that backed the Roman governor, Herod. Now they would try to get the government involved. They use the parable just taught in Matthew about not esteeming one man more than another. The three synoptic gospels have something to say:

Matthew:

Matthew 22:16 And they sent out unto him their disciples with the Herodians, saying, Master, we know that thou art true, and teachest the way of God in truth, neither carest thou for any man: for thou regardest not the person of men.

Matthew 22:17 Tell us therefore, What thinkest thou? Is it lawful to give tribute unto Caesar, or not?

Mark:

Mark 12:14 And when they were come, they say unto him, Master, we know that thou art true, and carest for no man: for thou regardest not the person of men, but teachest the way of God in truth: Is it lawful to give tribute to Caesar, or not?

Luke:

Luke 20:21 And they asked him, saying, Master, we know that thou sayest and teachest rightly, neither acceptest thou the person *of any*, but teachest the way of God truly:

Luke 20:22 Is it lawful for us to give tribute unto Caesar, or no?

But Jesus perceived their ungodly wickedness and craftiness and sent the Herodians away, marveling:

Matthew:

Matthew 22:18 But Jesus perceived their wickedness, and said, Why tempt ye me, *ye* hypocrites?

Matthew 22:19 Shew me the tribute money. And they brought unto him a penny.

Matthew 22:20 And he saith unto them, Whose *is* this image and superscription?

Matthew 22:21 They say unto him, Caesar's. Then saith he unto them, Render therefore unto Caesar the things which are Caesar's; and unto God the things that are God's.

Matthew 22:22 When they had heard *these words*, they marvelled, and left him, and went their way.

Mark:

Mark 12:15 Shall we give, or shall we not give? But he, knowing their hypocrisy, said unto them, Why tempt ye me? bring me a penny, that I may see *it*.

Mark 12:16 And they brought *it*. And he saith unto them, Whose *is* this image and superscription? And they said unto him, Caesar's.

Mark 12:17 And Jesus answering said unto them, Render to Caesar the things that are Caesar's, and to God the things that are God's. And they marvelled at him.

Luke:

Luke 20:23 But he perceived their craftiness, and said unto them, Why tempt ye me?

Luke 20:24 Shew me a penny. Whose image and superscription hath it? They answered and said, Caesar's.

Luke 20:25 And he said unto them, Render therefore unto Caesar the things which be Caesar's, and unto God the things which be God's.

Luke 20:26 And they could not take hold of his words before the people: and they marvelled at his answer, and held their peace.

10:00 a.m. on Saturday, the Tenth of Nisan

Up step the Sadducees. These are the religious leaders of the day who say there is no resurrection. The Sadducees have several beliefs different than the Pharisees:

Acts 23:8 For the Sadducees say that there is no resurrection, neither angel, nor spirit: but the Pharisees confess both.

The Sadducees do not believe in a resurrection but ask Jesus about the resurrection. This is nothing but a trick question! They try to stump Jesus by misquoting the verse from Moses in Deuteronomy 25:5:

Deuteronomy 25:5 If brethren dwell together, and one of them die, and have no child, the wife of the dead shall not marry without unto a stranger: her husband's brother shall go in unto her, and take her to him to wife, and perform the duty of an husband's brother unto her.

Matthew:

Matthew 22:23 The same day came to him the Sadducees, which say that there is no resurrection, and asked him,

Matthew 22:24 Saying, Master, Moses said, If a man die, having no children, his brother shall marry his wife, and raise up seed unto his brother.

Matthew 22:25 Now there were with us seven brethren: and the first, when he had married a wife, deceased, and, having no issue, left his wife unto his brother:

What a Finish! What a Start! The Month Jesus Met Man's Need

Fred A Kuypers

Matthew 22:26 Likewise the second also, and the third, unto the seventh.

Matthew 22:27 And last of all the woman died also.

Matthew 22:28 Therefore in the resurrection whose wife shall she be of the seven? for they all had her.

Mark:

Mark 12:18 Then come unto him the Sadducees, which say there is no resurrection; and they asked him, saying,

Mark 12:19 Master, Moses wrote unto us, If a man's brother die, and leave his wife behind him, and leave no children, that his brother should take his wife, and raise up seed unto his brother.

Mark 12:20 Now there were seven brethren: and the first took a wife, and dying left no seed.

Mark 12:21 And the second took her, and died, neither left he any seed: and the third likewise.

Mark 12:22 And the seven had her, and left no seed: last of all the woman died also.

Mark 12:23 In the resurrection therefore, when they shall rise, whose wife shall she be of them? for the seven had her to wife.

Luke:

Luke 20:27 Then came to *him* certain of the Sadducees, which deny that there is any resurrection; and they asked him,

Luke 20:28 Saying, Master, Moses wrote unto us, If any man's brother die, having a wife, and he die without children, that his brother should take his wife, and raise up seed unto his brother.

Luke 20:29 There were therefore seven brethren: and the first took a wife, and died without children.

Luke 20:30 And the second took her to wife, and he died childless.

Luke 20:31 And the third took her; and in like manner the seven also: and they left no children, and died.

Luke 20:32 Last of all the woman died also.

Luke 20:33 Therefore in the resurrection whose wife of them is she? for seven had her to wife.

Jesus gives an answer about marriage to the question that the Sadducees had asked. He set them straight by announcing to all in the temple this morning that they are in error. This must have really burned in the Sadducees' hearts with the entire temple congregation there to hear Jesus speak:

Matthew recorded:

Matthew 22:29 Jesus answered and said unto them, Ye do err, not knowing the scriptures, nor the power of God.

Matthew 22:30 For in the resurrection they neither marry, nor are given in marriage, but are as the angels of God in heaven.

Mark recorded:

Mark 12:24 And Jesus answering said unto them, Do ye not therefore err, because ye know not the scriptures, neither the power of God?

Mark 12:25 For when they shall rise from the dead, they neither marry, nor are given in marriage; but are as the angels which are in heaven.

Luke recorded:

Luke 20:34 And Jesus answering said unto them, The children of this world marry, and are given in marriage:

Luke 20:35 But they which shall be accounted worthy to obtain that world, and the resurrection from the dead, neither marry, nor are given in marriage:

Luke 20:36 Neither can they die any more: for they are equal unto the angels; and are the children of God, being the children of the resurrection.

Jesus will set the Sadducees straight by quoting scripture from Exodus:

Exodus 3:6 Moreover he said, I am the God of thy father, the God of Abraham, the God of Isaac, and the God of Jacob. And Moses hid his face; for he was afraid to look upon God.

Jesus explains what was really meant when He declared "I am the God of Abraham, The God of Isaac, and the God of Jacob" Our God is not the God of the dead but of the living!

Matthew says:

Matthew 22:31 But as touching the resurrection of the dead, have ye not read that which was spoken unto you by God, saying,

Matthew 22:32 I am the God of Abraham, and the God of Isaac, and the God of Jacob? God is not the God of the dead, but of the living.

Mark says:

Mark 12:26 And as touching the dead, that they rise: have ye not read in the book of Moses, how in the bush God spake unto him, saying, I am the God of Abraham, and the God of Isaac, and the God of Jacob?

Mark 12:27 He is not the God of the dead, but the God of the living: ye therefore do greatly err.

Luke says:

Luke 20:37 Now that the dead are raised, even Moses shewed at the bush, when he calleth the Lord the God of Abraham, and the God of Isaac, and the God of Jacob.

Luke 20:38 For he is not a God of the dead, but of the living: for all live unto him.

The crowds at the temple understand what Jesus said and are astonished at His answers:

Matthew 22:33 And when the multitude heard this, they were astonished at his doctrine.

Even the scribes understand what Jesus spoke, as recorded by Luke:

Luke 20:39 Then certain of the scribes answering said, Master, thou hast well said.

Luke 20:40 And after that they durst not ask him any question at all.

The Pharisees, who do not agree with the Sadducees but rather believe in the resurrection, come up to Jesus. Jesus gives an answer to a question that the Pharisees asked. They are trying to catch Jesus in a blasphemous statement:

What a Finish! What a Start! The Month Jesus Met Man's Need

Fred A Kuypers

Matthew:

Matthew 22:34 But when the Pharisees had heard that he had put the Sadducees to silence, they were gathered together.

Matthew 22:35 Then one of them, which was a lawyer, asked him a question, tempting him, and saying,

Matthew 22:36 Master, which is the great commandment in the law?

Matthew 22:37 Jesus said unto him, Thou shalt love the Lord thy God with all thy heart, and with all thy soul, and with all thy mind.

Matthew 22:38 This is the first and great commandment.

Matthew 22:39 And the second is like unto it, Thou shalt love thy neighbour as thyself.

Matthew 22:40 On these two commandments hang all the law and the prophets.

Mark:

Mark 12:28 And one of the scribes came, and having heard them reasoning together, and perceiving that he had answered them well, asked him, Which is the first commandment of all?

Mark 12:29 And Jesus answered him, The first of all the commandments is, Hear, O Israel; The Lord our God is one Lord:

Mark 12:30 And thou shalt love the Lord thy God with all thy heart, and with all thy soul, and with all thy mind, and with all thy strength: this is the first commandment.

Mark 12:31 And the second is like, namely this, Thou shalt love thy neighbour as thyself. There is none other commandment greater than these.

What happens next to this certain scribe, who Matthew called a lawyer, is extremely important to understand about repentance and faith.

Mark 12:32 And the scribe said unto him, Well, Master, thou hast said the truth: for there is one God; and there is none other but he:

Mark 12:33 And to love him with all the heart, and with all the understanding, and with all the soul, and with all the strength, and to love his neighbour as himself, is more than all whole burnt offerings and sacrifices.

Matthew records that a religious leader at first tempted Jesus in Matthew 22:35. Then he repented and acknowledged that Jesus spoke the truth. This was a sign of repentance by the scribe changing his mind about Jesus. Repentance is needed to lead to faith, but repentance will not save as Jesus points out to the scribe He is not far from the kingdom of God. He is not there yet with his repenting about Jesus speaking the truth. In order to reach the kingdom of God, he must believe, and this can only be accomplished by faith.

Mark 12:34 And when Jesus saw that he answered discreetly, he said unto him, Thou art not far from the kingdom of God. And no man after that durst ask him any question.

Jesus decides to turn the tables and asks the religious leaders a question to stump them. Jesus quotes from the Psalms again, showing that the Old Testament scriptures are the words of God. Notice the harmony of the synoptic Gospels here, with each narrative quoting Psalm 110:1; but each writer saying this passage in their own words:

Matthew:

Matthew 22:41 While the Pharisees were gathered together, Jesus asked them,

Matthew 22:42 Saying, What think ye of Christ? whose son is he? They say unto him, The Son of David.

Matthew 22:43 He saith unto them, How then doth David in spirit call him Lord, saying,

Matthew 22:44 The LORD said unto my Lord, Sit thou on my right hand, till I make thine enemies thy footstool?

Matthew 22:45 If David then call him Lord, how is he his son?

Mark:

Mark 12:35 And Jesus answered and said, while he taught in the temple, How say the scribes that Christ is the Son of David?

Mark 12:36 For David himself said by the Holy Ghost, The LORD said to my Lord, Sit thou on my right hand, till I make thine enemies thy footstool.

Mark 12:37 David therefore himself calleth him Lord; and whence is he then his son? And the common people heard him gladly.

Luke:

Luke 20:41 And he said unto them, How say they that Christ is David's son?

Luke 20:42 And David himself saith in the book of Psalms, The LORD said unto my Lord, Sit thou on my right hand,

Luke 20:43 Till I make thine enemies thy footstool.

Luke 20:44 David therefore calleth him Lord, how is he then his son?

Even back in His early childhood, Jesus had all knowledge of the scriptures. Remember when He was twelve years old and He was in the temple, hearing and asking questions about the scriptures? Of course, Jesus knew more about the Word of God than even the brightest Pharisee. He is the Logos and has taken the name "Word" as His own name. Jesus silences the Pharisees along with everyone else as He proves His divine wisdom again:

Matthew 22:46 And no man was able to answer him a word, neither durst any man from that day forth ask him any more questions.

10:30 a.m. on Saturday, the Tenth of Nisan

Jesus continually had a problem with religious leaders. It did not matter if they were preachers or leaders or even scribes and lawyers. Here He exposes the scribes who dress to impress and those who love the title of "Doctor" or "Reverend" or "Master Rabbi." They love to be seen and heard in their long prayer vigils and rituals.

Mark has quoted Jesus in unveiling them:

Mark 12:38 And he said unto them in his doctrine, Beware of the scribes, which love to go in long clothing, and love salutations in the marketplaces,

What a Finish! What a Start! The Month Jesus Met Man's Need

Fred A Kuypers

Mark 12:39 And the chief seats in the synagogues, and the uppermost rooms at feasts:

Mark 12:40 Which devour widows' houses, and for a pretence make long prayers: these shall receive greater damnation.

And Luke has quoted Jesus in exposing them:

Luke 20:45 Then in the audience of all the people he said unto his disciples,

Luke 20:46 Beware of the scribes, which desire to walk in long robes, and love greetings in the markets, and the highest seats in the synagogues, and the chief rooms at feasts;

Luke 20:47 Which devour widows' houses, and for a shew make long prayers: the same shall receive greater damnation.

11:00 a.m. on Saturday, the Tenth of Nisan

Jesus decides here and now to put the religious leaders in their place. They think that they sit in Moses's seat. It is not the seat but the keeping of the law that Jesus commands. Matthew becomes the only Gospel to expound on this:

Matthew 23:1 Then spake Jesus to the multitude, and to his disciples,

Matthew 23:2 Saying, The scribes and the Pharisees sit in Moses' seat:

Matthew 23:3 All therefore whatsoever they bid you observe, that observe and do; but do not ye after their works: for they say, and do not.

Matthew 23:4 For they bind heavy burdens and grievous to be borne, and lay them on men's shoulders; but they themselves will not move them with one of their fingers.

Matthew 23:5 But all their works they do for to be seen of men: they make broad their phylacteries, and enlarge the borders of their garments,

Matthew 23:6 And love the uppermost rooms at feasts, and the chief seats in the synagogues,

Matthew 23:7 And greetings in the markets, and to be called of men, Rabbi, Rabbi.

Matthew 23:8 But be not ye called Rabbi: for one is your Master, even Christ; and all ye are brethren.

Matthew continues to be the only Gospel to record the following truths. Jesus says that the title of Father is not to be used spiritually by anyone else but God who is the Father in heaven:

Matthew 23:9 And call no man your father upon the earth: for one is your Father, which is in heaven.

Matthew 23:10 Neither be ye called masters: for one is your Master, even Christ.

Jesus declares the importance of humbly serving:

Matthew 23:11 But he that is greatest among you shall be your servant.

Matthew 23:12 And whosoever shall exalt himself shall be abased; and he that shall humble himself shall be exalted.

11:15 a.m. on Saturday, the Tenth of Nisan

Jesus unleashes eight woes against the Pharisees.

➤ The first is that they block the true way to eternal life:

Matthew 23:13 But woe unto you, scribes and Pharisees, hypocrites! for ye shut up the kingdom of heaven against men: for ye neither go in yourselves, neither suffer ye them that are entering to go in.

➤ The second is that they add false doctrine to the way to eternal life:

Matthew 23:14 Woe unto you, scribes and Pharisees, hypocrites! for ye devour widows' houses, and for a pretence make long prayer: therefore ye shall receive the greater damnation.

➤ The third is that they lead people to hell:

Matthew 23:15 Woe unto you, scribes and Pharisees, hypocrites! for ye compass sea and land to make one proselyte, and when he is made, ye make him twofold more the child of hell than yourselves.

➤ The fourth is that they put material things ahead of God:

Matthew 23:16 Woe unto you, ye blind guides, which say, Whosoever shall swear by the temple, it is nothing; but whosoever shall swear by the gold of the temple, he is a debtor!

Matthew 23:17 Ye fools and blind: for whether is greater, the gold, or the temple that sanctifieth the gold?

Matthew 23:18 And, Whosoever shall swear by the altar, it is nothing; but whosoever sweareth by the gift that is upon it, he is guilty.

Matthew 23:19 Ye fools and blind: for whether is greater, the gift, or the altar that sanctifieth the gift?

Matthew 23:20 Whoso therefore shall swear by the altar, sweareth by it, and by all things thereon.

Matthew 23:21 And whoso shall swear by the temple, sweareth by it, and by him that dwelleth therein.

Matthew 23:22 And he that shall swear by heaven, sweareth by the throne of God, and by him that sitteth thereon.

➤ The fifth is that they keep trying to keep the law perfectly and miss the real matters of God's word:

Matthew 23:23 Woe unto you, scribes and Pharisees, hypocrites! for ye pay tithe of mint and anise and cummin, and have omitted the weightier matters of the law, judgment, mercy, and faith: these ought ye to have done, and not to leave the other undone.

Matthew 23:24 Ye blind guides, which strain at a gnat, and swallow a camel.

➤ The sixth is that they want to look clean and acceptable to God on the outside, but the inside is still dirty:

Matthew 23:25 Woe unto you, scribes and Pharisees, hypocrites! for ye make clean the outside of the cup and of the platter, but within they are full of extortion and excess.

Matthew 23:26 Thou blind Pharisee, cleanse first that which is within the cup and platter, that the outside of them may be clean also.

➢   The seventh is that they appear clean to men but are not acceptable to God:

Matthew 23:27 Woe unto you, scribes and Pharisees, hypocrites! for ye are like unto whited sepulchres, which indeed appear beautiful outward, but are within full of dead men's bones, and of all uncleanness.

Matthew 23:28 Even so ye also outwardly appear righteous unto men, but within ye are full of hypocrisy and iniquity.

➢   The eighth is that the Pharisees are no different than those that killed the prophets of the past and will seek to kill the one whom the prophets spoke of: "The Prophet"—the Lord Jesus Christ:

Matthew 23:29 Woe unto you, scribes and Pharisees, hypocrites! because ye build the tombs of the prophets, and garnish the sepulchres of the righteous,

Matthew 23:30 And say, If we had been in the days of our fathers, we would not have been partakers with them in the blood of the prophets.

Matthew 23:31 Wherefore ye be witnesses unto yourselves, that ye are the children of them which killed the prophets.

Matthew 23:32 Fill ye up then the measure of your fathers.

Matthew 23:33 Ye serpents, ye generation of vipers, how can ye escape the damnation of hell?

Matthew 23:34 Wherefore, behold, I send unto you prophets, and wise men, and scribes: and some of them ye shall kill and crucify; and some of them shall ye scourge in your synagogues, and persecute them from city to city:

Matthew 23:35 That upon you may come all the righteous blood shed upon the earth, from the blood of righteous Abel unto the blood of Zacharias son of Barachias, whom ye slew between the temple and the altar.

Matthew 23:36 Verily I say unto you, All these things shall come upon this generation.

11:30 a.m. on Saturday, the Tenth of Nisan

Jesus Christ will now lament over Jerusalem. It is always about Jerusalem. Jerusalem is God's city. It is mentioned over 600 times in the Bible but never mentioned in the Qur'an. The problem of course is not with the city. The city is inanimate. The problem is with the people of Jerusalem, God's chosen people. Their rebellious nature against God and God's attempt to be the Lord of His chosen people is what Jesus is lamenting over.

Matthew 23:37 O Jerusalem, Jerusalem, thou that killest the prophets, and stonest them which are sent unto thee, how often would I have gathered thy children together, even as a hen gathereth her chickens under her wings, and ye would not!

Matthew 23:38 Behold, your house is left unto you desolate.

Matthew 23:39 For I say unto you, Ye shall not see me henceforth, till ye shall say, Blessed is he that cometh in the name of the Lord.

Jesus Christ, who died for the sins of the whole world, would have all men come to Him in repentance and faith. But God stated in Isaiah that this marvelous work would be done:

Isaiah 29:13 Wherefore the Lord said, Forasmuch as this people draw near me with their mouth, and with their lips do honour me, but have removed their heart far from me, and their fear toward me is taught by the precept of men:

Isaiah 29:14 Therefore, behold, I will proceed to do a marvellous work among this people, even a marvellous work and a wonder: for the wisdom of their wise men shall perish, and the understanding of their prudent men shall be hid.

11:45 a.m. on Saturday, the Tenth of Nisan

Jesus sat over against the treasury and took note of a widow who had come to the temple on the Sabbath to pay her tribute to God. Jesus is about to explain the true essence of giving. The widow's mite has been used many times to teach the error of the love of money.

Mark describes giving:

Mark 12:41 And Jesus sat over against the treasury, and beheld how the people cast money into the treasury: and many that were rich cast in much.

Mark 12:42 And there came a certain poor widow, and she threw in two mites, which make a farthing.

Mark 12:43 And he called unto him his disciples, and saith unto them, Verily I say unto you, That this poor widow hath cast more in, than all they which have cast into the treasury:

Mark 12:44 For all they did cast in of their abundance; but she of her want did cast in all that she had, even all her living.

Luke describes giving:

Luke 21:1 And he looked up, and saw the rich men casting their gifts into the treasury.

Luke 21:2 And he saw also a certain poor widow casting in thither two mites.

Luke 21:3 And he said, Of a truth I say unto you, that this poor widow hath cast in more than they all:

Luke 21:4 For all these have of their abundance cast in unto the offerings of God: but she of her penury hath cast in all the living that she had.

12:00 noon on Saturday, the Tenth of Nisan
The Olivet Discourse Begins

Jesus leaves the temple and goes to the Mount of Olives for the Olivet Discourse. There are three eyewitness accounts of this, and all three are in harmony. As Jesus leaves the temple, He has some words for those who would hear:

Matthew:

Matthew 24:1 And Jesus went out, and departed from the temple: and his disciples came to *him* for to shew him the buildings of the temple.

What a Finish! What a Start! The Month Jesus Met Man's Need

Fred A Kuypers

Matthew 24:2 And Jesus said unto them, See ye not all these things? verily I say unto you, There shall not be left here one stone upon another, that shall not be thrown down.

Mark:

Mark 13:1 And as he went out of the temple, one of his disciples saith unto him, Master, see what manner of stones and what buildings are here!

Mark 13:2 And Jesus answering said unto him, Seest thou these great buildings? there shall not be left one stone upon another, that shall not be thrown down.

Luke:

Luke 21:5 And as some spake of the temple, how it was adorned with goodly stones and gifts, he said,

Luke 21:6 As for these things which ye behold, the days will come, in the which there shall not be left one stone upon another, that shall not be thrown down.

Jesus declared that the temple in Jerusalem would be totally destroyed again—not one stone left upon another. In the gospel of John verse 2:21 the temple is described to have a dual meaning so that it was not just the actual temple but also the temple of Christ's body. Both would be restored in the future. Remember that Nebuchadnezzar destroyed the temple and all of Jerusalem in 586 BC. Remember also that Nehemiah would receive the order to rebuild the city walls of Jerusalem from Artaxerxes (Nehemiah 2:6). The temple was rebuilt then headed up by Zerubbabel as written by Ezra. It was rebuilt, but Jesus is predicting the demise of it again. There will be a third time that the temple will be rebuilt, according to Daniel the prophet. But this third time will be a terrible time. The Antichrist will sit in this third temple and declare that he is God. This will take place in the middle of the seven-year tribulation period. And the seven-year tribulation period cannot take place until God is ready to deal with the Jews again, and the covenant (not necessarily a peace treaty as many have misstated in Daniel) between the Antichrist and many nations must be in place and confirmed with all nations turning against Israel.

Zechariah 14:2 For I will gather all nations against Jerusalem to battle; and the city shall be taken, and the houses rifled, and the women ravished; and half of the city shall go forth into captivity, and the residue of the people shall not be cut off from the city.

12:30 p.m. on Saturday, the Tenth of Nisan

Jesus arrives with His disciples on the Mount of Olives. Remember that the Mount of Olives is within a Sabbath's day journey from the temple mount. It is east, across the Kidron Valley. The Olivet Discourse begins. It is a rather lengthy sermon. The disciples have a very important question to ask Jesus as they arrive at the Mount of Olives. Matthew describes how the disciples start the questioning:

Matthew 24:3 And as he sat upon the mount of Olives, the disciples came unto him privately, saying, Tell us, when shall these things be? and what shall be the sign of thy coming, and of the end of the world?

The question needs some explanation. The "end of the world" here uses a different Greek word for "world."

> It is not the word *oikoumenē*,[18] the created earth or planet or globe. Interestingly the word *oikoumenē* is used in verse 14 of this chapter in Matthew, indicating that over the entire planet or to every corner of the inhabited earth. North, south, east, or west, the gospel of the kingdom will be preached:

Matthew 24:14 And this gospel of the kingdom shall be preached in all the world for a witness unto all nations; and then shall the end come.

> It is not the word *kosmos*,[19] meaning inhabitants or the adorning people on this globe. *Kosmos* is used in verse 21 of this chapter in Matthew, describing that the great tribulation that would come on the people will be greater than anything since Adam and Eve at the beginning of mankind.

Matthew 24:21 For then shall be great tribulation, such as was not since the beginning of the world to this time, no, nor ever shall be.

> It is not the word *ghay*,[20] meaning the solid part or the ground or land. *Ghay* is used in Revelation 13:3 where all the land wondered at the beast.

Revelation 13:3 And I saw one of his heads as it were wounded to death; and his deadly wound was healed: and all the world wondered after the beast.

> It is the word *aion*[21] or an "age" or a particular period of time. So, the disciples are questioning our Lord about *the end of the age of time* that will usher in His coming again, or as most call it the second coming of Jesus Christ. Putting this into perspective, what age is being talked about at this point? It cannot be the church age or the age of grace (the same age) because that age had not started at this time. It must be the age of law which began at the moment the Jews requested the law of God be given to them in Exodus 19:8:

Exodus 19:8 And all the people answered together, and said, All that the LORD hath spoken we will do. And Moses returned the words of the people unto the LORD.

From this moment forward, the Lord gave His chosen people commands even though He knew that they could not keep them just like Adam and Eve in the garden! God

---

18 Dr. James Strong, *Strongs Exhaustive Concordance of the Bible*. Dugan Publishers Inc. Gordonsville, TN. P. 1189
19 Dr. James Strong, *Strongs Exhaustive Concordance of the Bible*. Dugan Publishers Inc. Gordonsville, TN. P. 1189
20 Dr. James Strong, *Strongs Exhaustive Concordance of the Bible*. Dugan Publishers Inc. Gordonsville, TN. P. 1189
21 Dr. James Strong, *Strongs Exhaustive Concordance of the Bible*. Dugan Publishers Inc. Gordonsville, TN. P. 1189

really wanted man to have a heart to keep them: Deuteronomy 5:29 O that there were such an heart in them, that they would fear me, and keep all my commandments always, that it might be well with them, and with their children for ever!

The world or age that the disciples are talking about is their current period of time when God is dealing with the Jew as His chosen people to keep the law and obey all the commands of God. The answer Jesus gives to the Jew is all about the end of that age, which will now agree with Daniel chapter 9 and the final week of years, or seven years, that God has in store for the Jew. The last seven years will take place after Messiah is cut off in Daniel 9:26.

Can anyone guess what term is used in the most famous verse in the Bible? It is not the same as the word *world* used here in Matthew 24:3!

John 3:16 For God so loved the world, that he gave his only begotten Son, that whosoever believeth in him should not perish, but have everlasting life.

Here in John 3:16 *world* is the Greek word *kosmos*, meaning inhabitants!

Mark and Luke describe how the disciples start the questioning:

Mark:

Mark 13:3 And as he sat upon the mount of Olives over against the temple, Peter and James and John and Andrew asked him privately,

Mark 13:4 Tell us, when shall these things be? and what shall be the sign when all these things shall be fulfilled?

Luke:

Luke 21:7 And they asked him, saying, Master, but when shall these things be? and what sign will there be when these things shall come to pass?

12:45 p.m. on Saturday, the Tenth of Nisan

As the passages indicate, there is a moment in time when the three synoptic gospels are all in agreement as to this event known as the Olivet Discourse. John has still been silent here. John the apostle will not have anything to say until after this day of the Olivet Discourse.

If Jesus is presenting the end of an age, which is what the question really asks, then Matthew's account of the Olivet sermon begins with what to look for at the end of that age. At this point, the age in which Jesus was presenting this answer is the age of law as given through the Jewish nation of Israel. The end of this age is given precisely in the book of Daniel. At this moment, it is critical to know and understand that the time frame given to Daniel of seventy years was for "thy people," the Jews:

Daniel 9:24 Seventy weeks are determined upon thy people and upon thy holy city, to finish the transgression, and to make an end of sins, and to make reconciliation for iniquity, and to bring in everlasting righteousness, and to seal up the vision and prophecy, and to anoint the most Holy.

God did not say "My people." If He did, any assumption could be made here. Instead, God used the term "thy people" and in so doing referred to the Jews of Daniel's lineage. The prophecy Jesus is about to give will begin the seventieth week of Daniel's vision to the Jew and therefore does not speak of the church age or the end of it. The church age does parallel the time mentioned here but just as this church age began so will it end abruptly. When the disciples ask this question, there is no "church age." The church age began on the day of Pentecost with the giving of the Holy Spirit who continually dwells in each believer. The church age cannot end until the Holy Spirit ends this age by returning back to heaven bringing every believer with Him (the rapture).

The church age will end with the Holy Spirit back in heaven. The believer will immediately go to heaven because the Holy Spirit who indwells each believer will be home in heaven (which means the believer will be snatched up, too) on the day of the rapture. Then the last seven-year period of the age of law known as the tribulation can occur. First Thessalonians 4:16–18 says to comfort believers with these words.

Matthew's Olivet Discourse sermon begins:

Matthew 24:4 And Jesus answered and said unto them, Take heed that no man deceive you.

Matthew 24:5 For many shall come in my name, saying, I am Christ; and shall deceive many.

Matthew 24:6 And ye shall hear of wars and rumours of wars: see that ye be not troubled: for all these things must come to pass, but the end is not yet.

Matthew 24:7 For nation shall rise against nation, and kingdom against kingdom: and there shall be famines, and pestilences, and earthquakes, in divers places.

Matthew 24:8 All these *are* the beginning of sorrows.

Mark's Olivet Discourse sermon begins:

Mark 13:5 And Jesus answering them began to say, Take heed lest any man deceive you:

Mark 13:6 For many shall come in my name, saying, I am Christ; and shall deceive many.

Mark 13:7 And when ye shall hear of wars and rumours of wars, be ye not troubled: for such things must needs be; but the end shall not be yet.

Mark 13:8 For nation shall rise against nation, and kingdom against kingdom: and there shall be earthquakes in divers places, and there shall be famines and troubles: these are the beginnings of sorrows.

Luke's Olivet Discourse sermon begins:

Luke 21:8 And he said, Take heed that ye be not deceived: for many shall come in my name, saying, I am *Christ*; and the time draweth near: go ye not therefore after them.

Luke 21:9 But when ye shall hear of wars and commotions, be not terrified: for these things must first come to pass; but the end is not by and by.

Luke 21:10 Then said he unto them, Nation shall rise against nation, and kingdom against kingdom:

Luke 21:11 And great earthquakes shall be in divers places, and famines, and pestilences; and fearful sights and great signs shall there be from heaven.

Jesus explains some things to look for as the end of that age approaches. This age now gives way to the church age but the age of law has not ended. During this church age, God has switched from the Jew to the Gentile to call out a people for His name. The Jewish race was used to declare all of the events prophesied in the Old Testament. They were the ones who gave the oracles of God (Romans 3:2). Jesus will refer to one of the prophets, Daniel, who established the timeline for God to usher in His Son as King of kings and Lord of lords. The Olivet Discourse sermon expands on the time of the last of Daniel's seventy weeks known as the seven year tribulation week yet to occur. To fully understand this, you must know and read Daniel's book in the Old Testament along with the rest of the Old Testament books, as all the writings speak of the Lord Jesus Christ without saying His name.

1:00 p.m. on Saturday, the Tenth of Nisan

At this moment there is a quandary, a practical dilemma from each writer. Not one of the three synoptic gospels says anything similar. However the important thing to understand here is that there is no discrepancy either among the writers. Each gospel adds to a fulfillment of the final countdown of the age of the Jew and his time under the law. Remember this age began when the Jews asked God to give them all the laws that God wanted them to obey, recorded in Exodus 19:8. God then proceeded with the age of law given to the Jew and recorded by the Jew. The giving of the Ten Commandments immediately follows the statement by the Jews: "All that the LORD hath spoken we will do." In Exodus 19:8.

Matthew's next quote from Jesus:

Matthew 24:9 Then shall they deliver you up to be afflicted, and shall kill you: and ye shall be hated of all nations for my name's sake.

Matthew 24:10 And then shall many be offended, and shall betray one another, and shall hate one another.

Matthew 24:11 And many false prophets shall rise, and shall deceive many.

Matthew 24:12 And because iniquity shall abound, the love of many shall wax cold.

Matthew 24:13 But he that shall endure unto the end, the same shall be saved.

Matthew 24:14 And this gospel of the kingdom shall be preached in all the world for a witness unto all nations; and then shall the end come.

Notice Matthew says that "they shall deliver you up". You being spoken of here are also named by Daniel as *thy people* who are known today as the Jews. They would be delivered up to be afflicted and killed. No other Gospel presents this horror in such a way. Neither Mark nor Luke speaks of killing. But were the Jews killed because they were hated for Christ's name's sake? For many centuries, during the Crusades, they were mercilessly killed by the Roman authorities for having put Christ to death. They paid for their statement at the crucifixion of Christ that His blood was to be upon them and their children (Matthew 27:25).

Matthew exclusively says many shall be offended, iniquity shall abound, and the love of many shall wax cold. All this has happened to "thy people," the Jews, throughout this current age of grace. God has given grace that all may be saved by the blood of the Lamb, but man has shown his true colors by his hatred of the Jew. Matthew says the Gospel needs to be preached to the entire world for a witness before the end can come. The word *world* here means through all the inhabited land. Mark is next.

Mark's Olivet Discourse sermon continues:

Mark 13:9 But take heed to yourselves: for they shall deliver you up to councils; and in the synagogues ye shall be beaten: and ye shall be brought before rulers and kings for my sake, for a testimony against them.

Mark 13:10 And the gospel must first be published among all nations.

Mark 13:11 But when they shall lead *you*, and deliver you up, take no thought beforehand what ye shall speak, neither do ye premeditate: but whatsoever shall be given you in that hour, that speak ye: for it is not ye that speak, but the Holy Ghost.

Mark 13:12 Now the brother shall betray the brother to death, and the father the son; and children shall rise up against *their* parents, and shall cause them to be put to death.

Mark 13:13 And ye shall be hated of all *men* for my name's sake: but he that shall endure unto the end, the same shall be saved.

Mark discusses how the Jews are going to be put on trial over and over again. They will be "beaten" or flayed, a little harsher word than the word *afflicted*, which can mean pressure of a mental or a physical nature.[22] In Mark the gospel must be *published* among all nations for the end to come. This is the same Greek word that Matthew used in verse fourteen for *preached*. Published or preached is synoptic at this point. Mark is the only gospel that affirms the Holy Ghost will give you what to say when you are delivered up. Matthew does not talk about this at all. Luke mentions it but does not say the Holy Ghost but "I," referring to Jesus Christ. As Christians, it is understood that the Holy Ghost and Jesus are one. But in the last seven years of Daniel's prophecy, which is yet to be played out for the Jew, the Holy Ghost will work once again by coming and going as He did in the age of law, a different age than

---

22   Dr. James Strong, *Strongs Exhaustive Concordance of the Bible*. Dugan Publishers Inc. Gordonsville, TN. P. 102

the age of grace. Mark agrees with Matthew that he who endures to the end shall be saved. But Luke writes in his unique way.

Luke's Olivet Discourse sermon continues:

Luke 21:12 But before all these, they shall lay their hands on you, and persecute *you*, delivering *you* up to the synagogues, and into prisons, being brought before kings and rulers for my name's sake.

Luke 21:13 And it shall turn to you for a testimony.

Luke 21:14 Settle it therefore in your hearts, not to meditate before what ye shall answer:

Luke 21:15 For I will give you a mouth and wisdom, which all your adversaries shall not be able to gainsay nor resist.

Luke 21:16 And ye shall be betrayed both by parents, and brethren, and kinsfolks, and friends; and some of you shall they cause to be put to death.

Luke 21:17 And ye shall be hated of all *men* for my name's sake.

Luke 21:18 But there shall not an hair of your head perish.

Luke 21:19 In your patience possess ye your souls.

Luke has several different comments about this very important topic that the apostles are questioning Jesus about. He talks about the Jews' persecution. Jesus talks about giving a mouth (words to speak) and wisdom (right words), which none will be able to resist (words that can't be refuted). He talks about hatred of the Jew, for the name of Christ, and that not one hair of your head will perish (eternal life). This is different language. One of the strangest statements made during this discourse is here in Luke 21:19 where it says "in your patience possess ye your souls," which is the same word James used for patience. What Luke is saying is that our souls need to be controlled by God and that may take some time. The Bible interprets itself, as the book of James describes patience. Patience brings a person to the point of wanting nothing:

James 1:2 My brethren, count it all joy when ye fall into divers temptations;

James 1:3 Knowing *this*, that the trying of your faith worketh patience.

James 1:4 But let patience have *her* perfect work, that ye may be perfect and entire, wanting nothing.

James 1:5 If any of you lack wisdom, let him ask of God, that giveth to all *men* liberally, and upbraideth not; and it shall be given him.

Matthew's Olivet Discourse sermon builds up to the abomination of desolation, the height of blasphemy concerning God's Son, Jesus Christ. This comes from the book of Daniel and says that in the middle of the seven years of tribulation which is the final week of seven years from the book of Daniel (not accounted for as of this writing) when this abomination will take place. In the middle of this seven-year period, three and a half years after the rapture, the prince that shall come (this is a false prince called Satan and known as "the prince of the power of the air" in Ephesians 2:2) shall cause the sacrifice and oblation to cease. In the book of 2 Thessalonians 2:4

it states that this prince will sit in the temple of God and declare that he is God, which will be the abomination of desolation as spoken by Matthew and Mark.

Matthew:

Matthew 24:15 When ye therefore shall see the abomination of desolation, spoken of by Daniel the prophet, stand in the holy place, (whoso readeth, let him understand:)

Matthew 24:16 Then let them which be in Judaea flee into the mountains:

Mark:

Mark 13:14 But when ye shall see the abomination of desolation, spoken of by Daniel the prophet, standing where it ought not, (let him that readeth understand,) then let them that be in Judaea flee to the mountains

Luke does not mention the "abomination of desolation." Luke talks about the armies surrounding Jerusalem and talks about the "desolation" being near. This agrees with Zechariah 12:1–3, the minor prophet, who speaks of the whole world turning against Jerusalem at this time.

Luke 21:20 And when ye shall see Jerusalem compassed with armies, then know that the desolation thereof is nigh.

Luke 21:21 Then let them which are in Judaea flee to the mountains; and let them which are in the midst of it depart out; and let not them that are in the countries enter thereinto.

All three gospels are in agreement at this time. They are not dealing with the "saved" world because the Christians at this time are already home with the Lord, raptured. It is for the Jew back in the homeland, who has just had the blindness spoken of in Romans 11:25 lifted. Those Jews, who are the remnant God has called and has laid on their hearts to return to Him, are to flee the attack that will soon take place on Jerusalem. As it says in Revelation 7, God will take care of the one hundred and forty four thousand Jews whom He has sealed with His name—twelve thousand from each tribe.

These will be terrible times for all who remain on the earth at this time. Not only the Jew but over half the earth's inhabitants at this time will be killed. In just two events mentioned in the book of Revelation, the first in Revelation 6:7–8, one fourth of the world's population will be killed. There may be as many as eight billion people at that time (there are over seven billion on the earth at this time). That would be two billion people dying in just one event, which is the fourth seal. Second, in Revelation 9:14, the sixth trumpet sounds and one third of the world's population is destroyed. Eight billion minus two billion is six billion, and a third of six is two again, so in just two events of the seven-year tribulation period, four billion people out of eight billion will lose their lives. Many others will also die at the other judgments.

Jesus warns the disciples who are the same nationality as Daniel's people (Daniel 9:24), Jews, to flee from great tribulation that will take place on the earth. Remember this is the end of the age that Daniel speaks about that is appointed to Daniel's people, the Jews.

Matthew continues the discourse:

Matthew 24:17 Let him which is on the housetop not come down to take any thing out of his house:

Matthew 24:18 Neither let him which is in the field return back to take his clothes.

Matthew 24:19 And woe unto them that are with child, and to them that give suck in those days!

Matthew 24:20 But pray ye that your flight be not in the winter, neither on the sabbath day:

Matthew 24:21 For then shall be great tribulation, such as was not since the beginning of the world to this time, no, nor ever shall be.

Matthew 24:22 And except those days should be shortened, there should no flesh be saved: but for the elect's sake those days shall be shortened.

Matthew 24:23 Then if any man shall say unto you, Lo, here is Christ, or there; believe it not.

Matthew 24:24 For there shall arise false Christs, and false prophets, and shall shew great signs and wonders; insomuch that, if it were possible, they shall deceive the very elect.

Matthew 24:25 Behold, I have told you before.

Matthew 24:26 Wherefore if they shall say unto you, Behold, he is in the desert; go not forth: behold, he is in the secret chambers; believe it not.

Matthew 24:27 For as the lightning cometh out of the east, and shineth even unto the west; so shall also the coming of the Son of man be.

Matthew 24:28 For wheresoever the carcase is, there will the eagles be gathered together.

Matthew uses the term "great tribulation" here. This term has been used and misquoted many times. Even the very elect are being deceived by this. It will be a time of great tribulation, but the Christian will not see this time. The intensity of the events recorded in Revelation keeps getting worse and worse as each of the seven groups, (seven seals, seven trumpets, seven vials) are compacted into the seventh and last of each of the three groups. The seventh seal is the opening of the seven trumpets, and the seventh trumpet is the start of the pouring out of the seven vials, which are worse than all judgements before them. These seven vials begin in Revelation chapter 16 after Satan has set himself up to be God in the third temple that is still yet to be built. Remember this third temple is for Antichrist and not for Jesus Christ. This will not be a pleasant time to be alive on earth.

Mark's continuing Olivet Discourse sermon:

Mark 13:15 And let him that is on the housetop not go down into the house, neither enter therein, to take any thing out of his house:

Mark 13:16 And let him that is in the field not turn back again for to take up his garment.

Mark 13:17 But woe to them that are with child, and to them that give suck in those days!

Mark 13:18 And pray ye that your flight be not in the winter.

Mark 13:19 For *in* those days shall be affliction, such as was not from the beginning of the creation which God created unto this time, neither shall be.

Mark 13:20 And except that the Lord had shortened those days, no flesh should be saved: but for the elect's sake, whom he hath chosen, he hath shortened the days.

Mark 13:21 And then if any man shall say to you, Lo, here *is* Christ; or, lo, *he is* there; believe *him* not:

Mark 13:22 For false Christs and false prophets shall rise, and shall shew signs and wonders, to seduce, if *it were* possible, even the elect.

Mark 13:23 But take ye heed: behold, I have foretold you all things.

Mark 13:24 But in those days, after that tribulation, the sun shall be darkened, and the moon shall not give her light,

Mark 13:25 And the stars of heaven shall fall, and the powers that are in heaven shall be shaken.

Mark speaks of the sun being darkened and the moon not giving her light. This is in agreement with the fifth vial that the angels will pour out in Revelation 16:10. Heaven truly will be shaken at this time.

Luke's continuing Olivet Discourse sermon:

Luke 21:22 For these be the days of vengeance, that all things which are written may be fulfilled.

Luke 21:23 But woe unto them that are with child, and to them that give suck, in those days! for there shall be great distress in the land, and wrath upon this people.

Luke 21:24 And they shall fall by the edge of the sword, and shall be led away captive into all nations: and Jerusalem shall be trodden down of the Gentiles, until the times of the Gentiles be fulfilled.

Luke 21:25 And there shall be signs in the sun, and in the moon, and in the stars; and upon the earth distress of nations, with perplexity; the sea and the waves roaring;

Luke 21:26 Men's hearts failing them for fear, and for looking after those things which are coming on the earth: for the powers of heaven shall be shaken.

Daniel speaks of this time yet future. It is the final week of the seventy weeks of years that he wrote of:

Daniel 9:27 And he shall confirm the covenant with many for one week: and in the midst of the week he shall cause the sacrifice and the oblation to cease, and for the overspreading of abominations he shall make it desolate, even until the consummation, and that determined shall be poured upon the desolate.

In the midst of this seven years, or three and a half years into the tribulation, it is time for Antichrist to declare himself to be god. The entire world will worship Him whether you want to or not. If you don't, it will cost your life!

2:00 p.m. on Saturday, the Tenth of Nisan

This time frame that Jesus presents parallels perfectly the middle of the book of Revelation. It speaks of two great witnesses that have prophesied for 1260 days:

Revelation 11:3 And I will give power unto my two witnesses, and they shall prophesy a thousand two hundred and threescore days, clothed in sackcloth.

They are clothed in sackcloth. The number of days, 1260, divided by a thirty-day month is forty-two months. Forty-two months is three and half years. Another way to say this would be time (one year), and times (two years), and half a time (one-half year) as described here; it appears in Revelation 12:14.

Revelation 12:14 And to the woman were given two wings of a great eagle, that she might fly into the wilderness, into her place, where she is nourished for a time, and times, and half a time, from the face of the serpent.

How perfectly does this add up in God's timing! In the middle of the seven-year tribulation period, Revelation 13 will take place, which tells us that the dragon will reign for forty-two more months, again three and a half years or the second half of the seven-year tribulation period. Remember that the whole world at this point will be worshipping the dragon:

Revelation 13:4 And they worshipped the dragon which gave power unto the beast: and they worshipped the beast, saying, Who is like unto the beast? who is able to make war with him?

This will be three and a half years of the most dreadful time on this earth. The second half of the tribulation is the pouring out of the seven vials of Revelation. This will be the worst time of God's fury and wrath being poured out upon the world. This will happen because man has rejected God's plan of redemption.

Now the synoptic gospels announce Christ's second coming:

Matthew:

Matthew 24:29 Immediately after the tribulation of those days shall the sun be darkened, and the moon shall not give her light, and the stars shall fall from heaven, and the powers of the heavens shall be shaken:

Matthew 24:30 And then shall appear the sign of the Son of man in heaven: and then shall all the tribes of the earth mourn, and they shall see the Son of man coming in the clouds of heaven with power and great glory.

Matthew 24:31 And he shall send his angels with a great sound of a trumpet, and they shall gather together his elect from the four winds, from one end of heaven to the other.

Mark:

Mark 13:26 And then shall they see the Son of man coming in the clouds with great power and glory.

Mark 13:27 And then shall he send his angels, and shall gather together his elect from the four winds, from the uttermost part of the earth to the uttermost part of heaven.

Luke:

Luke 21:27 And then shall they see the Son of man coming in a cloud with power and great glory.

Luke 21:28 And when these things begin to come to pass, then look up, and lift up your heads; for your redemption draweth nigh.

Remember the fig tree Jesus cursed earlier this day. At this point He again speaks about it in a parable. Since the fig tree has represented the Jews as the "nation of Israel" and the figs represent the Jews themselves, Jesus gives this parable of the fig tree coming back. The nation of Israel would one day be restored, and when it is restored all the things spoken of by Jesus will be fulfilled. When was the nation of Israel restored? It was restored in 1948 with the UN resolution on May 14, 1948.[23] But the holy city that God has always dealt with is Jerusalem. Jerusalem is the key. The center of Jerusalem is the Temple Mount. Jerusalem was not taken control of by the Jews until the 1967 Six Day War. On June 7,1967,[24][25] the Jews regained control of Jerusalem for the first time since Nebuchadnezzar of Babylon destroyed it in BC 586. The generation that sees this, the fig tree budding again (Jerusalem back in the hands of God's chosen people), will be the generation that will see the second return that Jesus has described above.

Matthew:

Matthew 24:32 Now learn a parable of the fig tree; When his branch is yet tender, and putteth forth leaves, ye know that summer is nigh:

Matthew 24:33 So likewise ye, when ye shall see all these things, know that it is near, even at the doors.

Matthew 24:34 Verily I say unto you, This generation shall not pass, till all these things be fulfilled.

Matthew 24:35 Heaven and earth shall pass away, but my words shall not pass away.

Mark:

Mark 13:28 Now learn a parable of the fig tree; When her branch is yet tender, and putteth forth leaves, ye know that summer is near:

Mark 13:29 So ye in like manner, when ye shall see these things come to pass, know that it is nigh, even at the doors.

Mark 13:30 Verily I say unto you, that this generation shall not pass, till all these things be done.

Mark 13:31 Heaven and earth shall pass away: but my words shall not pass away.

Luke:

Luke 21:29 And he spake to them a parable; Behold the fig tree, and all the trees;

Luke 21:30 When they now shoot forth, ye see and know of your own selves that summer is now nigh at hand.

Luke 21:31 So likewise ye, when ye see these things come to pass, know ye that the kingdom of God is nigh at hand.

Luke 21:32 Verily I say unto you, This generation shall not pass away, till all be fulfilled.

Luke 21:33 Heaven and earth shall pass away: but my words shall not pass away.

Jesus announces some final instructions about the great and dreadful day of the Lord. This means that no one knows the *day* or the *hour* that Jesus will come again.

---

[23] "Independence Day (Israel)." *https://en.wikipedia.org/wiki/Independence_Day_(Israel)* viewed Dec 18, 2017

[24] "Six-Day War." *https://en.wikipedia.org/wiki/Six-Day_War* viewed Dec 18, 2017

Fred A Kuypers

He has just given signs to mark His return and what men are to look for preceding His return in power and great glory. The season or time is given by the fig tree (the nation of Israel) putting forth its leaves and shooting forth. Anyone who has even taken a breath in the past fifty years has seen the Jews established and shooting forth as a new nation. The season is here but the day or the hour is still unknown.

Matthew 24:36 But of that day and hour knoweth no man, no, not the angels of heaven, but my Father only.

Mark 13:32 But of that day and *that* hour knoweth no man, no, not the angels which are in heaven, neither the Son, but the Father.

Jesus has some final warnings about the last days before the great tribulation comes. The instructions are to watch. This is not easy to do. Christians need to come together and discuss what to watch and how to watch. The first day of the week is supposed to be the day that Christians assemble themselves together, which is Sunday (Acts 20:7 and 1 Corinthians 16:2). Look at the warning God has given about this assembly in Hebrews:

Hebrews 10:25 Not forsaking the assembling of ourselves together, as the manner of some is; but exhorting one another: and so much the more, as ye see the day approaching.

Schools are not allowing Bible study to take place. Many sporting events are scheduled on Sunday, which should be the day of assembled worship. Also, stores open to draw shoppers and make men and women work instead of going to a church to learn the Bible, God's holy Word. It is a hard thing to understand! But God has given fair warning of His soon and imminent return!

Matthew:

Matthew 24:37 But as the days of Noe *were*, so shall also the coming of the Son of man be.

Matthew 24:38 For as in the days that were before the flood they were eating and drinking, marrying and giving in marriage, until the day that Noe entered into the ark,

Matthew 24:39 And knew not until the flood came, and took them all away; so shall also the coming of the Son of man be.

Matthew 24:40 Then shall two be in the field; the one shall be taken, and the other left.

Matthew 24:41 Two *women shall be* grinding at the mill; the one shall be taken, and the other left.

Matthew 24:42 Watch therefore: for ye know not what hour your Lord doth come.

Matthew 24:43 But know this, that if the goodman of the house had known in what watch the thief would come, he would have watched, and would not have suffered his house to be broken up.

Matthew 24:44 Therefore be ye also ready: for in such an hour as ye think not the Son of man cometh.

Mark:

Mark 13:33 Take ye heed, watch and pray: for ye know not when the time is.

Mark 13:34 *For the Son of man is* as a man taking a far journey, who left his house, and gave authority to his servants, and to every man his work, and commanded the porter to watch.

Mark 13:35 Watch ye therefore: for ye know not when the master of the house cometh, at even, or at midnight, or at the cockcrowing, or in the morning:

Mark 13:36 Lest coming suddenly he find you sleeping. Mark 13:37 And what I say unto you I say unto all, Watch.

Luke:

Luke 21:34 And take heed to yourselves, lest at any time your hearts be overcharged with surfeiting, and drunkenness, and cares of this life, and so that day come upon you unawares.

Luke 21:35 For as a snare shall it come on all them that dwell on the face of the whole earth.

Luke 21:36 Watch ye therefore, and pray always, that ye may be accounted worthy to escape all these things that shall come to pass, and to stand before the Son of man.

What did Jesus command to watch for that we might escape from these things?

- To watch for the signs He has just given us.
- To watch for false Christs!
- To watch for war increasing!
- To watch for nation rising up against nation!
- To watch for famines, pestilences (plagues or diseases), earthquakes!
- To watch for the nation of Israel to return to the land!

Just follow the scriptures!

Why is it so important to watch as this time approaches? Keep in perspective that the disciples were the ones Jesus was addressing this to. However, the Bible is applicable for today and applies to all ages even the present age. It is not important anymore for the disciples of Jesus' day to watch. It is only important for those who are alive right now on Planet Earth to watch for His second coming.

3:00 p.m. on Saturday, the Tenth of Nisan

Matthew has some parables about the end of the age that was prophesied in the vision of Daniel and of the seventy weeks. Here are three parables about (1) the delayed, (2) the cry of, and (3) the reckoning of the imminent return of Christ!

In this first parable, the fact that the return of Jesus has been delayed for over two thousand years means many have begun to disregard the warnings that Jesus has given us and that He wants to see us doing the will of the Father:

Matthew 24:45 Who then is a faithful and wise servant, whom his lord hath made ruler over his household, to give them meat in due season?

Matthew 24:46 Blessed *is* that servant, whom his lord when he cometh shall find so doing.

Matthew 24:47 Verily I say unto you, That he shall make him ruler over all his goods.

Matthew 24:48 But and if that evil servant shall say in his heart, My lord delayeth his coming;

Matthew 24:49 And shall begin to smite *his* fellowservants, and to eat and drink with the drunken;

Matthew 24:50 The lord of that servant shall come in a day when he looketh not for *him*, and in an hour that he is not aware of,

Matthew 24:51 And shall cut him asunder, and appoint *him* his portion with the hypocrites: there shall be weeping and gnashing of teeth.

This second parable is about the ten virgins, again showing the secret coming of the Bridegroom, the Lord Jesus Christ, at the rapture. Notice the virgins with oil in their lamps. Oil has always been a symbol of the Holy Spirit. Who would have oil (the Holy Spirit) with them to fill their lamps and give light (Jesus Christ) to the truth? Only those who had oil were truly saved.

Matthew 25:1 Then shall the kingdom of heaven be likened unto ten virgins, which took their lamps, and went forth to meet the bridegroom.

Matthew 25:2 And five of them were wise, and five *were* foolish.

Matthew 25:3 They that *were* foolish took their lamps, and took no oil with them:

Matthew 25:4 But the wise took oil in their vessels with their lamps.

Matthew 25:5 While the bridegroom tarried, they all slumbered and slept.

Matthew 25:6 And at midnight there was a cry made, Behold, the bridegroom cometh; go ye out to meet him.

Matthew 25:7 Then all those virgins arose, and trimmed their lamps.

Matthew 25:8 And the foolish said unto the wise, Give us of your oil; for our lamps are gone out.

Matthew 25:9 But the wise answered, saying, *Not so;* lest there be not enough for us and you: but go ye rather to them that sell, and buy for yourselves.

Matthew 25:10 And while they went to buy, the bridegroom came; and they that were ready went in with him to the marriage: and the door was shut.

Matthew 25:11 Afterward came also the other virgins, saying, Lord, Lord, open to us.

Matthew 25:12 But he answered and said, Verily I say unto you, I know you not.

Matthew 25:13 Watch therefore, for ye know neither the day nor the hour wherein the Son of man cometh.

What about those without the oil (the Holy Spirit)? Those unsaved would not go at the midnight hour, and Jesus says to them, "I knew you not!" Sound familiar?

Matthew 7:22 Many will say to me in that day, Lord, Lord, have we not prophesied in thy name? and in thy name have cast out devils? and in thy name done many wonderful works?

Matthew 7:23 And then will I profess unto them, I never knew you: depart from me, ye that work iniquity.

The third parable is about the talents given to servants, again revealing the secret coming of the Lord Jesus Christ at the rapture. The timing of the rapture is similar to the timing of salvation. The rapture, just like the day of salvation, can occur at any time, so it is needful to be about the Father's business of using the talents a Christian is blessed with to win others to Christ.

Matthew is the only New Testament book to use the word *talent.*" As used, it means a weight or balanced measure, mainly speaking of money. How do you earn money? Working at your business or profession or the labor that you do is how to earn money. In serving the Lord Jesus Christ, Christians are not saved by their works but rather saved *for* good works (Ephesians 2:8–9). Matthew also spoke of knowing someone by their fruits or what they produce with their lives (Matthew 7:20).

Matthew 25:14 For the kingdom of heaven is as a man travelling into a far country, who called his own servants, and delivered unto them his goods.

Matthew 25:15 And unto one he gave five talents, to another two, and to another one; to every man according to his several ability; and straightway took his journey.

Matthew 25:16 Then he that had received the five talents went and traded with the same, and made them other five talents.

Matthew 25:17 And likewise he that had received two, he also gained other two.

Matthew 25:18 But he that had received one went and digged in the earth, and hid his lord's money.

Matthew 25:19 After a long time the lord of those servants cometh, and reckoneth with them.

Matthew 25:20 And so he that had received five talents came and brought other five talents, saying, Lord, thou deliveredst unto me five talents: behold, I have gained beside them five talents more.

Matthew 25:21 His lord said unto him, Well done, thou good and faithful servant: thou hast been faithful over a few things, I will make thee ruler over many things: enter thou into the joy of thy lord.

Matthew 25:22 He also that had received two talents came and said, Lord, thou deliveredst unto me two talents: behold, I have gained two other talents beside them.

Matthew 25:23 His lord said unto him, Well done, good and faithful servant; thou hast been faithful over a few things, I will make thee ruler over many things: enter thou into the joy of thy lord.

The first two servants have been judged equally. Jesus has rewarded according to the blessings bestowed on each servant and the return. However the result of the third servant is now seen. The real problem here is that this servant did not believe his master. He did not believe the reason that his master had him there was to serve the master. Because he did not believe and viewed his master as hard and demanding, the third servant demonstrated that he was not a true servant of his master at all. This again points to what Matthew has said in Matthew 7:22–23 that He never knew them or that they were not saved at all.

Matthew 25:24 Then he which had received the one talent came and said, Lord, I knew thee that thou art an hard man, reaping where thou hast not sown, and gathering where thou hast not strawed:

Matthew 25:25 And I was afraid, and went and hid thy talent in the earth: lo, there thou hast that is thine.

Matthew 25:26 His lord answered and said unto him, Thou wicked and slothful servant, thou knewest that I reap where I sowed not, and gather where I have not strawed:

Matthew 25:27 Thou oughtest therefore to have put my money to the exchangers, and then at my coming I should have received mine own with usury.

What a Finish! What a Start! The Month Jesus Met Man's Need

Fred A Kuypers

Matthew 25:28 Take therefore the talent from him, and give it unto him which hath ten talents.

Matthew 25:29 For unto every one that hath shall be given, and he shall have abundance: but from him that hath not shall be taken away even that which he hath.

Matthew 25:30 And cast ye the unprofitable servant into outer darkness: there shall be weeping and gnashing of teeth.

Jesus will come in His glory! He will reign for a thousand years, after which, everyone will be gathered before Him! This will take place at the great white throne judgment of Revelation 20.

Matthew 25:31 When the Son of man shall come in his glory, and all the holy angels with him, then shall he sit upon the throne of his glory:

Matthew 25:32 And before him shall be gathered all nations: and he shall separate them one from another, as a shepherd divideth his sheep from the goats:

Matthew 25:33 And he shall set the sheep on his right hand, but the goats on the left.

Remember when Mrs. Zebedee, the mother of James and John, asked that her two sons sit one on the left and one on the right of Jesus (Matthew 20:20–21)?

Matthew 25:34 Then shall the King say unto them on his right hand, Come, ye blessed of my Father, inherit the kingdom prepared for you from the foundation of the world:

Matthew 25:35 For I was an hungred, and ye gave me meat: I was thirsty, and ye gave me drink: I was a stranger, and ye took me in:

Matthew 25:36 Naked, and ye clothed me: I was sick, and ye visited me: I was in prison, and ye came unto me.

Matthew 25:37 Then shall the righteous answer him, saying, Lord, when saw we thee an hungred, and fed thee? or thirsty, and gave thee drink?

Matthew 25:38 When saw we thee a stranger, and took thee in? or naked, and clothed thee?

Matthew 25:39 Or when saw we thee sick, or in prison, and came unto thee?

Matthew 25:40 And the King shall answer and say unto them, Verily I say unto you, Inasmuch as ye have done it unto one of the least of these my brethren, ye have done it unto me.

Perhaps this is why Jesus denied her request:

Matthew 25:41 Then shall he say also unto them on the left hand, Depart from me, ye cursed, into everlasting fire, prepared for the devil and his angels:

Matthew 25:42 For I was an hungred, and ye gave me no meat: I was thirsty, and ye gave me no drink:

Matthew 25:43 I was a stranger, and ye took me not in: naked, and ye clothed me not: sick, and in prison, and ye visited me not.

Matthew 25:44 Then shall they also answer him, saying, Lord, when saw we thee an hungred, or athirst, or a stranger, or naked, or sick, or in prison, and did not minister unto thee?

Matthew 25:45 Then shall he answer them, saying, Verily I say unto you, Inasmuch as ye did it not to one of the least of these, ye did it not to me.

Matthew 25:46 And these shall go away into everlasting punishment: but the righteous into life eternal.

5:00 p.m. on Saturday, the Tenth of Nisan

Jesus Christ, without error and blemish, is selected to be killed by the authorities. He becomes the chosen Lamb on the tenth day of Nisan (Exodus 12:3).

Matthew explains that Jesus, after this long day of the Olivet Discourse, will have only two days before the Passover meal is eaten on Tuesday night. Jesus has just two full days until the Passover meal that He will eat with His disciples. What will He do? Time has run out for His teaching and instruction. Jesus knows that only a small number will hear His words and seek to follow Him. He also knows that all will deny Him at the trial and His torture. He foretells His betrayal by Judas. At this point, Judas had not yet made his deal with the Pharisees to betray Jesus with a kiss.

Matthew 26:1 And it came to pass, when Jesus had finished all these sayings, he said unto his disciples,

Matthew 26:2 Ye know that after two days is the feast of the passover, and the Son of man is betrayed to be crucified.

Jesus says that after two days is the feast of the Passover. "After" means that more than forty-eight hours need to go by, and any time after forty-eight hours from this point, the Passover can begin. That means all day Sunday and all day Monday need to go by, so some time Tuesday is the time to begin preparation for the Passover meal. Mark confirms this date after the Olivet Discourse:

Mark 14:1 After two days was the feast of the passover, and of unleavened bread: and the chief priests and the scribes sought how they might take him by craft, and put him to death.

Mark 14:2 But they said, Not on the feast day, lest there be an uproar of the people.

5:30 p.m. on Saturday, the Tenth of Nisan

The chief priests and scribes are worried about the Passover that is approaching and are concerned with killing Jesus but not on the feast day that is Passover. But God has another plan. God will bring about the crucifixion of His Son Jesus Christ on the day selected by God so many years earlier.

Matthew 26:3 Then assembled together the chief priests, and the scribes, and the elders of the people, unto the palace of the high priest, who was called Caiaphas,

Matthew 26:4 And consulted that they might take Jesus by subtilty, and kill him.

Matthew 26:5 But they said, Not on the feast day, lest there be an uproar among the people.

The chief priests and scribes select Jesus at the end of this day to kill Him. The tenth of Nisan must be the day that the lamb is selected, not the day the lamb is presented. The perfect Lamb of God who was presented just two days earlier is now chosen to be slain. He is without spot or blemish. He will be the perfect sacrifice for all of man. And at this point the chief priest has selected this Lamb on this day, the tenth of Nisan, to die on Mt. Calvary and pay the price for all sin.

By faith you must believe that Jesus was selected to die for you. Jesus was selected to die the cruel death on a cross on Mt. Calvary and pay the price for sin. If you have not repented of your old belief that you can do anything to save yourself please do so now. Then by faith turn to the work of Jesus on the cross and make Him your Lord.

Chapter 11

Nisan 11

Month of Nisan

1st day Yom Rishon Sunday	2nd day Yom Sheini Monday	3rd day Yom Shlishi Tuesday	4th day Yom R'vi'i Wednesday	5th day Yom Chamishi Thursday	6th day Yom Shishi Friday	Shabbat Yom Shabbat Saturday
						Nisan 11th 6:00pm Sunday begins
11th Nisan 12th 6:00am to 6:00pm Jesus is in the temple. Jesus prepares His disciples for the events of the crucifixion to take place in two days.						

This chapter includes:

Matthew	Mark	Luke	John
		21:37–21:38	12:20–12:50

What a Finish! What a Start! The Month Jesus Met Man's Need

Fred A Kuypers

Night on the Mount of Olives; Travel to Temple

Three days before Passover;

6:00 p.m. on Saturday, the Eleventh of Nisan

First Day of the Week Begins, Sunday

The Last day of the week Sabbath has ended. After two full days or another way to say this, in less than three days, the Passover meal will be prepared and eaten. This will be on the third day of the week, Tuesday to prepare the table ready for the supper by 6:00 p.m. Two full days yet to take place for the preparation of the Passover meal as discussed at the end of the last chapter. Luke is the only Gospel to reveal this night after the Olivet Discourse. Notice Saturday afternoon, yesterday the day of the Olivet Discourse, is the last time the Gospels are synoptic. All three synoptic gospels referred to the fig tree. They all said the same thing quoting Jesus: "Heaven and Earth shall pass away, but my words shall not pass away." This is a promise of preservation of the Words of God. The Words of God truly have been preserved for us today in the King James Bible. Luke explains how Jesus will spend this night resting as He was able on the Mount of Olives:

Luke 21:37 And in the day time he was teaching in the temple; and at night he went out, and abode in the mount that is called the mount of Olives.

9:00 a.m. on Sunday, the Eleventh of Nisan

Jesus had made such an impression on the people that many came early the next morning to hear Him. After Saturday night on the Mount of Olives, He is in the temple teaching again this Sunday morning. He is not afraid of those who are hunting for Him. He will give some sound wisdom as He speaks today.

Luke 21:38 And all the people came early in the morning to him in the temple, for to hear him.

10:00 a.m. on Sunday, the Eleventh of Nisan

In the temple again this morning as described in Luke above, many people have come early the next morning to hear Him. Certain Greeks who have come to worship for the feast of Passover are also there. Jesus at this time, is concentrating on what He is about to go through. He speaks of the hour or time that has come when He will be glorified.

John 12:20 And there were certain Greeks among them that came up to worship at the feast:

John 12:21 The same came therefore to Philip, which was of Bethsaida of Galilee, and desired him, saying, Sir, we would see Jesus.

John 12:22 Philip cometh and telleth Andrew: and again Andrew and Philip tell Jesus.

John 12:23 And Jesus answered them, saying, The hour is come, that the Son of man should be glorified.

Jesus uses the example of a seed planted to explain to his disciples that He must die:

John 12:24 Verily, verily, I say unto you, Except a corn of wheat fall into the ground and die, it abideth alone: but if it die, it bringeth forth much fruit.

Jesus gives his disciples an analogy comparing two things: love and hate. If you love the life that this world offers and live for gain in this present world system, denying the Lord Jesus Christ, you will lose your life in eternity. But to hate life in this world, which is this world system controlled by Satan, and believe in Christ you will keep your life eternally.

John 12:25 He that loveth his life shall lose it; and he that hateth his life in this world shall keep it unto life eternal.

John 12:26 If any man serve me, let him follow me; and where I am, there shall also my servant be: if any man serve me, him will my Father honour.

The proof of this is rather easy to see. The world looks at those who witness and go church-calling, and who want to talk about the Word of God as men who waste time, energy, resources, and knowledge. They want us to talk about sports, cars, material things, and possessions. Even family can come between your Christian stand and God.

12:00 noon on Sunday, the Eleventh of Nisan

Jesus speaks and says His soul is troubled. He knows what He is facing. It is not so much the cruel torture of the cross, although that is a terrible injustice that will happen to Him, but soon He will be separated (death on the cross) from the Father in heaven. It will be the only time in eternity that God the Father and God the Son will ever be separated.

What a Finish! What a Start! The Month Jesus Met Man's Need

Fred A Kuypers

John 12:27 Now is my soul troubled; and what shall I say? Father, save me from this hour: but for this cause came I unto this hour.

God the Father speaks from Heaven and glorifies His name:

John 12:28 Father, glorify thy name. Then came there a voice from heaven, saying, I have both glorified it, and will glorify it again.

John 12:29 The people therefore, that stood by, and heard it, said that it thundered: others said, An angel spake to him.

Why did some men hear God and others just hear noise? Why did God speak at this moment? Jesus does not have to hear God speak. He clarifies this by saying that God speaks for the sake of man:

John 12:30 Jesus answered and said, This voice came not because of me, but for your sakes.

Those who have followed the will of the Father can hear God clearly. Others just hear thunder and noise. Jesus is about to arrive at the appointed time, as first declared to Adam and Eve, to bruise the head of the serpent. Remember when God gave this great prophecy:

Genesis 3:15 And I will put enmity between thee and the woman, and between thy seed and her seed; it shall bruise thy head, and thou shalt bruise his heel.

The bruise to the head of the serpent (which is a death blow to the devil) is about to take place at the cross. Jesus will conquer and defeat Satan with God's plan of redemption at the cross. The upcoming death, burial, and resurrection, known as the Gospel, will cast Satan out forever. Man can be freed from his sin by the shed blood of the Savior.

John 12:31 Now is the judgment of this world: now shall the prince of this world be cast out.

Satan will bruise the heel of our Lord Jesus Christ at the cross. Jesus signifies crucifixion on the cross as the manner of death by saying He would be lifted up:

John 12:32 And I, if I be lifted up from the earth, will draw all men unto me.

John 12:33 This he said, signifying what death he should die.

This was not understood by all the people. They missed what the prophets said in the Old Testament that Jesus would come lowly as Zechariah 9:9 portrayed Him.

John 12:34 The people answered him, We have heard out of the law that Christ abideth for ever: and how sayest thou, The Son of man must be lifted up? who is this Son of man?

They missed what Isaiah said that He would be wounded for them:

Isaiah 53:5 But he was wounded for our transgressions, he was bruised for our iniquities: the chastisement of our peace was upon him; and with his stripes we are healed.

Jesus reveals that He will be with them for just a very short time and that He is the light of the world to all men. Jesus again says that the one and only way to become a child of that Light is through belief:

John 12:35 Then Jesus said unto them, Yet a little while is the light with you. Walk while ye have the light, lest darkness come upon you: for he that walketh in darkness knoweth not whither he goeth.

John 12:36 While ye have light, believe in the light, that ye may be the children of light. These things spake Jesus, and departed, and did hide himself from them.

God explains the real problem man has. The real problem man has is with God's plan. It is unbelief in His Word and in Jesus Christ and His finished work on the cross.

John 12:37 But though he had done so many miracles before them, yet they believed not on him:

The Gospels always parallel and perfect what God wanted to say in the Old Testament but would not because He did not want to reveal the name of the Savior.

Isaiah 53:1 Who hath believed our report? and to whom is the arm of the LORD revealed??

The Gospel of John mirrors this quote from Isaiah:

John 12:38 That the saying of Esaias the prophet might be fulfilled, which he spake, Lord, who hath believed our report? and to whom hath the arm of the Lord been revealed?

And again John quotes from Isaiah 6:10

Isaiah 6:10 Make the heart of this people fat, and make their ears heavy, and shut their eyes; lest they see with their eyes, and hear with their ears, and understand with their heart, and convert, and be healed.

Explaining why blindness came upon his people. Because they did not believe and were not converted:

John 12:39 Therefore they could not believe, because that Esaias said again,

John 12:40 He hath blinded their eyes, and hardened their heart; that they should not see with their eyes, nor understand with their heart, and be converted, and I should heal them.

John continues to quote from Isaiah 6:1

Isaiah 6:1 In the year that king Uzziah died I saw also the Lord sitting upon a throne, high and lifted up, and his train filled the temple.

The connection of the Old Testament to the New Testament is established between John and Isaiah and is cemented by the Holy Spirit:

John 12:41 These things said Esaias, when he saw his glory, and spake of him.

Some of the chief rulers would see the Lord Jesus as this light. He is that light that has come into the world. They would believe on Him but fear retribution.

John 12:42 Nevertheless among the chief rulers also many believed on him; but because of the Pharisees they did not confess him, lest they should be put out of the synagogue:

Fred A Kuypers

But the Pharisees would let the cares of this world occupy them. They would not hate this life but sought the "praise of men more than the praise of God"!

John 12:43 For they loved the praise of men more than the praise of God.

Jesus again declares His equal status with the Father:

John 12:44 Jesus cried and said, He that believeth on me, believeth not on me, but on him that sent me.

John 12:45 And he that seeth me seeth him that sent me.

The light of the world is Jesus:

John 12:46 I am come a light into the world, that whosoever believeth on me should not abide in darkness.

Jesus states a truth that rings forever. He did not come to judge the world but to save all who are in the world.

John 12:47 And if any man hear my words, and believe not, I judge him not: for I came not to judge the world, but to save the world.

At this point, He tells everyone that judgement has already been accomplished. It is the Ten Commandments, the law, that judge us. It is the Levitical law that no one can keep perfectly that judges us. It is our heart compared to the heart of God in the Psalms that judges us. Plainly speaking, it is the Bible that judges us! No man can say that he has kept the commands given in the Bible perfectly. So Jesus says:

John 12:48 He that rejecteth me, and receiveth not my words, hath one that judgeth him: the word that I have spoken, the same shall judge him in the last day.

All men are judged already and condemned according to the Bible:

John 3:18 He that believeth on him is not condemned: but he that believeth not is condemned already, because he hath not believed in the name of the only begotten Son of God.

All will be judged according to the Bible. The books of the Bible will be open on Judgment day, and every man's life will be judged and his name will be found either written in the book of life or not written in the book of life.

Revelation 20:11 And I saw a great white throne, and him that sat on it, from whose face the earth and the heaven fled away; and there was found no place for them.

Revelation 20:12 And I saw the dead, small and great, stand before God; and the books were opened: and another book was opened, which is the book of life: and the dead were judged out of those things which were written in the books, according to their works.

Notice what judges us, spoken again here in Revelation. Everyone will be judged by those things written in the books! That is the sixty-six books of the Bible. Jesus confirms this here and now, which is in total agreement with the Father.

John 12:49 For I have not spoken of myself; but the Father which sent me, he gave me a commandment, what I should say, and what I should speak.

John 12:50 And I know that his commandment is life everlasting: whatsoever I speak therefore, even as the Father said unto me, so I speak.

The eternal plan of God is given: life everlasting. Here Jesus is saying that you have one that judges you already, His Word, the Bible. God the Father is saying you can have His promise of life everlasting by believing in the Son of God, as He said in verse 46. And in First John God says it is this simple:

1 John 5:10 He that believeth on the Son of God hath the witness in himself: he that believeth not God hath made him a liar; because he believeth not the record that God gave of his Son.

1 John 5:11 And this is the record, that God hath given to us eternal life, and this life is in his Son.

1 John 5:12 He that hath the Son hath life; and he that hath not the Son of God hath not life.

1 John 5:13 These things have I written unto you that believe on the name of the Son of God; that ye may know that ye have eternal life, and that ye may believe on the name of the Son of God.

5:00 p.m. on Sunday, the Eleventh of Nisan

Now with less than two days left, there is a small amount of information given for the preparation of the Passover meal that takes place by Tuesday Evening. But this information is powerful. Today as Jesus was speaking in the temple according to John marks a different day than in Matthew and Mark. Jesus will then be in the house of Simon the leper, which is in Bethany. It is two different locations. It is two different nights. This past night on the Mount of Olives is Saturday night, and then tonight, He is at Simon the leper's house in Bethany.

Chapter 12

Nisan 12

Month of Nisan

1st day Yom Rishon Sunday	2nd day Yom Sheini Monday	3rd day Yom Shlishi Tuesday	4th day Yom R'vi'i Wednesday	5th day Yom Chamishi Thursday	6th day Yom Shishi Friday	Shabbat Yom Shabbat Saturday
Nisan 12th 6:00pm Monday begins	12th Nisan 13th 6:00am to 6:00pm Travel to Bethany to stay with Simon the leper. Judas's betrayal of Jesus is arranged for 30 pieces of silver.					

This chapter includes:

Matthew	Mark	Luke	John
26:6–26:16	14:3–14:11	22:1–22:6	

What a Finish! What a Start! The Month Jesus Met Man's Need

Fred A Kuypers

Night in Bethany; Travel to Jerusalem

Two days before Passover;

6:00 p.m. on Sunday, the Twelfth of Nisan

Second Day of the Week Begins

Jesus would retire tonight in Bethany at Simon house. After 6:00 p.m. it is now less than two days until the start of Passover. This is different than the previous night when Luke said He was on the Mount of Olives. He will go to the house of Simon the leper. Since Simon the leper lives in Bethany, which is a town on the southeast side of the Mount of Olives, his leprosy must have been healed. If it was not healed, he would have been an outcast and not allowed to live in any city, according to the book of Numbers:

Numbers 5:1 And the LORD spake unto Moses, saying,

Numbers 5:2 Command the children of Israel, that they put out of the camp every leper, and every one that hath an issue, and whosoever is defiled by the dead:

Numbers 5:3 Both male and female shall ye put out, without the camp shall ye put them; that they defile not their camps, in the midst whereof I dwell.

Though Simon was cleansed, he still was called Simon the leper. Those who are guilty of scandalous sins will oftentimes, though the sin be pardoned, bear the reproach of their sin. That sin will hardly be wiped away in people's eyes.

Proverbs 10:7 The memory of the just is blessed: but the name of the wicked shall rot.

Proverbs 22:1 A good name is rather to be chosen than great riches, and loving favour rather than silver and gold.

7:00 p.m. on Sunday, the Twelfth of Nisan

This night, Jesus goes to Bethany with his disciples. This is after the night He stayed on the Mount of Olives. Bethany, which is close to Jerusalem, is where Jesus would spend the night at Simon the leper's house. He is met by a woman with an alabaster box:

Matthew:

Matthew 26:6 Now when Jesus was in Bethany, in the house of Simon the leper,

Matthew 26:7 There came unto him a woman having an alabaster box of very precious ointment, and poured it on his head, as he sat at meat.

Mark:

Mark 14:3 And being in Bethany in the house of Simon the leper, as he sat at meat, there came a woman having an alabaster box of ointment of spikenard very precious; and she brake the box, and poured it on his head.

Many assume this woman with an alabaster box is Mary, Martha's sister. Some think it to be Mary Magdalene. But God has chosen not to reveal her. Instead God memorializes her!

Matthew's record of her:

Matthew 26:8 But when his disciples saw it, they had indignation, saying, To what purpose is this waste?

Matthew 26:9 For this ointment might have been sold for much, and given to the poor.

Matthew 26:10 When Jesus understood it, he said unto them, Why trouble ye the woman? for she hath wrought a good work upon me.

Matthew 26:11 For ye have the poor always with you; but me ye have not always.

Matthew 26:12 For in that she hath poured this ointment on my body, she did it for my burial.

Matthew 26:13 Verily I say unto you, Wheresoever this gospel shall be preached in the whole world, there shall also this, that this woman hath done, be told for a memorial of her.

And Mark's record of her:

Mark 14:4 And there were some that had indignation within themselves, and said, Why was this waste of the ointment made?

Mark 14:5 For it might have been sold for more than three hundred pence, and have been given to the poor. And they murmured against her.

Mark 14:6 And Jesus said, Let her alone; why trouble ye her? she hath wrought a good work on me.

Mark 14:7 For ye have the poor with you always, and whensoever ye will ye may do them good: but me ye have not always.

Mark 14:8 She hath done what she could: she is come aforehand to anoint my body to the burying.

Mark 14:9 Verily I say unto you, Wheresoever this gospel shall be preached throughout the whole world, this also that she hath done shall be spoken of for a memorial of her.

9:00 a.m. on Monday, the Twelfth of Nisan

As the day begins, His disciples are trying to understand what Jesus was talking about when He paid such an honor to the one who anointed Him. Judas did not understand. The chief priests did not understand. In just twenty-four hours, Jesus would advise His disciples to prepare for the Passover meal.

Luke 22:1 Now the feast of unleavened bread drew nigh, which is called the Passover.

He was selected as the sacrificial lamb two days ago by the chief priests. Now they began to scheme how to take Him.

Luke 22:2 And the chief priests and scribes sought how they might kill him; for they feared the people.

10:00 a.m. on Monday, the Twelfth of Nisan

But before that can happen, Judas went to the chief priests on this day to plot with them. He settled with them for thirty pieces of silver to betray Jesus at the earliest convenient time.

Matthew explains the betrayal of Jesus:

Matthew 26:14 Then one of the twelve, called Judas Iscariot, went unto the chief priests,

Matthew 26:15 And said unto them, What will ye give me, and I will deliver him unto you? And they covenanted with him for thirty pieces of silver.

Matthew 26:16 And from that time he sought opportunity to betray him.

Mark explains the betrayal of Jesus:

Mark 14:10 And Judas Iscariot, one of the twelve, went unto the chief priests, to betray him unto them.

Mark 14:11 And when they heard it, they were glad, and promised to give him money. And he sought how he might conveniently betray him.

Luke explains the betrayal of Jesus.

Luke 22:2 And the chief priests and scribes sought how they might kill him; for they feared the people.

Luke 22:3 Then entered Satan into Judas surnamed Iscariot, being of the number of the twelve.

Luke 22:4 And he went his way, and communed with the chief priests and captains, how he might betray him unto them.

Luke 22:5 And they were glad, and covenanted to give him money.

Luke 22:6 And he promised, and sought opportunity to betray him unto them in the absence of the multitude.

Satan is controlling Judas who has spent time and energy this day to find the chief priests and captains. He has communed with them, and they reached an agreement for money. Notice it is Matthew who gives the amount. This is again because Matthew is writing to the Jews, and they knew the amount as given in the Torah. Judas, after this day, will be back with the eleven so as to prepare for the supper tomorrow. This is in direct fulfillment of prophecy by Zechariah, as the chief priests and scribes weighed the value of Jesus' life:

Zechariah 11:12 And I said unto them, If ye think good, give me my price; and if not, forbear. So they weighed for my price thirty pieces of silver.

Zechariah 11:13 And the LORD said unto me, Cast it unto the potter: a goodly price that I was prised at of them. And I took the thirty pieces of silver, and cast them to the potter in the house of the LORD.

Many of the Psalms will be fulfilled as the day of our Lord's crucifixion approaches. In Psalm 40, Jesus is seen as obedient unto death. In fact, Jesus was delighted to do the Father's will:

Psalm 40:7 Then said I, Lo, I come: in the volume of the book it is written of me, Psalm 40:8 I delight to do thy will, O my God: yea, thy law is within my heart.

Psalm 41 is all about the betrayal of Jesus by Judas to the authorities who have the power to condemn Jesus.

Psalm 41:9 Yea, mine own familiar friend, in whom I trusted, which did eat of my bread, hath lifted up his heel against me.

All of the problems men have in not understanding that they need to be under the authority of the Son of God start with an attitude as seen in the heathen in Psalm 2. Men do not want the Lord to hold the reins (cords of control) over their life:

Psalm 2:1 Why do the heathen rage, and the people imagine a vain thing?

Psalm 2:2 The kings of the earth set themselves, and the rulers take counsel together, against the LORD, and against his anointed, saying,

Psalm 2:3 Let us break their bands asunder, and cast away their cords from us.

Psalm 2:4 He that sitteth in the heavens shall laugh: the Lord shall have them in derision.

Derision means that God shall laugh and mock at the attempt of man to rid himself of the control of the creator![25]Judas will have this day to make his deal with the chief priest and scribes. By tomorrow he will be back with the eleven; and by tomorrow night John writes that the Savior will tell him:

"That thou doest, do quickly."

5:00 p.m. on Monday, the Twelfth of Nisan

Judas has a place in history that is as low as one can go. But what does our pride mean to God? God created us. God gave us the ability to use our hands, our mouth, our feet, and the breath in our lungs. What can a man do that God does not already know? Nothing! If presenting our best works to God can improve our standing with Him, then Jesus did not have to go to the cross. But in less than two days from now, He will go to the cross and pay for my sins and not mine only but the sins of the whole world. Jesus would gladly bear that burden!

1John 2:1 My little children, these things write I unto you, that ye sin not. And if any man sin, we have an advocate with the Father, Jesus Christ the righteous:

---

[25]   Dr. James Strong, *Strongs Exhaustive Concordance of the Bible*. Dugan Publishers Inc. Gordonsville, TN. P.255

What a Finish! What a Start! The Month Jesus Met Man's Need

Fred A Kuypers

1John 2:2 And he is the propitiation for our sins: and not for ours only, but also for the sins of the whole world.

1John 2:3 And hereby we do know that we know him, if we keep his commandments.

1John 2:4 He that saith, I know him, and keepeth not his commandments, is a liar, and the truth is not in him.

1John 2:5 But whoso keepeth his word, in him verily is the love of God perfected: hereby know we that we are in him.

Chapter 13

Nisan 13

Month of Nisan

1st day Yom Rishon Sunday	2nd day Yom Sheini Monday	3rd day Yom Shlishi Tuesday	4th day Yom R'vi'i Wednesday	5th day Yom Chamishi Thursday	6th day Yom Shishi Friday	Shabbat Yom Shabbat Saturday
	Nisan 13th 6:00pm Tuesday begins	13th Nisan 14th 6:00am to 6:00pm Jesus and His disciples will go to Jerusalem and prepare for the Passover meal at 6:00 p.m. this night.				

This chapter includes:

Matthew	Mark	Luke	John
26:17–26:20	14:12–14:16	22:7–22:13	13:1

What a Finish! What a Start! The Month Jesus Met Man's Need

Fred A Kuypers

Night in Bethany and Travel in the Day to Jerusalem

Final day before Passover;

6:00 p.m. on Monday, the Thirteenth of Nisan

Twenty Four Hours until the Last Supper

After this night will be the day Jesus requests the Passover meal to be prepared. The upper room will need to be prepared. The supper will need to be readied. In exactly twenty-four hours, the Passover supper would begin. The Passover meal is an important meal. To understand this meal, one must understand the Jewish seder.[26] This meal is very holy to the Jew. It is a time when a place setting is set at the table for Elijah, and a cup of juice, known as the fruit of the vine, is prepared and set at the table for him. Elijah will herald the coming of the Messiah according to Malachi:

Malachi 4:5 Behold, I will send you Elijah the prophet before the coming of the great and dreadful day of the LORD:

Malachi 4:6 And he shall turn the heart of the fathers to the children, and the heart of the children to their fathers, lest I come and smite the earth with a curse.

Of course, the Bible declares this day has already occurred. It was declared to Zacharias and Elizabeth:

Luke 1:17 And he shall go before him in the spirit and power of Elias, to turn the hearts of the fathers to the children, and the disobedient to the wisdom of the just; to make ready a people prepared for the Lord.

Malachi describes the messenger who will prepare the way before the Lord:

Malachi 3:1 Behold, I will send my messenger, and he shall prepare the way before me: and the Lord, whom ye seek, shall suddenly come to his temple, even the messenger of the covenant, whom ye delight in: behold, he shall come, saith the LORD of hosts.

This messenger was John the Baptist as Jesus declared:

Luke 7:27 This is he, of whom it is written, Behold, I send my messenger before thy face, which shall prepare thy way before thee.

Luke 7:28 For I say unto you, Among those that are born of women there is not a greater prophet than John the Baptist: but he that is least in the kingdom of God is greater than he.

---

[26] Rabbi YY Kazen, Chabad-Lubavitch Media Center. http://www.chabad.org/holidays/passover/pesach_cdo/aid/1751/jewish/What-Is-a-Seder.htm Viewed 12–18–2017

This messenger, John the Baptist, was killed; beheaded by the Roman authorities. These same Roman authorities will order Jesus to be put to death by crucifixion:

Matthew 17:10 And his disciples asked him, saying, Why then say the scribes that Elias must first come?

Matthew 17:11 And Jesus answered and said unto them, Elias truly shall first come, and restore all things.

Matthew 17:12 But I say unto you, That Elias is come already, and they knew him not, but have done unto him whatsoever they listed. Likewise shall also the Son of man suffer of them.

Elijah (Elias) and Moses had a special relationship with Jesus. They are the two witnesses that appeared with the Lord on the Mount of Transfiguration:

Matthew 17:3 And, behold, there appeared unto them Moses and Elias talking with him.

Mark 9:4 And there appeared unto them Elias with Moses: and they were talking with Jesus.

After the rapture, during the seven-year tribulation, Elijah and Moses will appear again; three and a half years before the "great and dreadful" second coming of our Lord which is yet to take place. Elijah is one of the two witnesses who witnessed Jesus Christ at the Mount of Transfiguration pictured in Revelation:

Revelation 11:3 And I will give power unto my two witnesses, and they shall prophesy a thousand two hundred and threescore days, clothed in sackcloth.

Revelation 11:4 These are the two olive trees, and the two candlesticks standing before the God of the earth.

Revelation 11:5 And if any man will hurt them, fire proceedeth out of their mouth, and devoureth their enemies: and if any man will hurt them, he must in this manner be killed.

Revelation 11:6 These have power to shut heaven, that it rain not in the days of their prophecy: and have power over waters to turn them to blood, and to smite the earth with all plagues, as often as they will.

9:00 a.m. on Tuesday, the Thirteenth of Nisan

Here Luke gives some insight as to the timeframe of the days of unleavened bread. The Feast of Unleavened Bread drew near. This feast begins with the Passover day, sometimes called the "preparation day" for the "high Sabbath" first day of unleavened bread. It is better explained in Luke 22:7:

Luke 22:7 Then came the day of unleavened bread, when the passover must be killed.

It would start at 6:00 p.m. this Tuesday night. This entire feast begins with the Passover day, which is the day that the lamb is to be killed. The Passover day is not a Sabbath day. It is a day when work can and would be done.

1. The Lamb will have to be killed.

2. The Passover meal will have to be prepared.

3. The blood was applied to the doorposts at the first Passover (there was work to do).

4. The Lamb would have to be roasted with fire and shared with all in the house.

The Passover, or as it is sometimes called the beginning of the Feast of Unleavened Bread, or the preparation day (that is to prepare for the high Sabbath), is on the fourteenth of Nisan. This first day called Passover, which begins at 6:00 p.m. this night is the day before the seven days of unleavened bread. This may make the Feast of Unleavened Bread a total of eight days.

It is time to explain and to understand the Jewish feast of Passover as given in Exodus.

Exodus 12:1 And the LORD spake unto Moses and Aaron in the land of Egypt, saying,

Exodus 12:2 This month shall be unto you the beginning of months: it shall be the first month of the year to you.

Exodus 12:3 Speak ye unto all the congregation of Israel, saying, In the tenth day of this month they shall take to them every man a lamb, according to the house of their fathers, a lamb for an house:

Exodus 12:4 And if the household be too little for the lamb, let him and his neighbour next unto his house take it according to the number of the souls; every man according to his eating shall make your count for the lamb.

Exodus 12:5 Your lamb shall be without blemish, a male of the first year: ye shall take it out from the sheep, or from the goats:

Exodus 12:6 And ye shall keep it up until the fourteenth day of the same month: and the whole assembly of the congregation of Israel shall kill it in the evening.

Here is the timing for the start of the entire Feast of Unleavened Bread which goes for eight days: The first day of the Feast of Unleavened Bread will be called the Passover day and is on the fourteenth of Nisan. On this day, the male lamb, which was selected on the tenth of Nisan, will be killed. The timing of this is precisely accurate along with the timing of Christ's crucifixion as recorded in Mark 14:12. This is the same as Matthew 26:17: the first day of the Feast of Unleavened Bread as seen later this day. All four gospels will attest to this day leading up to the most important day of all time. In Exodus again, the seven-day Feast of Unleavened Bread is described:

Exodus 12:15 Seven days shall ye eat unleavened bread; even the first day ye shall put away leaven out of your houses: for whosoever eateth leavened bread from the first day until the seventh day, that soul shall be cut off from Israel.

Exodus 12:16 And in the first day there shall be an holy convocation, and in the seventh day there shall be an holy convocation to you; no manner of work shall be done in them, save that which every man must eat, that only may be done of you.

Exodus 12:17 And ye shall observe the feast of unleavened bread; for in this selfsame day have I brought your armies out of the land of Egypt: therefore shall ye observe this day in your generations by an ordinance for ever.

Exodus 12:18 In the first month, on the fourteenth day of the month at even, ye shall eat unleavened bread, until the one and twentieth day of the month at even.

The start of the fifteenth day which would be 6:00 p.m. on the day Passover ends (because Jews begin their day on the night before), a new holy convocation day would begin called a high Sabbath. Notice no manner of work. Again, nothing can be done on this high Sabbath. If this is followed yearly, then the day after the Passover will always be a high Sabbath or a day of holy convocation where no manner of work can be done. Following this, on the last day of unleavened bread it is another high Sabbath with no manner of work being done. That makes eight total days, which is, Passover and seven days of unleavened bread with the first and last day of unleavened bread being high Sabbaths. Since this is true, then it will be expected to see some special activity leading up to 6:00 p.m. this night, the beginning of the Passover day.

12:00 noon on Tuesday, the Thirteenth of Nisan

John makes a short but powerful and loving statement just a short time before the Passover meal. For it will be at this time, during the Passover meal, that Jesus will spend His last free moments with His disciples. Later this upcoming night, He would be betrayed:

John 13:1 Now before the feast of the passover, when Jesus knew that his hour was come that he should depart out of this world unto the Father, having loved his own which were in the world, he loved them unto the end.

The fourteenth of Nisan has several identities.

1. Passover

2. First day of unleavened bread when the lamb is slain.

3. First day of the Feast of Unleavened Bread, eight days total.

4. This day is also called the day of preparation for the high Sabbath.

5. It is the day before the high Sabbath. The high Sabbath is a day of holy convocation; no manner of work shall be done in them, as explained in Exodus 12:16, which is the first day of the seven days of unleavened bread.

3:00 p.m. on Tuesday, the Thirteenth of Nisan

As the 6:00 p.m. hour approaches, Matthew states that Passover is called the first day of the Feast of Unleavened Bread. This makes for an eight-day period of unleavened bread. The Passover day is part of the eight days, with the seven days of unleavened bread included.

Matthew 26:17 Now the first day of the feast of unleavened bread the disciples came to Jesus, saying unto him, Where wilt thou that we prepare for thee to eat the passover?

The Gospel of Mark states that Passover, the day that the lamb is to be slain, is the start of unleavened bread. This day called Passover cannot be the high Sabbath day, the first day of unleavened bread as that day is a day of no servile work as explained in Leviticus:

Leviticus 23:4 These are the feasts of the LORD, even holy convocations, which ye shall proclaim in their seasons.

Leviticus 23:5 In the fourteenth day of the first month at even is the LORD'S passover.

Leviticus 23:6 And on the fifteenth day of the same month is the feast of unleavened bread unto the LORD: seven days ye must eat unleavened bread.

Therefore Mark must be referring to the entire eight days of Passover and unleavened bread. On this day, the Passover lamb was to be killed and that would be a work not allowed on the high Sabbath.

Mark 14:12 And the first day of unleavened bread, when they killed the passover, his disciples said unto him, Where wilt thou that we go and prepare that thou mayest eat the passover?

Jesus instructed the apostles to make the Passover meal ready.

Luke 22:8 And he sent Peter and John, saying, Go and prepare us the passover, that we may eat.

There are three accounts of the preparation of the last supper in the synoptic Gospels.

Matthew's view of the preparation of the Passover meal:

Matthew 26:18 And he said, Go into the city to such a man, and say unto him, The Master saith, My time is at hand; I will keep the passover at thy house with my disciples.

Matthew 26:19 And the disciples did as Jesus had appointed them; and they made ready the passover.

Mark's view of the preparation of the Passover meal:

Mark 14:13 And he sendeth forth two of his disciples, and saith unto them, Go ye into the city, and there shall meet you a man bearing a pitcher of water: follow him.

Mark 14:14 And wheresoever he shall go in, say ye to the goodman of the house, The Master saith, Where is the guestchamber, where I shall eat the passover with my disciples?

Mark 14:15 And he will shew you a large upper room furnished and prepared: there make ready for us.

Mark 14:16 And his disciples went forth, and came into the city, and found as he had said unto them: and they made ready the passover.

Mark 14:17 And in the evening he cometh with the twelve.

Luke's view of the preparation of the Passover meal:

Luke 22:9 And they said unto him, Where wilt thou that we prepare?

Luke 22:10 And he said unto them, Behold, when ye are entered into the city, there shall a man meet you, bearing a pitcher of water; follow him into the house where he entereth in.

Luke 22:11 And ye shall say unto the goodman of the house, The Master saith unto thee, Where is the guestchamber, where I shall eat the passover with my disciples?

Luke 22:12 And he shall shew you a large upper room furnished: there make ready.

Luke 22:13 And they went, and found as he had said unto them: and they made ready the passover.

5:00 p.m. on Tuesday, the Thirteenth of Nisan

Jesus is about to begin the most important day in history. The fourteenth of Nisan is the day that Jesus would become the perfect substitute Lamb required by God to give a blood atonement for our sins. This is so clearly stated in Hebrews:

Hebrews 9:22 And almost all things are by the law purged with blood; and without shedding of blood is no remission.

There is no need to sacrifice Jesus again. Any religion that crucifies or claims to sacrifice Jesus again is committing horrible blasphemy against God.

Hebrews 9:28 So Christ was once offered to bear the sins of many; and unto them that look for him shall he appear the second time without sin unto salvation.

Jesus Christ is about to be offered up as the sacrificial lamb to God. This only had to happen once as the above verse states. This sacrifice was made complete by the supreme cost of the Savior, our Lord Jesus Christ. God will not allow this to happen again. Any religion that allows for a re-crucifixion of Jesus Christ is the ultimate insult to God Almighty.

Jesus begins the most important day in history! The day my sins were paid for.

Matthew 26:20 Now when the even was come, he sat down with the twelve.

Chapter 14

Nisan 14

Month of Nisan

1st day Yom Rishon Sunday	2nd day Yom Sheini Monday	3rd day Yom Shlishi Tuesday	4th day Yom R'vi'i Wednesday	5th day Yom Chamishi Thursday	6th day Yom Shishi Friday	Shabbat Yom Shabbat Saturday
		Nisan 14th 6:00pm Wednesday begins	14th Nisan 15th 6:00am to 6:00pm Jesus the Lamb of God is cut off and is placed in the grave before 6:00 p.m. when the high Sabbath begins.			

This chapter includes:

Matthew	Mark	Luke	John
26:21–27:61	14:17–15:47	22:14–23:55	13:2–19:42

What a Finish! What a Start! The Month Jesus Met Man's Need

Fred A Kuypers

Last Supper Tonight; then to the Garden of Gethsemane; The Trials of Christ; Daytime in Jerusalem to Mt. Calvary and the Death of Jesus Christ.

6:00 p.m. on Tuesday, the Fourteenth of Nisan

Passover Begins

This day the supper, which today is called the Seder, is eaten. The traditional Seder of today has more rituals than any other Jewish ceremonial meal. Most important, participants are expected to read through the Haggada, a short book detailing the story of the Jewish Exodus from Egypt.[27] The religious leaders will come later this day and bring Jesus to Pilate and admit that the Passover could have been eaten already as described by John 18:28. This meal would not be when the lamb was eaten. The lamb will be slain later this day and eaten through the night if the passage from Exodus 12 is followed.

John Gill explained as quoted in the preface of this book the Evening of this day would begin at 3:00pm:

Exodus 12:6 And ye shall keep it up until the fourteenth day of the same month: and the whole assembly of the congregation of Israel shall kill it in the evening.

Exodus 12:7 And they shall take of the blood, and strike it on the two side posts and on the upper door post of the houses, wherein they shall eat it.

They were to eat of the lamb that night with bitter herbs and unleavened bread:

Exodus 12:8 And they shall eat the flesh in that night, roast with fire, and unleavened bread; and with bitter herbs they shall eat it.

They were to cook it well and roast it with all its parts:

Exodus 12:9 Eat not of it raw, nor sodden at all with water, but roast with fire; his head with his legs, and with the purtenance thereof.

They were to eat it throughout the night of the high Sabbath the 15th of Nisan (Abib).

Exodus 12:10 And ye shall let nothing of it remain until the morning; and that which remaineth of it until the morning ye shall burn with fire.

---

[27]   Telushkin, Joseph Rabbi. Jewish Literacy. William Morrow and Company Inc. New York. C1991. P585

They were to eat it fully clothed and prepared for what was to come, not sitting at the table with their shoes off.

Exodus 12:11 And thus shall ye eat it; with your loins girded, your shoes on your feet, and your staff in your hand; and ye shall eat it in haste: it is the LORD'S passover.

6:01 p.m. on Tuesday, the Fourteenth of Nisan

Passover

The Gospel of Luke describes the start of this most important day. Just a few minutes after the hour was come that the day changed from the thirteenth of Nisan to the fourteenth at 6:00 p.m.:

Luke 22:14 And when the hour was come, he sat down, and the twelve apostles with him.

Luke 22:15 And he said unto them, With desire I have desired to eat this passover with you before I suffer:

Luke 22:16 For I say unto you, I will not any more eat thereof, until it be fulfilled in the kingdom of God.

As they began to eat, Jesus declares this prophecy about Judas' betrayal. After Supper Luke will describe this betrayer sitting at the table. However, Matthew and Mark describe him before the supper.

Matthew's view of the betrayal:

Matthew 26:21 And as they did eat, he said, Verily I say unto you, that one of you shall betray me.

Matthew 26:22 And they were exceeding sorrowful, and began every one of them to say unto him, Lord, is it I?

Matthew 26:23 And he answered and said, He that dippeth his hand with me in the dish, the same shall betray me.

Matthew 26:24 The Son of man goeth as it is written of him: but woe unto that man by whom the Son of man is betrayed! it had been good for that man if he had not been born.

Matthew 26:25 Then Judas, which betrayed him, answered and said, Master, is it I? He said unto him, Thou hast said.

Mark's view of the betrayal:

Mark 14:18 And as they sat and did eat, Jesus said, Verily I say unto you, One of you which eateth with me shall betray me.

Mark 14:19 And they began to be sorrowful, and to say unto him one by one, Is it I? and another said, Is it I?

Mark 14:20 And he answered and said unto them, It is one of the twelve, that dippeth with me in the dish.

Mark 14:21 The Son of man indeed goeth, as it is written of him: but woe to that man by whom the Son of man is betrayed! good were it for that man if he had never been born.

After the meal, Jesus will once again point out the hand of the betrayer as quoted by Luke just a few minutes after the Lord's Supper.

6:15 p.m. on Tuesday, the Fourteenth of Nisan
Passover

The Lord's Supper was instituted to remind everyone that Jesus did come. That He did suffer on the cross for our sins as the synoptic gospels declare:

The Gospel of Matthew:

Matthew 26:26 And as they were eating, Jesus took bread, and blessed it, and brake it, and gave it to the disciples, and said, Take, eat; this is my body.

Matthew 26:27 And he took the cup, and gave thanks, and gave it to them, saying, Drink ye all of it;

Matthew 26:28 For this is my blood of the new testament, which is shed for many for the remission of sins.

Matthew 26:29 But I say unto you, I will not drink henceforth of this fruit of the vine, until that day when I drink it new with you in my Father's kingdom.

The Gospel of Mark:

Mark 14:22 And as they did eat, Jesus took bread, and blessed, and brake it, and gave to them, and said, Take, eat: this is my body.

Mark 14:23 And he took the cup, and when he had given thanks, he gave it to them: and they all drank of it.

Mark 14:24 And he said unto them, This is my blood of the new testament, which is shed for many.

Mark 14:25 Verily I say unto you, I will drink no more of the fruit of the vine, until that day that I drink it new in the kingdom of God.

The Gospel of Luke:

Luke 22:17 And he took the cup, and gave thanks, and said, Take this, and divide it among yourselves:

Luke 22:18 For I say unto you, I will not drink of the fruit of the vine, until the kingdom of God shall come.

Luke 22:19 And he took bread, and gave thanks, and brake it, and gave unto them, saying, This is my body which is given for you: this do in remembrance of me.

Luke 22:20 Likewise also the cup after supper, saying, This cup is the new testament in my blood, which is shed for you.

The Lord's Supper is the second of two orders that are to be carried out by the local churches. The first order is to baptize those who have made a decision in their heart to follow Jesus Christ as their Lord and Master. Members in the local church are to first go into the area where they live and win the lost to Christ. As the lost become saved and are now new Christians, they grow and realize that to follow Christ; they must first follow Him in baptism. The church is ordered to carry this out. It is by immersion.

Matthew 28:19 Go ye therefore, and teach all nations, baptizing them in the name of the Father, and of the Son, and of the Holy Ghost:

Matthew 28:20 Teaching them to observe all things whatsoever I have commanded you: and, lo, I am with you alway, even unto the end of the world. Amen.

To win souls is a wise thing to do:

Proverbs 11:30 The fruit of the righteous is a tree of life; and he that winneth souls is wise.

Winning is an old Scottish term used in mining such as to "win the coal" or to discover and dig the coal out from a coal mine. It would mean to go in and find the coal that already existed, locate it, dig it out, and transport it out of the mine. That is witnessing in a nutshell. Christians are to go into the world, locate a lost soul, dig them out of the clutches of Satan and hell, and bring them to Jesus! Once this is accomplished, those who have been won need to be baptized to join a local church. This public display of baptism shows all who witness it that the new believer is following Christ in His death, burial, and resurrection. The second ordinance of the Lord's Supper is then carried out by the local church according to the direction given to the church, such as in Corinth:

1 Corinthians 11:23 For I have received of the Lord that which also I delivered unto you, That the Lord Jesus the same night in which he was betrayed took bread:

1 Corinthians 11:24 And when he had given thanks, he brake it, and said, Take, eat: this is my body, which is broken for you: this do in remembrance of me.

1 Corinthians 11:25 After the same manner also he took the cup, when he had supped, saying, This cup is the new testament in my blood: this do ye, as oft as ye drink it, in remembrance of me.

1 Corinthians 11:26 For as often as ye eat this bread, and drink this cup, ye do shew the Lord's death till he come.

This order is followed as often as a church sees the need of reminding its members to examine their lives and to look forward to the soon return of Jesus.

Following the Lord's Supper, Jesus again points out the hand of the betrayer at the table. It is given by Luke's account. Notice there are two different accounts. Earlier Matthew and Mark state the disciples were asking Jesus "is it I". However the disciples discuss it among themselves. After the meal, the disciples are still questioning what is happening and now it is Luke's turn to write about the betrayer:

Luke 22:21 But, behold, the hand of him that betrayeth me is with me on the table.

Luke 22:22 And truly the Son of man goeth, as it was determined: but woe unto that man by whom he is betrayed!

Luke 22:23 And they began to enquire among themselves, which of them it was that should do this thing.

6:30 p.m. on Tuesday, the Fourteenth of Nisan

Passover

It doesn't take long for the disciples to go off topic and argue again as to who is the greatest among them. At the supper table, the apostles are once again striving with each other over who is the best and should be number one with Jesus. Luke is the only Gospel to record this exchange between the apostles:

Luke 22:24 And there was also a strife among them, which of them should be accounted the greatest.

Luke 22:25 And he said unto them, The kings of the Gentiles exercise lordship over them; and they that exercise authority upon them are called benefactors.

Luke 22:26 But ye shall not be so: but he that is greatest among you, let him be as the younger; and he that is chief, as he that doth serve.

Luke 22:27 For whether is greater, he that sitteth at meat, or he that serveth? is not he that sitteth at meat? but I am among you as he that serveth.

Jesus declares He came to serve and, in a few moments, will wash the feet of them with Him. Jesus tells His twelve that they are in a special position to sit at the table with Jesus at this time:

Luke 22:28 Ye are they which have continued with me in my temptations.

Luke 22:29 And I appoint unto you a kingdom, as my Father hath appointed unto me;

Luke 22:30 That ye may eat and drink at my table in my kingdom, and sit on thrones judging the twelve tribes of Israel.

Jesus has something special to say to Peter. He reveals that Peter is not yet surrendered to Him. Peter is not yet converted.

Luke 22:31 And the Lord said, Simon, Simon, behold, Satan hath desired to have you, that he may sift you as wheat:

Luke 22:32 But I have prayed for thee, that thy faith fail not: and when thou art converted, strengthen thy brethren.

However, Peter shows his desire to follow the Lord. Remember that desire or dedication or sincerity will not save a person from eternal damnation in hell. Repentance leading to belief in the heart; and that belief is what saves a man:

Luke 22:33 And he said unto him, Lord, I am ready to go with thee, both into prison, and to death.

Jesus at this time predicts the denial of Peter for the first time. This prediction happened three times. This first time before they went to Gethsemane, as described here in Luke. It happens again shortly after they leave for the Mount of Olives, as it says in Matthew and Mark, and a third time in John.

Luke 22:34 And he said, I tell thee, Peter, the cock shall not crow this day, before that thou shalt thrice deny that thou knowest me.

Jesus adds something here describing what His apostles were to take with them. A weapon is ordered for each apostle to have. It is so necessary that Jesus even says to sell your garment to obtain it:

Luke 22:35 And he said unto them, When I sent you without purse, and scrip, and shoes, lacked ye any thing? And they said, Nothing.

Luke 22:36 Then said he unto them, But now, he that hath a purse, let him take it, and likewise his scrip: and he that hath no sword, let him sell his garment, and buy one.

Luke 22:37 For I say unto you, that this that is written must yet be accomplished in me, And he was reckoned among the transgressors: for the things concerning me have an end.

The weapon in those days of course was a sword. Jesus said everyone should have one. Certainly, this was not for attacking, not for offense or each disciple would have more than one. This is obviously for defensive measures as a deterrent. When you have something valuable and worth defending, such as a wife, children, and personal beliefs, Jesus says to take a weapon:

Luke 22:38 And they said, Lord, behold, here are two swords. And he said unto them, It is enough.

6:45 p.m. on Tuesday, the Fourteenth of Nisan

Passover

The washing of the feet of the apostles by Jesus is about to take place. However certain things at this time do not follow the scriptures. Several of the Exodus commands given are not followed by Jesus at this last supper meal. This meal is different from the meal of the Exodus Passover in the following ways:

- The meal is the first thing at the start of the Passover day
- Jesus does not have His loins girded but undresses.
- All are barefoot and not with shoes as Jesus washes their feet.
- The lamb that is to be killed has not taken place yet. It is a small part—one-sixth of the Passover meal today—which includes six items. Back when God gave this to Moses, they were to eat three things: (1) Bitter herbs; (2) unleavened bread; and (3) the lamb itself.

Jews today have added several things to the Seder or Passover meal.[28] But mainly there is:

1. *Shmurah matzah-* Unleavened Bread

---

[28]   Telushkin, Joseph Rabbi. Jewish Literacy. William Morrow and Company Inc. New York. C1991. P585

2. *Maror*- Bitter herbs (horseradish or something as strong) to bring tears to remind them of the bondage in Egypt. Sometimes Lettuce symbolizes the bitter enslavement of Jewish fathers in Egypt is used. The leaves of romaine lettuce are not bitter, but the stem, when left to grow in the ground, turns hard and bitter.

3. *Kharoset*- The paste which is a mixture of apples, nuts, and wine, which resembles the mortar and brick made by the Jews when they toiled for Pharaoh.

4. *Zeroa*- A piece of roasted meat (shankbone) represents the lamb that was the special Paschal sacrifice on the eve of the exodus from Egypt, and annually, on the afternoon before Passover, in the holy temple. The meat of this animal constituted the main part of the Passover meal[29].

5. *Karpas*- A vegetable or non-bitter root vegetable (parsley) alludes to the backbreaking work of the Jews as slaves.

6. *Chagigah*- A hard-boiled egg represents the holiday offering brought in the days of the holy temple

For this Passover unleavened bread was at the table. Bitter herbs could have been prepared by the "Goodman of the house" or by the disciples in the upper room prior to 6:00 p.m. However, there is no mention of the lamb being slain. The Lamb, known as Jesus Christ the Lamb of God, would not be slain until God's proper time, the evening or 3:00 p.m. on this fourteenth day of the month.

Jesus washes the disciple's feet. Why does the church not practice this today? First because no church followed it in scripture and secondly no further instruction is given for it, unlike the Lord's Supper, which is repeated with further instructions to the church in Corinth.

John 13:2 And supper being ended, the devil having now put into the heart of Judas Iscariot, Simon's son, to betray him;

John 13:3 Jesus knowing that the Father had given all things into his hands, and that he was come from God, and went to God;

John 13:4 He riseth from supper, and laid aside his garments; and took a towel, and girded himself.

John 13:5 After that he poureth water into a bason, and began to wash the disciples' feet, and to wipe them with the towel wherewith he was girded.

John 13:6 Then cometh he to Simon Peter: and Peter saith unto him, Lord, dost thou wash my feet?

John 13:7 Jesus answered and said unto him, What I do thou knowest not now; but thou shalt know hereafter.

---

29   "The Seder Plate ". https://www.chabad.org/holidays/passover/pesach_cdo/aid/1998/jewish/The-Seder-Plate.htm. Viewed Feb 21, 2 019.

John 13:8 Peter saith unto him, Thou shalt never wash my feet. Jesus answered him, If I wash thee not, thou hast no part with me.

John 13:9 Simon Peter saith unto him, Lord, not my feet only, but also my hands and my head.

John 13:10 Jesus saith to him, He that is washed needeth not save to wash his feet, but is clean every whit: and ye are clean, but not all.

John 13:11 For he knew who should betray him; therefore said he, Ye are not all clean.

John describes what the washing of feet is all about. It is about loving and serving others. Today foot washing is not a necessity in public as it was in Jesus' time. But helping others with transportation or house chores or yard raking or sitting with elderly in need are services we can do for each other. Here John quotes the Lord as Jesus speaks of the example He is setting:

John 13:12 So after he had washed their feet, and had taken his garments, and was set down again, he said unto them, Know ye what I have done to you?

John 13:13 Ye call me Master and Lord: and ye say well; for so I am.

John 13:14 If I then, your Lord and Master, have washed your feet; ye also ought to wash one another's feet.

John 13:15 For I have given you an example, that ye should do as I have done to you.

John 13:16 Verily, verily, I say unto you, The servant is not greater than his lord; neither he that is sent greater than he that sent him.

John 13:17 If ye know these things, happy are ye if ye do them.

John gives his view of the betrayal after the washing of the feet. John spoke of the betrayal at dinner in verse 2, prior to the washing of the feet, but here John further elaborates on the betrayal:

John 13:18 I speak not of you all: I know whom I have chosen: but that the scripture may be fulfilled, He that eateth bread with me hath lifted up his heel against me.

John 13:19 Now I tell you before it come, that, when it is come to pass, ye may believe that I am he.

John 13:20 Verily, verily, I say unto you, He that receiveth whomsoever I send receiveth me; and he that receiveth me receiveth him that sent me.

John 13:21 When Jesus had thus said, he was troubled in spirit, and testified, and said, Verily, verily, I say unto you, that one of you shall betray me.

John 13:22 Then the disciples looked one on another, doubting of whom he spake.

John 13:23 Now there was leaning on Jesus' bosom one of his disciples, whom Jesus loved.

This is the first time that the phrase mentioning of the disciple "whom Jesus loved" appears. This phrase is agreed by all to be none other than John the Apostle who is writing this gospel. This phrase only appears five times in the Bible, and every time it is by John as he describes his closeness to Jesus.

Simon Peter asks John to question Jesus to name the one who would betray Him.

John 13:24 Simon Peter therefore beckoned to him, that he should ask who it should be of whom he spake.

John 13:25 He then lying on Jesus' breast saith unto him, Lord, who is it?

Jesus responds without naming the betrayer. This would have caused an ugly scene between all the disciples, so Jesus just gives a clue:

John 13:26 Jesus answered, He it is, to whom I shall give a sop, when I have dipped it. And when he had dipped the sop, he gave it to Judas Iscariot, the son of Simon.

John 13:27 And after the sop Satan entered into him. Then said Jesus unto him, That thou doest, do quickly.

The clue is not fully understood by John or any of the disciples. But just as Jesus said it, Judas went immediately out of the upper room:

John 13:28 Now no man at the table knew for what intent he spake this unto him.

John 13:29 For some of them thought, because Judas had the bag, that Jesus had said unto him, Buy those things that we have need of against the feast; or, that he should give something to the poor.

John 13:30 He then having received the sop went immediately out: and it was night.

7:00 p.m. on Tuesday, the Fourteenth of Nisan
Passover

"And it was night." This would be dark after twilight, maybe 7:00 or 8:00 p.m. Judas leaves to find the chief priests and scribes to tell them where Jesus could be located. Judas knows that they will be heading to where Jesus liked to pray. The disciples sing a hymn together before departing for the Garden of Gethsemane, located on the Mount of Olives:

Matthew and Mark together:

Matthew 26:30 And when they had sung an hymn, they went out into the mount of Olives.

Mark 14:26 And when they had sung an hymn, they went out into the mount of Olives.

It must have been routine that after a meal like this, Jesus would go where He liked to pray to His heavenly Father. Judas must have known this for he would soon lead Malchus and the others to the garden of Gethsemane where Jesus would go. As they are ready to leave, Jesus speaks to them about what is going to take place shortly.

John 13:31 Therefore, when he was gone out, Jesus said, Now is the Son of man glorified, and God is glorified in him.

Christ is removing the veil surrounding His death. Jesus states that both He and his Father would be glorified by it. He begins to open his desire to explain to His disciples and acquaint them with His death.

John 13:32 If God be glorified in him, God shall also glorify him in himself, and shall straightway glorify him.

First, Jesus points out that all will be offended with Him. Matthew and Mark will say that Jesus quotes from the Old Testament, from the book of Zechariah:

Zechariah 13:7 Awake, O sword, against my shepherd, and against the man that is my fellow, saith the LORD of hosts: smite the shepherd, and the sheep shall be scattered: and I will turn mine hand upon the little ones.--

Matthew:

Matthew 26:31 Then saith Jesus unto them, All ye shall be offended because of me this night: for it is written, I will smite the shepherd, and the sheep of the flock shall be scattered abroad.

Mark:

Mark 14:27 And Jesus saith unto them, All ye shall be offended because of me this night: for it is written, I will smite the shepherd, and the sheep shall be scattered.

Then Jesus tells the disciples that after He is raised, He will appear unto them in Galilee, which is a four-day trip to the north, up to the area around the Sea of Galilee. Peter and the others would not fully understand what Jesus is telling them:

Matthew:

Matthew 26:32 But after I am risen again, I will go before you into Galilee.

Mark:

Mark 14:28 But after that I am risen, I will go before you into Galilee.

Secondly, He addresses them in the most tender, affectionate way as "little children," expressing the relationship that existed between them. Jesus gives His new command that His followers love one another. They have just left the upper chamber and are about to walk to the garden of Gethsemane:

John 13:33 Little children, yet a little while I am with you. Ye shall seek me: and as I said unto the Jews, Whither I go, ye cannot come; so now I say to you.

John 13:34 A new commandment I give unto you, That ye love one another; as I have loved you, that ye also love one another.

John 13:35 By this shall all men know that ye are my disciples, if ye have love one to another.

This is the message of feet washing! The disciples, like all of us, must learn to love one another.

Peter will address what Jesus said earlier about his denial. It is still bothering him. If Peter will deny Jesus three times before the cock crows, perhaps Jesus will warn Peter three times this night. Notice this statement Peter made recorded in John is slightly different than how Matthew and Mark recorded Peter at this time when they are preparing to walk to the garden:

John 13:36 Simon Peter said unto him, Lord, whither goest thou? Jesus answered him, Whither I go, thou canst not follow me now; but thou shalt follow me afterwards.

John 13:37 Peter said unto him, Lord, why cannot I follow thee now? I will lay down my life for thy sake.

In John, the reply from Jesus is stated. Again, it is about the fact that Peter will deny Him three times:

John 13:38 Jesus answered him, Wilt thou lay down thy life for my sake? Verily, verily, I say unto thee, The cock shall not crow, till thou hast denied me thrice.

This is what Peter had to say as given by Matthew and Mark:

Matthew:

Matthew 26:33 Peter answered and said unto him, Though all men shall be offended because of thee, yet will I never be offended.

Mark:

Mark 14:29 But Peter said unto him, Although all shall be offended, yet will not I.

Earlier, Luke said for the first time in Luke 22:34 that Peter would deny Him three times. When Luke declared this they were still at supper. Then the Scripture says in John 13:31-38 that they were out of the upper room and preparing to walk to Gethsemane, and Jesus tells Peter again that he will deny Him. In Matthew Christ narrows it down to this very day; even this very night!

Matthew:

Matthew 26:34 Jesus said unto him, Verily I say unto thee, That this night, before the cock crow, thou shalt deny me thrice.

Mark adds that the cock will crow twice. This will be addressed in a few hours when daybreak occurs:

Mark 14:30 And Jesus saith unto him, Verily I say unto thee, That this day, even in this night, before the cock crow twice, thou shalt deny me thrice.

Remember, it is not just Peter that says I will never deny thee! Matthew writes that all the disciples say they will not deny him:

Matthew 26:35 Peter said unto him, Though I should die with thee, yet will I not deny thee. Likewise also said all the disciples.

Mark writes that all the disciples say they will not deny Him also:

Mark 14:31 But he spake the more vehemently, If I should die with thee, I will not deny thee in any wise. Likewise also said they all.

7:15 p.m. on Tuesday, the Fourteenth of Nisan

Passover

The words from John chapters 14–17, are spoken by Jesus as they prepare to leave the goodman's house. It is west of the temple mount area, and they walk heading east through Jerusalem and to the Mount of Olives where the Garden of Gethsemane is located. *If* Jesus walked on the Via Dolorosa, it would be at this point, leaving the goodman's house and heading to the temple mount and onward to the garden of Gethsemane, not later during the crucifixion. This walk will be a very intimate and enlightening time for the disciples. Jesus will comfort and unveil many truths that are about to take place in the apostles' lives. One of the most comforting statements in the entire Bible is about to be spoken by Jesus himself:

John 14:1 Let not your heart be troubled: ye believe in God, believe also in me.

John 14:2 In my Father's house are many mansions: if *it were* not *so*, I would have told you. I go to prepare a place for you.

John 14:3 And if I go and prepare a place for you, I will come again, and receive you unto myself; that where I am, *there* ye may be also.

John 14:4 And whither I go ye know, and the way ye know.

"Doubting Thomas" will speak up at this point:

John 14:5 Thomas saith unto him, Lord, we know not whither thou goest; and how can we know the way?

The statement to end all statements was made by Jesus Himself!

John 14:6 Jesus saith unto him, I am the way, the truth, and the life: no man cometh unto the Father, but by me.

Jesus will restate His claims in the past, not because He was vague or unclear but because His followers were "of little faith," lacking confidence in what Jesus had taught them.

John 14:7 If ye had known me, ye should have known my Father also: and from henceforth ye know him, and have seen him.

John 14:8 Philip saith unto him, Lord, shew us the Father, and it sufficeth us.

John 14:9 Jesus saith unto him, Have I been so long time with you, and yet hast thou not known me, Philip? he that hath seen me hath seen the Father; and how sayest thou *then*, Shew us the Father?

John 14:10 Believest thou not that I am in the Father, and the Father in me? the words that I speak unto you I speak not of myself: but the Father that dwelleth in me, he doeth the works.

John 14:11 Believe me that I *am* in the Father, and the Father in me: or else believe me for the very works' sake.

Jesus gives two things to assure them:
   (1.) That they should do works such as He has done and
   (2.) That they should do greater works than these.

What a Finish! What a Start! The Month Jesus Met Man's Need

Fred A Kuypers

John 14:12 Verily, verily, I say unto you, He that believeth on me, the works that I do shall he do also; and greater *works* than these shall he do; because I go unto my Father.

What can Christians do today that Jesus did and even in greater abundance? Win souls to Christ!

John 14:13 And whatsoever ye shall ask in my name, that will I do, that the Father may be glorified in the Son.

John 14:14 If ye shall ask any thing in my name, I will do *it*.

How important is it to keep God's commandments?

➢ The first of seven signs of a believer is given. It is one who keeps His commandments:

John 14:15 If ye love me, keep my commandments.

The first promise to the believer that Jesus would reveal was that He would not leave us comfortless or without aid. It was the promise of the abiding and indwelling of the Holy Spirit of God:

John 14:16 And I will pray the Father, and he shall give you another Comforter, that he may abide with you for ever;

John 14:17 *Even* the Spirit of truth; whom the world cannot receive, because it seeth him not, neither knoweth him: but ye know him; for he dwelleth with you, and shall be in you.

John 14:18 I will not leave you comfortless: I will come to you.

John 14:19 Yet a little while, and the world seeth me no more; but ye see me: because I live, ye shall live also.

John 14:20 At that day ye shall know that I *am* in my Father, and ye in me, and I in you.

➢ Second, Jesus mentions the sign of a believer is one who keeps His commandments:

John 14:21 He that hath my commandments, and keepeth them, he it is that loveth me: and he that loveth me shall be loved of my Father, and I will love him, and will manifest myself to him.

John 14:22 Judas saith unto him, not Iscariot, Lord, how is it that thou wilt manifest thyself unto us, and not unto the world?

➢ Third, Jesus mentions the sign of a believer is one who keeps His words (commandments):

John 14:23 Jesus answered and said unto him, If a man love me, he will keep my words: and my Father will love him, and we will come unto him, and make our abode with him.

➢ Fourth, Jesus mentions the sign of a believer is one who keeps His sayings (commandments) and the believer's relationship with Jesus:

John 14:24 He that loveth me not keepeth not my sayings: and the word which ye hear is not mine, but the Father's which sent me.

John 14:25 These things have I spoken unto you, being *yet* present with you.

Fred A Kuypers

Jesus puts a huge emphasis on the gift that God the Father will send to each one who has put their faith and trust in Jesus Christ. That gift is the Comforter, otherwise known as the Holy Ghost, the third part of the Godhead. His work on earth will be as our accountability partner. Today many organizations want to replace the accountability partner with another person. This is not what Jesus teaches here. The Holy Ghost is everyone's accountability partner. He will teach and instruct. He will remind and comfort.

John 14:26 But the Comforter, *which is* the Holy Ghost, whom the Father will send in my name, he shall teach you all things, and bring all things to your remembrance, whatsoever I have said unto you.

Christians often talk about a peace "which passes all understanding" (Philippians 4:7). It is the peace that only Jesus can give. Jesus speaks of that peace here:

John 14:27 Peace I leave with you, my peace I give unto you: not as the world giveth, give I unto you. Let not your heart be troubled, neither let it be afraid.

John 14:28 Ye have heard how I said unto you, I go away, and come *again* unto you. If ye loved me, ye would rejoice, because I said, I go unto the Father: for my Father is greater than I.

John 14:29 And now I have told you before it come to pass, that, when it is come to pass, ye might believe.

The "accuser of our brethren" (Revelation 12:10) also known as the prince of this world, Satan, has nothing on Jesus!

John 14:30 Hereafter I will not talk much with you: for the prince of this world cometh, and hath nothing in me.

John 14:31 But that the world may know that I love the Father; and as the Father gave me commandment, even so I do. Arise, let us go hence.

During the walk from the upper chamber to the garden of Gethsemane, Jesus had much to say about the trinity. He spoke to His disciples about God's Holy Spirit known as the Holy Ghost. He would soon come down from heaven on the day of Pentecost. Jesus begins with the relationship Christians will be having with the Godhead:

John 15:1 I am the true vine, and my Father is the husbandman.

Jesus uses a metaphor familiar to the disciples. Isaiah, Jeremiah, and Zechariah all use the name *Branch*, and it points to an intimate relationship that one would have with the main part of the tree or vine. Jesus would declare Himself to be the vine, and Jesus says those who are saved are the branches. The job of the branch is to bear fruit. Jesus steps this up by saying fruit, then more fruit and in verse 5, much fruit.

John 15:2 Every branch in me that beareth not fruit he taketh away: and every *branch* that beareth fruit, he purgeth it, that it may bring forth more fruit.

John 15:3 Now ye are clean through the word which I have spoken unto you.

John 15:4 Abide in me, and I in you. As the branch cannot bear fruit of itself, except it abide in the vine; no more can ye, except ye abide in me.

What a Finish! What a Start! The Month Jesus Met Man's Need

Fred A Kuypers

John 15:5 I am the vine, ye *are* the branches: He that abideth in me, and I in him, the same bringeth forth much fruit: for without me ye can do nothing.

The branch of a vine is worthless once it is cut from the vine. You cannot make furniture from it. It is not structural at all. No lumber can be made from it. It is worthless! Only good for kindling!

John 15:6 If a man abide not in me, he is cast forth as a branch, and is withered; and men gather them, and cast *them* into the fire, and they are burned.

John 15:7 If ye abide in me, and my words abide in you, ye shall ask what ye will, and it shall be done unto you.

John 15:8 Herein is my Father glorified, that ye bear much fruit; so shall ye be my disciples.

John 15:9 As the Father hath loved me, so have I loved you: continue ye in my love.

➤ Fifth, Jesus mentions the sign of a believer is one who keeps His commandments:

John 15:10 If ye keep my commandments, ye shall abide in my love; even as I have kept my Father's commandments, and abide in his love.

John 15:11 These things have I spoken unto you, that my joy might remain in you, and *that* your joy might be full.

John 15:12 This is my commandment, That ye love one another, as I have loved you.

John 15:13 Greater love hath no man than this, that a man lay down his life for his friends.

➤ Sixth, Jesus mentions the sign of a believer is one who keeps His commandments, and now the intimate term *friend* is used:

John 15:14 Ye are my friends, if ye do whatsoever I command you.

John 15:15 Henceforth I call you not servants; for the servant knoweth not what his lord doeth: but I have called you friends; for all things that I have heard of my Father I have made known unto you.

John 15:16 Ye have not chosen me, but I have chosen you, and ordained you, that ye should go and bring forth fruit, and *that* your fruit should remain: that whatsoever ye shall ask of the Father in my name, he may give it you.

➤ Seventh, Jesus mentions the sign of a believer is one who keeps His commandments and loves one another:

John 15:17 These things I command you, that ye love one another.

John 15:18 If the world hate you, ye know that it hated me before *it hated* you.

It is one of many marks of a believer if you see someone who is keeping God's commandments.
Believers are also to be marked by the love they have for one another.

John 15:19 If ye were of the world, the world would love his own: but because ye are not of the world, but I have chosen you out of the world, therefore the world hateth you.

John 15:20 Remember the word that I said unto you, The servant is not greater than his lord. If they have persecuted me, they will also persecute you; if they have kept my saying, they will keep yours also.

John 15:21 But all these things will they do unto you for my name's sake, because they know not him that sent me.

John 15:22 If I had not come and spoken unto them, they had not had sin: but now they have no cloke for their sin.

John 15:23 He that hateth me hateth my Father also.

John 15:24 If I had not done among them the works which none other man did, they had not had sin: but now have they both seen and hated both me and my Father.

John 15:25 But *this cometh to pass*, that the word might be fulfilled that is written in their law, They hated me without a cause.

John 15:26 But when the Comforter is come, whom I will send unto you from the Father, *even* the Spirit of truth, which proceedeth from the Father, he shall testify of me:

John 15:27 And ye also shall bear witness, because ye have been with me from the beginning.

As John 16 begins, Jesus reveals the work of the Holy Spirit through the believer. He continues His message with a warning to His disciples:

John 16:1 These things have I spoken unto you, that ye should not be offended.

John 16:2 They shall put you out of the synagogues: yea, the time cometh, that whosoever killeth you will think that he doeth God service.

The real problem is that the one who does not know Christ as Savior never knew the Father, either.

John 16:3 And these things will they do unto you, because they have not known the Father, nor me.

Jesus admonishes the disciples with several "flipside" (but) statements at this moment:

John 16:4 But these things have I told you, that when the time shall come, ye may remember that I told you of them. And these things I said not unto you at the beginning, because I was with you.

John 16:5 But now I go my way to him that sent me; and none of you asketh me, Whither goest thou?

John 16:6 But because I have said these things unto you, sorrow hath filled your heart.

But is there sorrow in their hearts? Just a moment earlier Jesus had said "These things have I spoken unto you, that my joy might remain in you, and that your joy might be full" in John 15:11. How quickly sorrow can fill a heart even after the joy that Jesus gives. Jesus again describes how He will never leave us nor forsake us (Hebrews 13:5) by sending the Comforter that is the Holy Spirit.

John 16:7 Nevertheless I tell you the truth; It is expedient for you that I go away: for if I go not away, the Comforter will not come unto you; but if I depart, I will send him unto you.

John 16:8 And when he is come, he will reprove the world of sin, and of righteousness, and of judgment:

The Holy Spirit reproves of these three items, sin, righteousness, and judgment. He rebukes the sinner for not believing God:

John 16:9 Of sin, because they believe not on me;

Then He admonishes the sinner to receive Christ while he can:

John 16:10 Of righteousness, because I go to my Father, and ye see me no more;

What a Finish! What a Start! The Month Jesus Met Man's Need

Fred A Kuypers

Then He cautions us that judgment is coming:

John 16:11 Of judgment, because the prince of this world is judged.

Jesus gives more good information about the Holy Spirit to come:

John 16:12 I have yet many things to say unto you, but ye cannot bear them now.

John 16:13 Howbeit when he, the Spirit of truth, is come, he will guide you into all truth: for he shall not speak of himself; but whatsoever he shall hear, *that* shall he speak: and he will shew you things to come.

The Holy Spirit will not speak of Himself but will always direct to the Lord Jesus Christ:

John 16:14 He shall glorify me: for he shall receive of mine, and shall shew *it* unto you.

John 16:15 All things that the Father hath are mine: therefore said I, that he shall take of mine, and shall shew *it* unto you.

Jesus declares again His death, burial, and resurrection by telling all that they would see Him again:

John 16:16 A little while, and ye shall not see me: and again, a little while, and ye shall see me, because I go to the Father.

Sometimes when witnessing to others, they have no comprehension of what is being said. The disciples were no different:

John 16:17 Then said *some* of his disciples among themselves, What is this that he saith unto us, A little while, and ye shall not see me: and again, a little while, and ye shall see me: and, Because I go to the Father?

John 16:18 They said therefore, What is this that he saith, A little while? we cannot tell what he saith.

Jesus understands all our inabilities.

John 16:19 Now Jesus knew that they were desirous to ask him, and said unto them, Do ye enquire among yourselves of that I said, A little while, and ye shall not see me: and again, a little while, and ye shall see me?

John 16:20 Verily, verily, I say unto you, That ye shall weep and lament, but the world shall rejoice: and ye shall be sorrowful, but your sorrow shall be turned into joy.

Why do women who have had a child want another? Here Jesus gives some insight. It will be the same for the believer.

John 16:21 A woman when she is in travail hath sorrow, because her hour is come: but as soon as she is delivered of the child, she remembereth no more the anguish, for joy that a man is born into the world.

John 16:22 And ye now therefore have sorrow: but I will see you again, and your heart shall rejoice, and your joy no man taketh from you.

John 16:23 And in that day ye shall ask me nothing. Verily, verily, I say unto you, Whatsoever ye shall ask the Father in my name, he will give *it* you.

John 16:24 Hitherto have ye asked nothing in my name: ask, and ye shall receive, that your joy may be full.

Jesus tells the disciples that He has been speaking in proverbs. But very soon they will see the reality of what He has been teaching them.

John 16:25 These things have I spoken unto you in proverbs: but the time cometh, when I shall no more speak unto you in proverbs, but I shall shew you plainly of the Father.

John 16:26 At that day ye shall ask in my name: and I say not unto you, that I will pray the Father for you:

It is no doubt that the disciples loved the one they were following. He is leading them to His place of prayer, the garden of Gethsemane. They continued to follow Him up until this point. But before this day would be over all would forsake Him.

John 16:27 For the Father himself loveth you, because ye have loved me, and have believed that I came out from God.

John 16:28 I came forth from the Father, and am come into the world: again, I leave the world, and go to the Father.

John 16:29 His disciples said unto him, Lo, now speakest thou plainly, and speakest no proverb.

John 16:30 Now are we sure that thou knowest all things, and needest not that any man should ask thee: by this we believe that thou camest forth from God.

As they approach the temple mount area, Jesus tells His followers that even after they profess that they believe in Him that the time has come that they will scatter from Him and leave Him alone:

John 16:31 Jesus answered them, Do ye now believe?

John 16:32 Behold, the hour cometh, yea, is now come, that ye shall be scattered, every man to his own, and shall leave me alone: and yet I am not alone, because the Father is with me.

Jesus gave the promise of peace and the warning of tribulation in the world. This is not the great tribulation but is true for every believer that there will be trouble as they walk in this world. It is needful to totally come to Jesus in prayer to deal with these problems in the world!

John 16:33 These things I have spoken unto you, that in me ye might have peace. In the world ye shall have tribulation: but be of good cheer; I have overcome the world.

7:30 p.m. on Tuesday, the Fourteenth of Nisan

Passover

As Jesus approaches the temple area where the Holy of Holies is located, perhaps He prays to His Father. This could be as He walks by the temple after coming from the western side of Jerusalem heading east to the garden of Gethsemane. He prays this prayer of John 17.

This is the most complete prayer Jesus has prayed in talking with the Father. His concern was for those He loved here on Earth. It is a good example for us to follow. God gave each one of us family, friends, and neighbors to pray for and to turn to God for salvation.

What a Finish! What a Start! The Month Jesus Met Man's Need

Fred A Kuypers

This prayer should be read in its entirety, so I will withhold comment until the finish:

John 17:1 These words spake Jesus, and lifted up his eyes to heaven, and said, Father, the hour is come; glorify thy Son, that thy Son also may glorify thee:

John 17:2 As thou hast given him power over all flesh, that he should give eternal life to as many as thou hast given him.

John 17:3 And this is life eternal, that they might know thee the only true God, and Jesus Christ, whom thou hast sent.

John 17:4 I have glorified thee on the earth: I have finished the work which thou gavest me to do.

John 17:5 And now, O Father, glorify thou me with thine own self with the glory which I had with thee before the world was.

John 17:6 I have manifested thy name unto the men which thou gavest me out of the world: thine they were, and thou gavest them me; and they have kept thy word.

John 17:7 Now they have known that all things whatsoever thou hast given me are of thee.

John 17:8 For I have given unto them the words which thou gavest me; and they have received *them*, and have known surely that I came out from thee, and they have believed that thou didst send me.

John 17:9 I pray for them: I pray not for the world, but for them which thou hast given me; for they are thine.

John 17:10 And all mine are thine, and thine are mine; and I am glorified in them.

John 17:11 And now I am no more in the world, but these are in the world, and I come to thee. Holy Father, keep through thine own name those whom thou hast given me, that they may be one, as we *are*.

John 17:12 While I was with them in the world, I kept them in thy name: those that thou gavest me I have kept, and none of them is lost, but the son of perdition; that the scripture might be fulfilled.

John 17:13 And now come I to thee; and these things I speak in the world, that they might have my joy fulfilled in themselves.

John 17:14 I have given them thy word; and the world hath hated them, because they are not of the world, even as I am not of the world.

John 17:15 I pray not that thou shouldest take them out of the world, but that thou shouldest keep them from the evil.

John 17:16 They are not of the world, even as I am not of the world.

John 17:17 Sanctify them through thy truth: thy word is truth.

John 17:18 As thou hast sent me into the world, even so have I also sent them into the world.

John 17:19 And for their sakes I sanctify myself, that they also might be sanctified through the truth.

John 17:20 Neither pray I for these alone, but for them also which shall believe on me through their word;

John 17:21 That they all may be one; as thou, Father, art in me, and I in thee, that they also may be one in us: that the world may believe that thou hast sent me.

John 17:22 And the glory which thou gavest me I have given them; that they may be one, even as we are one:

John 17:23 I in them, and thou in me, that they may be made perfect in one; and that the world may know that thou hast sent me, and hast loved them, as thou hast loved me.

John 17:24 Father, I will that they also, whom thou hast given me, be with me where I am; that they may behold my glory, which thou hast given me: for thou lovedst me before the foundation of the world.

John 17:25 O righteous Father, the world hath not known thee: but I have known thee, and these have known that thou hast sent me.

John 17:26 And I have declared unto them thy name, and will declare *it*: that the love wherewith thou hast loved me may be in them, and I in them.

After a sermon, it is proper to close in prayer. Jesus had finished His preaching about this soon and eminent gift to be given to them, which is the Holy Ghost (Acts 2:38). He would come down and indwell them not many days hence. As Jesus continued His trek to the Mount of Olives (to the garden of Gethsemane), He would close with this prayer to God the Father to confirm and seal what He had just preached. This prayer has several things completely different than the sermon Jesus had just preached to the disciples.

1. He directed His prayer to God the Father. However, He prayed as if He was on equal ground with the Father. This is done with a different type of language tone than what is used in everyday language. When talking with peers, it is a level language. Commands or direction can be given with a certain tone. No one is superior. It is different than talking to a child or children. The talk is with a commanding voice to give instruction or direction with superior knowledge. When prayer is offered to the Father above, it is with an asking voice or a voice showing respect and honor. Jesus switched here to a level command voice. When Jesus said "The hour is come; glorify thy Son," it is with a level voice commanding the Father only as one could do if they were equals or peers. This entire prayer is in that tense. Jesus was equal with the Father and could pray that way.

2. It was all about His disciples and those He loved and would hope that they would follow him. His sermon (John 17:8) was given to the disciples because it was given to Jesus by the Father.

3. Jesus describes here the enmity between God and the world that is unsaved. To reject the free gift of the Son of God, Jesus will not pray for and is spoken of by Jesus in verses 9–12.

4. In verse 12, the reference to the "son of perdition" is to Judas Iscariot who betrayed Jesus. This phrase is an adjective phrase describing the fact that someone is damned to hell. It is the same adjective phrase used to describe Satan in 2 Thessalonians 2:3:

   2 Thessalonians 2:3 Let no man deceive you by any means: for *that day shall not come*, except there come a falling away first, and that man of sin be revealed, the son of perdition;

What a Finish! What a Start! The Month Jesus Met Man's Need

Fred A Kuypers

5. Joy comes from hearing the truth and the truth setting us free (John 8:32–36). In verses 13–17, Jesus gives the truth again, and it is in His Word as verse 17 declares.

6. Did you know that Jesus actually prayed here to the Father for you in particular? Verse 20 is a command to the Father for you and for me.
    God wants us to be one. Verses 21–23 say we are to be as one—together in thought and in direction and in truth and in love. This is the fruit to look for that Jesus spoke of as a proper way to discern if someone is following Christ. The scripture says that by their fruits, they shall be known:

    Matthew 7:14 Because strait *is* the gate, and narrow *is* the way, which leadeth unto life, and few there be that find it.

    Matthew 7:15 Beware of false prophets, which come to you in sheep's clothing, but inwardly they are ravening wolves.

    Matthew 7:16 Ye shall know them by their fruits. Do men gather grapes of thorns, or figs of thistles?

    Matthew 7:17 Even so every good tree bringeth forth good fruit; but a corrupt tree bringeth forth evil fruit.

    Matthew 7:18 A good tree cannot bring forth evil fruit, neither *can* a corrupt tree bring forth good fruit.

    Matthew 7:19 Every tree that bringeth not forth good fruit is hewn down, and cast into the fire.

    Matthew 7:20 Wherefore by their fruits ye shall know them.

7. To be filled with the fruits of righteousness is commanded by the scriptures:

    Philippians 1:11 Being filled with the fruits of righteousness, which are by Jesus Christ, unto the glory and praise of God.

It is most important now, today, that each one declares the name of the Father and tells others about Jesus. This is the sign of real love. To give the Gospel message of Jesus is the only way to save someone for eternity! That is real love. Jesus declares the only way to do this is by love in verses 24–26. Jesus wants the love of the Father to be in each one of us.

7:45 p.m. on Tuesday, the Fourteenth of Nisan

Passover

As John 18 opens, it is explained that Jesus and the disciples are near the Kidron valley (spelled Cedron here) which is what separates the Mount of Olives from that part of Mount Moriah known as the temple mount. On the western slope of the Mount of Olives is the garden called the garden of Gethsemane. It should take less than an hour to walk from the upper chamber, even if it is west of the temple, and head toward the temple and past the most holy place and the Holy of Holies: then out the Eastern Gate and down Kidron valley over the brook Cedron, and up the west slope of the Mount of Olives, where the Garden of Gethsemane is. Leaving the upper room where the Lord's Supper was prepared and walking to the garden of Gethsemane is taking this amount of time.

Today, the garden of Gethsemane is marked by a beautiful Russian Orthodox Church. The church of Saint Mary Magdalene is built on the western slope of the Mount of Olives in the Garden of Gethsemane and is one of the most recognizable landmarks of Jerusalem. This beautiful example of Russian architecture was built in the Muscovite style with golden onion domes sometimes called cupolas[3031].

Matthew's view of entering the garden of Gethsemane:

Matthew 26:36 Then cometh Jesus with them unto a place called Gethsemane, and saith unto the disciples, Sit ye here, while I go and pray yonder.

Mark's view of entering the garden of Gethsemane:

Mark 14:32 And they came to a place which was named Gethsemane: and he saith to his disciples, Sit ye here, while I shall pray.

Luke's view of entering the garden of Gethsemane:

Luke 22:39 And he came out, and went, as he was wont, to the mount of Olives; and his disciples also followed him.

Entering the garden of Gethsemane "as he was wont" means it was His custom or manner to do so. This is why Judas knew exactly where to go when the time came.

John's view of entering the Garden of Gethsemane:

John 18:1 When Jesus had spoken these words, he went forth with his disciples over the brook Cedron, where was a garden, into the which he entered, and his disciples.

This must have been a place familiar to His disciples as Jesus would come to the garden often. John confirms the fact that Judas would know where Jesus would be and could lead the band of men directly to Him.

John 18:2 And Judas also, which betrayed him, knew the place: for Jesus ofttimes resorted thither with his disciples.

When Jesus arrived, He would begin to do what He always did in this place, and that would be to go to prayer. He also instructed His disciples to do likewise. Luke

---

30   "Convent of Saint Mary Magdalene-the Garden of Gethsemane," Russian Ecclesiastical Mission. http://jerusalem-mission.org/convent_magdalene.html. Viewed Feb 21, 2019.

What a Finish! What a Start! The Month Jesus Met Man's Need

Fred A Kuypers

says that Jesus instructed His disciples to pray using the words of the Lord's Prayer from Luke 11:4:

Luke 22:40 And when he was at the place, he said unto them, Pray that ye enter not into temptation.

Jesus would ask His inner three disciples, Peter, James, and John, to go off and pray with Him. The same three who were with Him at the Mount of Transfiguration (Matthew 17:1; Mark 9:2):

Matthew 26:37 And he took with him Peter and the two sons of Zebedee, and began to be sorrowful and very heavy.

Matthew 26:38 Then saith he unto them, My soul is exceeding sorrowful, even unto death: tarry ye here, and watch with me.

Matthew uses the term "began to be sorrowful" meaning "to be in distress" or "to cause to grieve." Every part of the Lord Jesus Christ knew what was to come upon Him shortly; and the torment He was about to bear. Mark also said Jesus took His inner three, His core disciples, Peter, James and John, to pray:

Mark 14:33 And he taketh with him Peter and James and John, and began to be sore amazed, and to be very heavy;

Mark 14:34 And saith unto them, My soul is exceeding sorrowful unto death: tarry ye here, and watch.

Mark uses the term "sore amazed" to describe Jesus' emotions. This means Jesus was utterly astonished so that every living cell of Jesus was focused on the time that had come. The sins of the whole world were about to come on Him. When He left to pray, He had asked His disciples to wait behind for Him, but to watch also. Even today the command to do this, to tarry in this world, means to wait on the Lord for His good pleasure and timing and to watch for the soon and imminent return of the Lord Jesus Christ!

8:00 p.m. on Tuesday, the Fourteenth of Nisan
Passover

Jesus would go off by Himself and pray. The pressure of the cross was upon Him. He felt the cruel weight of my sin upon Him as He prepared to give His all for me.

Matthew describes what occurred next in the garden:

Matthew 26:39 And he went a little further, and fell on his face, and prayed, saying, O my Father, if it be possible, let this cup pass from me: nevertheless not as I will, but as thou wilt.

Mark includes the statement that Jesus separated Himself even from the three by a little distance.

Mark 14:35 And he went forward a little, and fell on the ground, and prayed that, if it were possible, the hour might pass from him.

Mark 14:36 And he said, Abba, Father, all things are possible unto thee; take away this cup from me: nevertheless not what I will, but what thou wilt.

Luke gives his narrative about Jesus as He goes off with His inner core of three disciples; Peter, James, and John. They are about a stone's throw away, says Luke. This is the "little further" as stated by Matthew and Mark.

Luke 22:41 And he was withdrawn from them about a stone's cast, and kneeled down, and prayed,

Luke 22:42 Saying, Father, if thou be willing, remove this cup from me: nevertheless not my will, but thine, be done.

Luke includes in his intense narrative the appearance of an angel from heaven to strengthen Jesus.

Luke 22:43 And there appeared an angel unto him from heaven, strengthening him.

Is Jesus strengthened here? He is strengthened Only in His human form. Being God, Jesus certainly did not need an angel to strengthen Him. After all He created the angels:

Revelation 4:11 Thou art worthy, O Lord, to receive glory and honour and power: for thou hast created all things, and for thy pleasure they are and were created.

Each believer should know God cares enough to have guardian angels watching over us continually.

Luke also describes the great drops of blood falling to the ground. Jesus sweats "as it were great drops of blood" because He is at the height of His concern about the soon separation that would occur between Him and His Father who is in heaven above. Again, it is Luke the physician who describes the events of the human side of Jesus as He sweats blood." This is holy blood. It is the beginning of the longest, hardest day in history and the continual shedding of blood for man's sins!

Luke 22:44 And being in an agony he prayed more earnestly: and his sweat was as it were great drops of blood falling down to the ground.

This key verse in Luke has four uniquely used words that only occur once in the New Testament. They are 1-agony, 2-more earnestly, 3-sweat, and 4-great drops. It is a tremendously emotional passage proving Jesus was manifested in the flesh:

1 John 3:5 And ye know that he was manifested to take away our sins; and in him is no sin.

The shedding of Christ's blood begins. This is the price of my redemption as it says in Colossians. The blood is declared clearly in the King James Version but not as clear in many others:

Colossians 1:14 In whom we have redemption through his blood, even the forgiveness of sins:

This would be when He takes upon Himself the sins of each one of us as it says in Galatians:

Galatians 1:4 Who gave himself for our sins, that he might deliver us from this present evil world, according to the will of God and our Father

And again in 1 John, it says Jesus paid for the sins of the whole world:

1 John 2:2 And he is the propitiation for our sins: and not for ours only, but also for the sins of the whole world.

9:00 p.m. on Tuesday, the Fourteenth of Nisan
Passover

Christ returns to His inner three apostles, and finding them asleep, He talks to Peter.

Matthew says:

Matthew 26:40 And he cometh unto the disciples, and findeth them asleep, and saith unto Peter, What, could ye not watch with me one hour?

Matthew 26:41 Watch and pray, that ye enter not into temptation: the spirit indeed is willing, but the flesh is weak.

Mark says:

Mark 14:37 And he cometh, and findeth them sleeping, and saith unto Peter, Simon, sleepest thou? couldest not thou watch one hour?

Mark 14:38 Watch ye and pray, lest ye enter into temptation. The spirit truly is ready, but the flesh is weak.

Jesus would go the second time to pray.

Matthew:

Matthew 26:42 He went away again the second time, and prayed, saying, O my Father, if this cup may not pass away from me, except I drink it, thy will be done.

Mark:

Mark 14:39 And again he went away, and prayed, and spake the same words.

10:00 p.m. on Tuesday, the Fourteenth of Nisan
Passover

Jesus would come back a second time to see His followers sleeping.

Matthew:

Matthew 26:43 And he came and found them asleep again: for their eyes were heavy.

Mark:

Mark 14:40 And when he returned, he found them asleep again, (for their eyes were heavy,) neither wist they what to answer him.

Jesus would go a third time to pray according to Matthew:

Matthew 26:44 And he left them, and went away again, and prayed the third time, saying the same words.

11:00 p.m. on Tuesday, the Fourteenth of Nisan
Passover

Matthew and Mark have a narrative about the third time Jesus comes back to His disciples and finds them sleeping.

Matthew:

Matthew 26:45 Then cometh he to his disciples, and saith unto them, Sleep on now, and take your rest: behold, the hour is at hand, and the Son of man is betrayed into the hands of sinners.

Mark:

Mark 14:41 And he cometh the third time, and saith unto them, Sleep on now, and take your rest: it is enough, the hour is come; behold, the Son of man is betrayed into the hands of sinners.

After some time of sleep, the synoptic Gospels say that Jesus was aware that the time was at hand. That time being Judas and his band of men and officers, a multitude of men had come, and so Jesus tells His disciples to rise up!

Matthew:

Matthew 26:46 Rise, let us be going: behold, he is at hand that doth betray me.

Mark:

Mark 14:42 Rise up, let us go; lo, he that betrayeth me is at hand.

Luke:

Luke 22:45 And when he rose up from prayer, and was come to his disciples, he found them sleeping for sorrow,

Luke 22:46 And said unto them, Why sleep ye? rise and pray, lest ye enter into temptation.

11:10 p.m. on Tuesday, the Fourteenth of Nisan
Passover

Judas and a great multitude of men referred to as a "band of men and officers" in the Gospel of John arrive at the garden and approach Jesus. In Psalm 41 it states:

Psalm 41:9 Yea, mine own familiar friend, in whom I trusted, which did eat of my bread, hath lifted up his heel against me.

John gives his view of Judas and the band of men entering the garden:

John 18:3 Judas then, having received a band *of men* and officers from the chief priests and Pharisees, cometh thither with lanterns and torches and weapons.

The synoptic gospels all call this group of men a great "multitude."

Matthew's view of Judas and the band of men entering the garden:

Matthew 26:47 And while he yet spake, lo, Judas, one of the twelve, came, and with him a great multitude with swords and staves, from the chief priests and elders of the people.

Mark's view of Judas and the band of men entering the garden:

Mark 14:43 And immediately, while he yet spake, cometh Judas, one of the twelve, and with him a great multitude with swords and staves, from the chief priests and the scribes and the elders.

Luke's view of Judas and the band of men entering the garden:

Luke 22:47 And while he yet spake, behold a multitude, and he that was called Judas, one of the twelve, went before them, and drew near unto Jesus to kiss him.

Luke says that Judas drew near to Jesus to kiss Him. Matthew and Mark each will give an account of Judas who will at this point betray Jesus with the kiss.

Matthew's view of Judas betraying Him with a kiss:

Matthew 26:48 Now he that betrayed him gave them a sign, saying, Whomsoever I shall kiss, that same is he: hold him fast.

Matthew 26:49 And forthwith he came to Jesus, and said, Hail, master; and kissed him.

Mark's view of Judas betraying Him with a kiss:

Mark 14:44 And he that betrayed him had given them a token, saying, Whomsoever I shall kiss, that same is he; take him, and lead him away safely.

Mark 14:45 And as soon as he was come, he goeth straightway to him, and saith, Master, master; and kissed him.

Jesus responds to this kiss with words that bring conviction to the heart of Judas. And in Matthew, He will still refer to Judas as His friend.

Matthew 26:50 And Jesus said unto him, Friend, wherefore art thou come? Then came they, and laid hands on Jesus, and took him.

Luke describes how Jesus questions Judas about this secret sign he has given to the band of men. How Jesus phrases this brings all the conviction down on Judas. God prophesied of this moment in Psalms:

Psalm 55:12 For it was not an enemy that reproached me; then I could have borne it: neither was it he that hated me that did magnify himself against me; then I would have hid myself from him:

Psalm 55:13 But it was thou, a man mine equal, my guide, and mine acquaintance.

Psalm 55:14 We took sweet counsel together, and walked unto the house of God in company.

It was not an enemy that would reproach Him but a man of His acquaintance.

Luke 22:48 But Jesus said unto him, Judas, betrayest thou the Son of man with a kiss?

Judas steps back and rejoins the band of men, and Jesus brings the whole matter to a pinnacle by asking, "Who do you seek?"

John 18:4 Jesus therefore, knowing all things that should come upon him, went forth, and said unto them, Whom seek ye?

One of the bands of men makes it clear. It is "Jesus of Nazareth" that they are seeking:

John 18:5 They answered him, Jesus of Nazareth. Jesus saith unto them, I am *he*. And Judas also, which betrayed him, stood with them.

Three times Jesus will say "I AM". In verse five He says "I am" and notice the "*he*" is in italics meaning it was inserted by the translators for proper English and clarity. Three times in verses five, six, and eight Jesus declares that He is the great "I AM" that appeared to Moses at the burning bush in Exodus chapter three. Judas and the band of men show fear because they located this Jesus who showed no fear. Jesus, with His love for you and me, was not about to hide from them on this special night:

John 18:6 As soon then as he had said unto them, I am *he*, they went backward, and fell to the ground.

Jesus would ask the band of men a second time as they were so startled about the fact that He was not running and hiding.

John 18:7 Then asked he them again, Whom seek ye? And they said, Jesus of Nazareth.

John 18:8 Jesus answered, I have told you that I am *he*: if therefore ye seek me, let these go their way

John quotes the statement Jesus made earlier this night about His ability not to lose one soul:

John 17:12 While I was with them in the world, I kept them in thy name: those that thou gavest me I have kept, and none of them is lost, but the son of perdition; that the scripture might be fulfilled.

John quotes this statement again that Jesus spoke, which leads to the belief that Judas, though Jesus loved him, was never saved to begin with:

John 18:9 That the saying might be fulfilled, which he spake, Of them which thou gavest me have I lost none.

11:15 p.m. on Tuesday, the Fourteenth of Nisan

Passover

There is a skirmish with the band of men brought by Judas Iscariot. They asked for Jesus of Nazareth! They found Him! There must have been a scuffle, and a servant's ear is cut off by someone's sword.

Matthew does not name the disciple and does not describe the skirmish:

Matthew 26:51 And, behold, one of them which were with Jesus stretched out his hand, and drew his sword, and struck a servant of the high priest's, and smote off his ear.

Mark does not name the disciple but gives a little more information about the skirmish:

Mark 14:46 And they laid their hands on him, and took him.

Mark 14:47 And one of them that stood by drew a sword, and smote a servant of the high priest, and cut off his ear.

Luke does not name the disciple but discusses human strategy and the disciples fighting spirit:

Luke 22:49 When they which were about him saw what would follow, they said unto him, Lord, shall we smite with the sword?

Luke 22:50 And one of them smote the servant of the high priest, and cut off his right ear.

John names the disciple, Peter, and describes in detail the cutting off of the right ear and names the servant, Malchus:

John 18:10 Then Simon Peter having a sword drew it, and smote the high priest's servant, and cut off his right ear. The servant's name was Malchus.

Jesus orders Peter to sheath his weapon:

Matthew 26:52 Then said Jesus unto him, Put up again thy sword into his place: for all they that take the sword shall perish with the sword.

Remember at the Last Supper earlier this night at 6:30 p.m., Jesus said to sell your garment to purchase a weapon? The Lord explains that it is not to be used as an offensive weapon but as a deterrent. John describes in his gospel that Jesus turns to Peter and gives him a direct order to put up his sword:

John 18:11 Then said Jesus unto Peter, Put up thy sword into the sheath: the cup which my Father hath given me, shall I not drink it?

Luke is the only Gospel that declares Jesus healing Malchus's ear. He does not name Malchus. However once again, Luke being a physician takes note of the healing process:

Luke 22:51 And Jesus answered and said, Suffer ye thus far. And he touched his ear, and healed him.

Matthew's gospel adds that He could have called twelve legions of angels:

Matthew 26:53 Thinkest thou that I cannot now pray to my Father, and he shall presently give me more than twelve legions of angels?

How many angels? Perhaps the best look at what one angel can do:

2Kings 19:35 And it came to pass that night, that the angel of the LORD went out, and smote in the camp of the Assyrians an hundred fourscore and five thousand: and when they arose early in the morning, behold, they were all dead corpses.

There was one angel that destroyed one hundred and eighty-five thousand men. A legion in the Roman army at the time of Christ was approximately six thousand men, not counting officers and leaders. Twelve legions of six thousand angels, each with the capability of killing that many—well, you do the math!

Scripture must be fulfilled. The Old Testament prophesies of the first advent of Christ are being fulfilled. Matthew speaking of Messiah coming and as a rejected servant must all come to pass as Jesus makes clear.

Matthew 26:54 But how then shall the scriptures be fulfilled, that thus it must be?

The scripture Jesus is referring to here is recorded by Isaiah. It begins with Jesus having to stand alone for sins He never committed.

Isaiah 53:3 He is despised and rejected of men; a man of sorrows, and acquainted with grief: and we hid as it were our faces from him; he was despised, and we esteemed him not.

Jesus stood innocent before the band of men:

Matthew:

Matthew 26:55 In that same hour said Jesus to the multitudes, Are ye come out as against a thief with swords and staves for to take me? I sat daily with you teaching in the temple, and ye laid no hold on me.

What a Finish! What a Start! The Month Jesus Met Man's Need

Fred A Kuypers

Mark:

Mark 14:48 And Jesus answered and said unto them, Are ye come out, as against a thief, with swords and with staves to take me?

Mark 14:49 I was daily with you in the temple teaching, and ye took me not: but the scriptures must be fulfilled.

He speaks of the power of darkness mentioned here in Luke, that being Satan who is the prince of the power of the air:

Luke 22:52 Then Jesus said unto the chief priests, and captains of the temple, and the elders, which were come to him, Be ye come out, as against a thief, with swords and staves?

Luke 22:53 When I was daily with you in the temple, ye stretched forth no hands against me: but this is your hour, and the power of darkness.

Isaiah has much to say about this time as Jesus is taken on this longest day. The prophecy in Isaiah declares that Jesus will go it alone:

Isaiah 63:3 I have trodden the winepress alone; and of the people there was none with me:

Matthew says that all the disciples forsook Him at this time, and Jesus would stand alone:

Matthew 26:56 But all this was done, that the scriptures of the prophets might be fulfilled. Then all the disciples forsook him, and fled.

However, Mark says not just the disciples but "all" forsook Him:

Mark 14:50 And they all forsook him, and fled.

Jesus says that the scriptures of the prophets must be fulfilled. Again, the scripture referred to is in Isaiah, which reads:

Isaiah 53:6 All we like sheep have gone astray; we have turned every one to his own way; and the LORD hath laid on him the iniquity of us all.

Even this certain young man forsook Him. Many believe this young man to be John Mark who was not one of the twelve but was most certainly a young associate with them. This young man, who wrote the Gospel of Mark, was an eyewitness to the life of Jesus Christ:

Mark 14:51 And there followed him a certain young man, having a linen cloth cast about his naked body; and the young men laid hold on him:

Mark 14:52 And he left the linen cloth, and fled from them naked.

Jesus stood innocent before the band of men but is now taken and bound:

John 18:12 Then the band and the captain and officers of the Jews took Jesus, and bound him,

11:30 p.m. on Tuesday, the Fourteenth of Nisan

Passover

Jesus is led to Annas first. The Gospel of John will describe the relationship here of Annas and Caiaphas. Annas is father-in-law to the current high priest, Caiaphas. Many of the council laws will be broken, but the religious leaders follow protocol by bringing Jesus first to the high priest emeritus:

John 18:13 And led him away to Annas first; for he was father in law to Caiaphas, which was the high priest that same year.

John 18:14 Now Caiaphas was he, which gave counsel to the Jews, that it was expedient that one man should die for the people.

Earlier on Nisan 7 (that is chapter 7 of this book) Caiaphas stepped up and spoke with the authority of the high priest:

John 11:49 And one of them, named Caiaphas, being the high priest that same year, said unto them, Ye know nothing at all,

John 11:50 Nor consider that it is expedient for us, that one man should die for the people, and that the whole nation perish not.

John 11:51 And this spake he not of himself: but being high priest that year, he prophesied that Jesus should die for that nation;

Caiaphas predicted this day would occur, and now it was materializing right before him. Jesus was quickly shuffled first to Annas's house and then over to Caiaphas's house.

12:00 Midnight on Wednesday, the Fourteenth of Nisan

Passover

As Jesus is moved from Annas's house to where Caiaphas is waiting, Caiaphas readies himself and is prepared for this moment. Caiaphas has already hired Judas for thirty pieces of silver. He has sent a band of men, a great multitude, with him to find Jesus. He has all the religious leaders gathered at his residence: scribes, chief priests, and elders are all assembled at the palace. This is the real assembly of those who want to condemn Jesus as Matthew and Mark declare:

Matthew:

Matthew 26:57 And they that had laid hold on Jesus led him away to Caiaphas the high priest, where the scribes and the elders were assembled.

Mark:

Mark 14:53 And they led Jesus away to the high priest: and with him were assembled all the chief priests and the elders and the scribes.

Dealing with a young man's pride! Even at a crucial time such as this, God in all His mercy will deal one on one with any person at any time. Are there any followers more faithful than Peter? Would it be possible knowing what Peter knew, and also having just witnessed the miracle of reattaching the ear of Malchus that he had so carelessly chopped off, that Peter could deny the Lord Jesus Christ at this moment? Peter, who just a few hours earlier said to Jesus; "Though all men shall be offended because of thee, yet will I never be offended," is now keeping his distance. He looks for the comfort of the warm fire and has forsaken Jesus already in his heart. Also in just a few short hours, he will verbally deny Jesus three times.

Matthew says that Peter actually sat with the servants to see what would happen to Jesus:

Matthew 26:58 But Peter followed him afar off unto the high priest's palace, and went in, and sat with the servants, to see the end.

Mark adds that Peter actually warmed himself at the fire:

Mark 14:54 And Peter followed him afar off, even into the palace of the high priest: and he sat with the servants, and warmed himself at the fire.

Luke adds that it was the house called the palace of Caiaphas that Jesus was brought to:

Luke 22:54 Then took they him, and led him, and brought him into the high priest's house. And Peter followed afar off.

John adds that Peter actually went into the house:

John 18:15 And Simon Peter followed Jesus, and so did another disciple: that disciple was known unto the high priest, and went in with Jesus into the palace of the high priest.

As Peter was in the house of Caiaphas and then retreated to sit by the fire with the servants to warm himself, the council of chief priests did all they could to locate a witness to testify against Jesus. This council to condemn Jesus was thrown together by Caiaphas. So the scriptures have a truth declared in that:

Proverbs 16:27 An ungodly man diggeth up evil: and in his lips there is as a burning fire.

This whole council was an illegal council by Jewish law to dig up evil against the Lord Jesus Christ. This nighttime trial was illegal, according to the Sanhedrin's laws and regulations. According to Jewish law, all criminal trials must be in the daylight. The Jewish Mishna explains:

Let a capital offense be tried during the day but suspended at night.[31]

Caiaphas already made the decision to condemn Jesus, so the religious leaders would conduct a second trial in daylight which will take place at 6:00 a.m. as Luke explains shortly. These leaders knew this first trial had no legal standing. Matthew and Mark will both declare that false witnesses were sought to condemn Jesus to death. However, they could not find any witnesses who would collaborate or band together, and they could not get their stories straight!

Matthew:

Matthew 26:59 Now the chief priests, and elders, and all the council, sought false witness against Jesus, to put him to death;

Matthew 26:60 But found none: yea, though many false witnesses came, yet found they none. At the last came two false witnesses,

Mark:

Mark 14:55 And the chief priests and all the council sought for witness against Jesus to put him to death; and found none.

Mark 14:56 For many bare false witness against him, but their witness agreed not together.

The scripture declared what was required to condemn in Deuteronomy:

Deuteronomy 17:6 At the mouth of two witnesses, or three witnesses, shall he that is worthy of death be put to death; but at the mouth of one witness he shall not be put to death.

12:15 a.m. on Wednesday, the Fourteenth of Nisan

Passover

Both Matthew and Mark are clear that the chief priest's witnesses do not agree. Matthew adds that two false witnesses at last step up and these two collaborate on a statement made by Jesus. The two are going to claim that Jesus spoke two years earlier as recorded in John 2 about raising up the temple in three days. John's account in chapter two says Jesus just went up to Jerusalem for the first Passover during His public ministry. Jesus was angered at this point with a cause:

John 2:13 And the Jews' passover was at hand, and Jesus went up to Jerusalem,

John 2:14 And found in the temple those that sold oxen and sheep and doves, and the changers of money sitting:

John 2:15 And when he had made a scourge of small cords, he drove them all out of the temple, and the sheep, and the oxen; and poured out the changers' money, and overthrew the tables;

---

31   Walter M Chandler. The trial of *Jesus from a Lawyer's standpoint*. Empire Publishing Company. New York. C1908. p.255

John 2:16 And said unto them that sold doves, Take these things hence; make not my Father's house an house of merchandise.

In the verses above it was the first of two times that Jesus would drive out the money changers. The second time occurred just a few days ago in chapter 9 on the ninth of Nisan. This first time took place two years earlier when the Jews asked for a sign:

John 2:17 And his disciples remembered that it was written, The zeal of thine house hath eaten me up.

John 2:18 Then answered the Jews and said unto him, What sign shewest thou unto us, seeing that thou doest these things?

At this point, the scriptures made it clear that the sign Jesus spoke of was the temple of His body:

John 2:19 Jesus answered and said unto them, Destroy this temple, and in three days I will raise it up.

John 2:20 Then said the Jews, Forty and six years was this temple in building, and wilt thou rear it up in three days?

John 2:21 But he spake of the temple of his body.

This statement made in John 2 was a full two years before this trial. No wonder the witnesses could not agree with each other. But Caiaphas would hear the matter:

Matthew:

Matthew 26:61 And said, This fellow said, I am able to destroy the temple of God, and to build it in three days.

Mark:

Mark 14:57 And there arose certain, and bare false witness against him, saying,

Mark 14:58 We heard him say, I will destroy this temple that is made with hands, and within three days I will build another made without hands.

Mark 14:59 But neither so did their witness agree together.

Caiaphas starts to really get annoyed. He stands and accuses Jesus. However, Jesus says nothing! Caiaphas will then ask Jesus a direct question, "Art thou the Christ" (Greek for the word *Messiah*).[32]

Matthew:

Matthew 26:62 And the high priest arose, and said unto him, Answerest thou nothing? what is it which these witness against thee?

Matthew 26:63 But Jesus held his peace. And the high priest answered and said unto him, I adjure thee by the living God, that thou tell us whether thou be the Christ, the Son of God.

---

[32]   Dr. James Strong, *Strongs Exhaustive Concordance of the Bible.* Dugan Publishers Inc. Gordonsville, TN. P.190

Mark:

Mark 14:60 And the high priest stood up in the midst, and asked Jesus, saying, Answerest thou nothing? what is it which these witness against thee?

Mark 14:61 But he held his peace, and answered nothing. Again the high priest asked him, and said unto him, Art thou the Christ, the Son of the Blessed?

Jesus states the truth that all scripture centers on Jesus Christ as Lord and that He is the I AM. Some have called this a discrepancy between Matthew and Mark. The two statements actually complement each other beautifully.

Matthew:

Matthew 26:64 Jesus saith unto him, Thou hast said: nevertheless I say unto you, Hereafter shall ye see the Son of man sitting on the right hand of power, and coming in the clouds of heaven.

Mark:

Mark 14:62 And Jesus said, I am: and ye shall see the Son of man sitting on the right hand of power, and coming in the clouds of heaven.

There are many ways that this could have been stated. Jesus could have said this twice. Jesus could have said all the words from both gospels. Jesus could have said something like this:

Nevertheless I say unto you, I AM, and hereafter shall ye see the Son of man sitting on the right hand of power, and coming in the clouds of heaven.

But each gospel says this in different ways to be exact and to the point. Once again, this would prove in today's courts that there was no collaboration between Matthew and Mark. Jesus Christ is the I AM of the Old Testament. Caiaphas could have asked Jesus twice with Matthew and Mark recording the responses. Jesus then declares with no uncertainty that He is God by using the name God took at the burning bush with Moses: Exodus 3:13 And Moses said unto God, Behold, when I come unto the children of Israel, and shall say unto them, The God of your fathers hath sent me unto you; and they shall say to me, What is his name? what shall I say unto them?

Exodus 3:14 And God said unto Moses, I AM THAT I AM: and he said, Thus shalt thou say unto the children of Israel, I AM hath sent me unto you.

Caiaphas the high priest knows exactly what Jesus meant! He is so infuriated by Jesus' statement that he tears his clothes off. He begins to rage and to declare that Jesus has blasphemed. No more eyewitnesses are needed:

Matthew:

Matthew 26:65 Then the high priest rent his clothes, saying, He hath spoken blasphemy; what further need have we of witnesses? behold, now ye have heard his blasphemy.

Mark:

Mark 14:63 Then the high priest rent his clothes, and saith, What need we any further witnesses?

It is amazing what some will do when they think they are right and will accept no other view. Later, recorded in the Acts of the Apostles in chapter seven, is what the religious leaders did to Stephen, one of the first deacons as they put Him to death:

Acts 7:54 When they heard these things, they were cut to the heart, and they gnashed on him with their teeth.

Acts 7:55 But he, being full of the Holy Ghost, looked up stedfastly into heaven, and saw the glory of God, and Jesus standing on the right hand of God,

Acts 7:56 And said, Behold, I see the heavens opened, and the Son of man standing on the right hand of God.

Acts 7:57 Then they cried out with a loud voice, and stopped their ears, and ran upon him with one accord,

Acts 7:58 And cast him out of the city, and stoned him: and the witnesses laid down their clothes at a young man's feet, whose name was Saul.

Acts 7:59 And they stoned Stephen, calling upon God, and saying, Lord Jesus, receive my spirit.

Acts 7:60 And he kneeled down, and cried with a loud voice, Lord, lay not this sin to their charge. And when he had said this, he fell asleep.

This scene in the book of Acts of the Apostles is the only time that scripture records Jesus standing in heaven (verse 56). Jesus accepts the arrival of the first martyr, Stephen who is the first church-age martyr, by standing as he enters heaven. This is quite an honor!

1:00 a.m. on Wednesday, the Fourteenth of Nisan

Passover

Jesus is declared guilty by all the religious leaders assembled on this night:

Matthew:

Matthew 26:66 What think ye? They answered and said, He is guilty of death.

Mark:

Mark 14:64 Ye have heard the blasphemy: what think ye? And they all condemned him to be guilty of death.

Jesus was spit upon and buffeted by the religious leaders of their day. These also will stand in judgment for eternity because of this atrocity of spitting in the face of the Savior, which if they died unsaved will surely come to pass:

Matthew:

Matthew 26:67 Then did they spit in his face, and buffeted him; and others smote him with the palms of their hands,

Matthew 26:68 Saying, Prophesy unto us, thou Christ, Who is he that smote thee?

Mark:

Mark 14:65 And some began to spit on him, and to cover his face, and to buffet him, and to say unto him, Prophesy: and the servants did strike him with the palms of their hands.

As awful as this was, these men could have repented of their sin, confessed it, turned to the Lord Jesus Christ, and asked Him to save them. Believing in their hearts that Jesus died on the cross, was buried, and rose again the third day just as the scriptures say, they would be saved. Our God knows exactly who hit Him and would forgive and remember this event no more! If only they would repent of this evil sin and turn from it and turn to by faith the Lord Jesus Christ!

2:00 a.m. on Wednesday, the Fourteenth of Nisan

Passover

The insults would continue to be hurled at Jesus. As the night continues, Peter has been in an area where some are gathered around a fire, warming themselves. He is trying to blend in with the crowd. He had the opportunity to be with Jesus and come forward as a witness to defend Christ. But He chose to just stay back and out of sight. He finally walks in by the door led by John, that other disciple, and walks past the one who kept the door. John must have known her for he speaks to her, and she allows Peter to enter the palace as John's gospel says:

John 18:16 But Peter stood at the door without. Then went out that other disciple, which was known unto the high priest, and spake unto her that kept the door, and brought in Peter.

What a Finish! What a Start! The Month Jesus Met Man's Need

Fred A Kuypers

3:00 a.m. on Wednesday, the Fourteenth of Nisan
Passover

Now a damsel, a maid of the high priest, spots him. She confronts Peter and all four of the Gospels have something to say about Peter's first denial. Note that all four quote Peter differently. This does not mean the gospels are conflicting. It only shows once again that there was no collaboration between the witnesses.

First denial of Peter from Matthew:

Matthew 26:69 Now Peter sat without in the palace: and a damsel came unto him, saying, Thou also wast with Jesus of Galilee.

Matthew 26:70 But he denied before them all, saying, I know not what thou sayest.

The first denial of Peter as stated by Mark adds that Peter does not understand what she is saying: Mark adds that the cock crowed at this time. Remember earlier this night around 7:00 p.m. that Mark was the only gospel that said the cock would crow twice. Surely this happened. The other writers just did not document it like Mark did.

Mark 14:66 And as Peter was beneath in the palace, there cometh one of the maids of the high priest:

Mark 14:67 And when she saw Peter warming himself, she looked upon him, and said, And thou also wast with Jesus of Nazareth.

Mark 14:68 But he denied, saying, I know not, neither understand I what thou sayest. And he went out into the porch; and the cock crew.

First denial of Peter from Luke:

Luke 22:55 And when they had kindled a fire in the midst of the hall, and were set down together, Peter sat down among them.

Luke 22:56 But a certain maid beheld him as he sat by the fire, and earnestly looked upon him, and said, This man was also with him.

Luke 22:57 And he denied him, saying, Woman, I know him not.

First denial of Peter from John who tells us that the maid was actually the one who kept the door:

John 18:17 Then saith the damsel that kept the door unto Peter, Art not thou also *one* of this man's disciples? He saith, I am not.

John 18:18 And the servants and officers stood there, who had made a fire of coals; for it was cold: and they warmed themselves: and Peter stood with them, and warmed himself.

The questioning of Jesus continues at Caiaphas' home. John's gospel has more information about this illegal trial at Caiaphas' house:

John 18:19 The high priest then asked Jesus of his disciples, and of his doctrine.

The illegal trial of Jesus by Caiaphas the high priest has progressed. Caiaphas has settled down after tearing his clothes and asks Jesus of his disciples. Just imagine Peter shaking in his boots. He has just denied Jesus for the first time. Jesus could have said, "You were with me, Peter, you dirty rat! Why do you deny me now?" But instead of being in silence as before recorded in Matthew and Mark, Jesus replies to Caiaphas's questions:

John 18:20 Jesus answered him, I spake openly to the world; I ever taught in the synagogue, and in the temple, whither the Jews always resort; and in secret have I said nothing.

John 18:21 Why askest thou me? ask them which heard me, what I have said unto them: behold, they know what I said.

Jesus is buffeted for disrespect to Caiaphas. Little does the officer know that he commits one of the most disrespectful acts in history and for eternity. Can you imagine this officer standing before Jesus in judgment having to answer for this slap? If this officer becomes saved after Pentecost, perhaps as part of the three thousand that joined the church, this slap will be remembered no more. If this officer died unsaved, he will reply that he slapped God in the face for eternity:

John 18:22 And when he had thus spoken, one of the officers which stood by struck Jesus with the palm of his hand, saying, Answerest thou the high priest so?

John 18:23 Jesus answered him, If I have spoken evil, bear witness of the evil: but if well, why smitest thou me?

Earlier, Annas had had enough. He had sent Jesus to his son-in-law Caiaphas. John wants to make it clear that this trial was taking place at the home of Caiaphas, the current high priest:

John 18:24 Now Annas had sent him bound unto Caiaphas the high priest.

Caiaphas has now had enough! This night, the abuse continued as Caiaphas was getting no answers he wanted to hear from the Lord Jesus Christ.

4:00 a.m. on Wednesday, the Fourteenth of Nisan

Passover

The second denial from Peter is attested to by three of the Gospels. John is silent as to this denial. Peter leaves the inside of the palace and goes out on the porch. A maid of the high priest sees him and confronts him.

Second denial of Peter from Matthew. Notice a different maid, not the door keeper, confronts Peter:

Matthew 26:71 And when he was gone out into the porch, another maid saw him, and said unto them that were there, This fellow was also with Jesus of Nazareth.

Matthew 26:72 And again he denied with an oath, I do not know the man.

Second denial of Peter from Mark:

Mark 14:69 And a maid saw him again, and began to say to them that stood by, This is one of them.

Mark 14:70a And he denied it again.

Second denial of Peter from Luke:

Luke 22:58 And after a little while another saw him, and said, Thou art also of them. And Peter said, Man, I am not.

5:00 a.m. on Wednesday, the Fourteenth of Nisan
Passover

One hour goes by after the second denial. This is explained by the gospel of Luke.

Luke 22:59 And about the space of one hour after another confidently affirmed, saying, Of a truth this fellow also was with him: for he is a Galilaean.

The third denial of Peter from Matthew explains that Peter is before a group of people. This group of people referred to as "they" are standing and or sitting on the porch of the palace. The crowd says his speech makes it evident that Peter was with Jesus in the garden. Peter is from Galilee. Jesus, being from Nazareth, also would have a Galilean accent though maybe a little different than Peter. There must have been a Galilean accent that would make his language different from the Judean dialect down around Jerusalem. "Thy speech betrayeth thee" means his speech banded him together with others, and the crowd would say he was from Galilee.

Matthew 26:73 And after a while came unto him they that stood by, and said to Peter, Surely thou also art one of them; for thy speech bewrayeth thee.

Matthew 26:74 Then began he to curse and to swear, saying, I know not the man. And immediately the cock crew.

The third denial of Peter from Mark tells us that a group of people were gathered outside on the porch of the palace. They say to Peter that his accent is giving him away as one of the disciples.

Mark 14:70b And a little after, they that stood by said again to Peter, Surely thou art one of them: for thou art a Galilaean, and thy speech agreeth thereto.

Mark 14:71 But he began to curse and to swear, saying, I know not this man of whom ye speak.

The third denial of Peter from Luke tells us that as Peter looked this man in the eye, he would stand on his lie of not knowing who Jesus Christ is. Peter was denying the Lord, and the words were coming out of his mouth when the cock would crow:

Luke 22:60 And Peter said, Man, I know not what thou sayest. And immediately, while he yet spake, the cock crew.

Notice that Luke tells us while he spoke the cock crowed. If something can bring conviction to a man, it is the precision of the Holy Spirit. There would be no doubt in Peter's mind that the sound of the cock crowing was meant for him.

John recorded Peter's third denial but adds some more details to it. First, the group of people who were on the porch will confront Peter. They will ask him, and he will deny that he was with Jesus. A relative of Malchus, whose ear was cut off and miraculously healed by Jesus, steps up and says he personally witnessed Peter with Jesus in the garden. It is much harder to look an accuser in the eye and flatly tell a lie. God brings Peter to that point. Peter has the opportunity here for the last time to tell the truth or just continue with his lie.

John 18:25 And Simon Peter stood and warmed himself. They said therefore unto him, Art not thou also *one* of his disciples? He denied *it,* and said, I am not.

John 18:26 One of the servants of the high priest, being *his* kinsman whose ear Peter cut off, saith, Did not I see thee in the garden with him?

John writes the cock crowed immediately also.

John 18:27 Peter then denied again: and immediately the cock crew.

5:10 a.m. on Wednesday, the Fourteenth of Nisan
Passover

It is close to sunrise. Anyone who has lived on a farm knows that the cock will start to crow at the first sight of sunrise. Before you can see any daylight, the cock will sound off. This was also the time when Peter committed his final denial of Christ, and he repented of this denial.

A cock will start to crow and then will usually crow again very soon after the first crow. Luke records the cock crowing this way: "And immediately, while he yet spake, the cock crew." However, Matthew writes and does not include "while he yet spake" but says "And immediately the cock crew." This is not a contradiction but a different way of expressing the exact same time.

Matthew writes that Peter realized what Jesus said about denying Him three times. This became apparent when the cock had crowed.

Matthew 26:75 And Peter remembered the word of Jesus, which said unto him, Before the cock crow, thou shalt deny me thrice. And he went out, and wept bitterly.

Mark tells us the cock crowed twice, and all this can be easily understood. It is interesting to see that the only writer of the Gospels who does not use the word *immediately* is Mark who has used this word many times throughout his Gospel to describe the service and attitude of Jesus. Mark did not use the word *immediately* because an act of denial of Christ is not an act of service.

Mark 14:72 And the second time the cock crew. And Peter called to mind the word that Jesus said unto him, Before the cock crow twice, thou shalt deny me thrice. And when he thought thereon, he wept.

Luke is the only writer to add to Peter's third denial. This moment is forever recorded as Jesus turns and looks at Peter. This is a moment in time that will live in infamy.

Luke 22:61 And the Lord turned, and looked upon Peter. And Peter remembered the word of the Lord, how he had said unto him, Before the cock crow, thou shalt deny me thrice.

Luke 22:62 And Peter went out, and wept bitterly.

5:30 a.m. on Wednesday, the Fourteenth of Nisan
Passover

As the cock crows at the first sign of daylight, people would know about what time it is. There is still a little time before daybreak. That is before the morning officially begins at 6 a.m. Jesus was still being held and mocked as a criminal by those holding Him during this illegal trial. They continue to ridicule Him by blindfolding Him and slapping Him in the face, telling Him to miraculously discern who hit Him while He was blindfolded:

Luke 22:63 And the men that held Jesus mocked him, and smote him.

Luke 22:64 And when they had blindfolded him, they struck him on the face, and asked him, saying, Prophesy, who is it that smote thee?

Luke 22:65 And many other things blasphemously spake they against him.

6:00 a.m. on Wednesday, the Fourteenth of Nisan
Passover

Now it is daylight. Officially 6:00am when the morning begins. Jesus is questioned by the chief priests for the last time. The leaders want to clear their conscience about an illegal trial that took place during the night. The leaders meet and determine at this daylight trial that Jesus is already guilty of death as Matthew records:

Matthew 27:1 When the morning was come, all the chief priests and elders of the people took counsel against Jesus to put him to death:

Caiaphas and a council of religious leaders ask Him after 6:00 a.m. one last time if He is truly the Messiah according to the Gospel of Luke:

Luke 22:66 And as soon as it was day, the elders of the people and the chief priests and the scribes came together, and led him into their council, saying,

Luke 22:67 Art thou the Christ? tell us. And he said unto them, If I tell you, ye will not believe:

Luke 22:68 And if I also ask you, ye will not answer me, nor let me go.

Luke 22:69 Hereafter shall the Son of man sit on the right hand of the power of God.

Luke 22:70 Then said they all, Art thou then the Son of God? And he said unto them, Ye say that I am.

The council is illegal again, for there are no witnesses. They just want to condemn Jesus!

Luke 22:71 And they said, What need we any further witness? for we ourselves have heard of his own mouth.

Mark then records that after the council meets and after the denial of witnesses recorded in Luke, Jesus is bound and carried away:

Mark 15:1 And straightway in the morning the chief priests held a consultation with the elders and scribes and the whole council, and bound Jesus, and carried him away, and delivered him to Pilate.

Matthew tells the same, and He is lead away to the judgment hall of Pontius Pilate.

Matthew 27:2 And when they had bound him, they led him away, and delivered him to Pontius Pilate the governor.

A very important statement is made here. The chief priests know that this day is the Passover day. They have not eaten the Passover meal as of yet. They do not want to defile themselves by entering into a Gentile meeting area before they eat the Passover. Jesus and His disciples ate of the Passover meal the night before when Passover began at 6:00 p.m. on Tuesday night. Passover would continue until 6:00 p.m. Wednesday night, when the first day of unleavened bread would begin, which is a high Sabbath day according to Exodus chapter twelve.

John 18:28 Then led they Jesus from Caiaphas unto the hall of judgment: and it was early; and they themselves went not into the judgment hall, lest they should be defiled; but that they might eat the passover.

8:00 a.m. on Wednesday, the Fourteenth of Nisan

Passover

Conviction comes upon Judas, and he begins to realize the awful thing he did by betraying Jesus. His remorse is more than he can bear. This act of repentance alone does not save him. It is important to understand this. You can change your mind or repent about your sin, but if you could do this perfectly and become sinless then you do not need Christ. When repentance takes place, a person turns from something.

Faith is what God requires for a man to turn to something. Since it is man's nature to sin, man should be in constant repentance.

Understand that man is not a sinner because he sins; man sins because he is a sinner! The strain of constantly having to repent because of our sin by our old nature would kill us. It did Judas!

Matthew 27:3 Then Judas, which had betrayed him, when he saw that he was condemned, repented himself, and brought again the thirty pieces of silver to the chief priests and elders,

Matthew 27:4 Saying, I have sinned in that I have betrayed the innocent blood. And they said, What is that to us? see thou to that.

Matthew 27:5 And he cast down the pieces of silver in the temple, and departed, and went and hanged himself.

Repentance will not save a man. It did not save Judas. Sincerity will not save a man. Humility will not save a man. Though repentance is an important first step, along with sincerity and humility, the only way to be saved is to come to Jesus Christ by faith, to ask Him to personally save you and by believing the gospel. The gospel is the good news that Jesus Christ came and that He died and that He was buried, and that He rose again from the grave on the first day of the week, which is contained in the Bible, the Word of God. Repentance means to "turn from," and faith means to "turn to." Ye have not because ye ask not!

James 4:2 Ye lust, and have not: ye kill, and desire to have, and cannot obtain: ye fight and war, yet ye have not, because ye ask not.

The chief priests were afraid of what to do with this money. It was cast at their feet, and they decide to buy a plot in the potter's field. A potter's field is a place where clay is removed for making pottery. It then is useless to build on and commonly is referred to as a burial site for unknown or indigent people.

Matthew 27:6 And the chief priests took the silver pieces, and said, It is not lawful for to put them into the treasury, because it is the price of blood.

Matthew 27:7 And they took counsel, and bought with them the potter's field, to bury strangers in. Matthew 27:8 Wherefore that field was called, The field of blood, unto this day.

Again Bible prophesies are fulfilled, this time by Jeremiah:

Matthew 27:9 Then was fulfilled that which was spoken by Jeremy the prophet, saying, And they took the thirty pieces of silver, the price of him that was valued, whom they of the children of Israel did value;

Matthew 27:10 And gave them for the potter's field, as the Lord appointed me.

What a minute! This specific Bible prophesy is in Zechariah not in Jeremiah.

Zechariah 11:12 And I said unto them, If ye think good, give me my price; and if not, forbear. So they weighed for my price thirty pieces of silver.

Zechariah 11:13 And the LORD said unto me, Cast it unto the potter: a goodly price that I was prised at of them. And I took the thirty pieces of silver, and cast them to the potter in the house of the LORD.

However, the book of Jeremiah is where God really points out the problem of a people who have never turned to God and His Word. God used a comparison of the potter and the clay.

Jeremiah 18:1 The word which came to Jeremiah from the LORD, saying,

Jeremiah 18:2 Arise, and go down to the potter's house, and there I will cause thee to hear my words.

The potter's house would be the house of God. Where it is appropriate to hear the words of God.

Jeremiah 18:3 Then I went down to the potter's house, and, behold, he wrought a work on the wheels.

Who is the potter? Scripture tells us that God represents Himself as the Potter and that all of mankind is the clay. He formed man out of the dust of the ground.

Isaiah 64:8 But now, O LORD, thou art our father; we are the clay, and thou our potter; and we all are the work of thy hand.

God created Adam. He was the first vessel. He became marred with sin. God could not rework the old Adam. He had to create a new vessel. God would have to regenerate man. This was done to his spirit. Adam's spirit became new. God did not just change the old Adam but made him a new work via the new birth in Christ.

Jeremiah 18:4 And the vessel that he made of clay was marred in the hand of the potter: so he made it again another vessel, as seemed good to the potter to make it.

God says through this prophesy in Jeremiah that these chief priests have totally forgotten the Messiah who they should have been looking for. Now that they have caused others to stumble including all of God's people, the Jews will be scattered and all they will see is God's back:

Jeremiah 18:15 Because my people hath forgotten me, they have burned incense to vanity, and they have caused them to stumble in their ways from the ancient paths, to walk in paths, in a way not cast up;

Jeremiah 18:16 To make their land desolate, and a perpetual hissing; every one that passeth thereby shall be astonished, and wag his head.

Jeremiah 18:17 I will scatter them as with an east wind before the enemy; I will shew them the back, and not the face, in the day of their calamity.

The two-thousand-year Jewish calamity was about to begin. A calamity like no other was about to take place. In just forty short years, Jerusalem would be destroyed, and the Jews would be scattered and hated even to this very day. God showed them His back and not His face, and it has been a horrible time for their race. But God is not through with the Jews as of yet. There is still the matter of the seven-year period or one week left from Daniel's seventy weeks to come to pass, and God will continue dealing with His people, the Jews at that time.

What a Finish! What a Start! The Month Jesus Met Man's Need

Fred A Kuypers

9:00 a.m. on Wednesday, the Fourteenth of Nisan
Passover, First encounter with Pilate

Jesus is taken to the governor, Pilate.

Luke 23:1 And the whole multitude of them arose, and led him unto Pilate.

The chief priests condemn themselves according to the prophecy above by Jeremiah. They claim Jesus perverted the nation, causing the people of Israel to stumble and not accept the Messiah.

Luke 23:2 And they began to accuse him, saying, We found this fellow perverting the nation, and forbidding to give tribute to Caesar, saying that he himself is Christ a King.

On this first appearance before Pilate, Jesus will simply state His case. Jesus will answer Pilate just one time. He will declare what Pilate says is true and correct!

Matthew records:

Matthew 27:11 And Jesus stood before the governor: and the governor asked him, saying, Art thou the King of the Jews? And Jesus said unto him, Thou sayest.

Mark records:

Mark 15:2 And Pilate asked him, Art thou the King of the Jews? And he answering said unto him, Thou sayest it.

Luke records:

Luke 23:3 And Pilate asked him, saying, Art thou the King of the Jews? And he answered him and said, Thou sayest it.

From this moment, Jesus stands and says nothing. He will not speak to Pilate until He returns from Herod.

Matthew:

Matthew 27:12 And when he was accused of the chief priests and elders, he answered nothing.

Matthew 27:13 Then said Pilate unto him, Hearest thou not how many things they witness against thee?

Matthew 27:14 And he answered him to never a word; insomuch that the governor marvelled greatly.

Mark:

Mark 15:3 And the chief priests accused him of many things: but he answered nothing.

Mark 15:4 And Pilate asked him again, saying, Answerest thou nothing? behold how many things they witness against thee.

Mark 15:5 But Jesus yet answered nothing; so that Pilate marvelled.

Isaiah also prophesied of this time:

Isaiah 53:7 He was oppressed, and he was afflicted, yet he opened not his mouth: he is brought as a lamb to the slaughter, and as a sheep before her shearers is dumb, so he openeth not his mouth.

This first meeting with Pilate is about to come to an end. Pilate is looking for an easy way out. He does not want to make a decision. He does not believe there is enough evidence against Jesus to convict Him by Roman law.

Luke 23:4 Then said Pilate to the chief priests and to the people, I find no fault in this man.

Luke 23:5 And they were the more fierce, saying, He stirreth up the people, teaching throughout all Jewry, beginning from Galilee to this place.

Pilate hears the key word *Galilee*. He determines that Jesus is not part of his jurisdiction.

Luke 23:6 When Pilate heard of Galilee, he asked whether the man were a Galilaean.

9:05 a.m. on Wednesday, the Fourteenth of Nisan
Passover

Herod is in town. He is the tetrarch of the Galilean area. Pilate sends Jesus to Herod. Herod and Pilate did not see eye to eye, but Pilate sees this as an opportunity. He will either turn Herod against him, or Pilate will please Herod by seeking his higher judgement.

Luke 23:7 And as soon as he knew that he belonged unto Herod's jurisdiction, he sent him to Herod, who himself also was at Jerusalem at that time.

9:10 a.m. on Wednesday, the Fourteenth of Nisan
Passover

Herod accepts Jesus for an entirely different reason. Herod was excited to see Jesus, not to hear the message of eternal life, but for the entertainment he hoped Jesus would perform. Today the lukewarm church of Laodicea is full of this type of people who are only in church for one thing: the show, entertainment that will produce that lukewarm feeling. But the house of God is not about feelings. Feelings are damnable. They can damn a person to hell.

Luke 23:8 And when Herod saw Jesus, he was exceeding glad: for he was desirous to see him of a long season, because he had heard many things of him; and he hoped to have seen some miracle done by him.

Luke 23:9 Then he questioned with him in many words; but he answered him nothing.

Again the chief priests condemn themselves according to the prophecy read earlier in Jeremiah. They continue to cause the people of Israel to stumble by accusing the Messiah.

Luke 23:10 And the chief priests and scribes stood and vehemently accused him.

Herod must have enjoyed this time of mocking and humiliating Christ:

Luke 23:11 And Herod with his men of war set him at nought, and mocked him, and arrayed him in a gorgeous robe, and sent him again to Pilate.

Herod and Pilate become good friends through this encounter with the Messiah.

Luke 23:12 And the same day Pilate and Herod were made friends together: for before they were at enmity between themselves.

9:20 a.m. on Wednesday, the Fourteenth of Nisan
Passover, Second encounter with Pilate

Jesus is back before Pilate for the second time as Luke says:

Luke 23:13 And Pilate, when he had called together the chief priests and the rulers and the people,

The chief priests attempt to have Pilate say the actual Jeremiah prophecy that Jesus has done a horrible thing:

Jeremiah 18:13 Therefore thus saith the LORD; Ask ye now among the heathen, who hath heard such things: the virgin of Israel hath done a very horrible thing.

Pilate has the opportunity to tell the chief priests that Jesus has done a very horrible thing. But instead Pilate answers this way:

Luke 23:14 Said unto them, Ye have brought this man unto me, as one that perverteth the people: and, behold, I, having examined him before you, have found no fault in this man touching those things whereof ye accuse him:

God makes the comparison of Jesus and what He gave up by leaving the Father, to pure snow in the mountains of Lebanon or cold flowing water and describes how Jesus will be forsaken.

Jeremiah 18:14 Will a man leave the snow of Lebanon which cometh from the rock of the field? or shall the cold flowing waters that come from another place be forsaken?

Pilate says that not even his new friend, Herod, sees anything wrong with the "Virgin of Israel" Jesus Christ.

Luke 23:15 No, nor yet Herod: for I sent you to him; and, lo, nothing worthy of death is done unto him.

Jesus has stood before Pilate earlier this morning. Pilate asked Jesus, "Art thou the King of the Jews?" Jesus answered with two words "Thou Sayest." After sending Jesus to Herod, Jesus is returned to Pilate. Pilate decides to punish Jesus and then just release Him. A whipping will punish Him enough.

Luke 23:16 I will therefore chastise him, and release him.

Jesus is before Pilate to discuss His fate. The Jews do not wish to just punish Jesus. They want Him dead! However, Pilate knows that on the Passover, it is customary to release a prisoner back to the people as the synoptic gospels agree.

Matthew 27:15 Now at that feast the governor was wont to release unto the people a prisoner, whom they would

Mark 15:6 Now at that feast he released unto them one prisoner, whomsoever they desired.

Luke 23:17 (For of necessity he must release one unto them at the feast.)

Having to release a prisoner, Pilate wanted the crowd to direct him to release Jesus. But the crowd was stirred up by the chief priests not to release Jesus. Pilate would bring Barabbas who was a notable prisoner, a murderer. Pilate thought who would want to release a murderer? This would make Jesus the obvious alternative.

Matthew 27:16 And they had then a notable prisoner, called Barabbas.

Mark 15:7 And there was one named Barabbas, which lay bound with them that had made insurrection with him, who had committed murder in the insurrection.

The crowd was beginning to get vocal. They wanted to see some action by the governor. Today it is no different. As crowds gather they just want to see heads roll.

Mark 15:8 And the multitude crying aloud began to desire him to do as he had ever done unto them.

Pilate was thinking between Jesus and Barabbas, the crowd will surely pick Jesus to be released. After all they were just envious of Him.

Matthew on Pilate's decision:

Matthew 27:17 Therefore when they were gathered together, Pilate said unto them, Whom will ye that I release unto you? Barabbas, or Jesus which is called Christ?

Matthew 27:18 For he knew that for envy they had delivered him.

Mark on Pilate's decision:

Mark 15:9 But Pilate answered them, saying, Will ye that I release unto you the King of the Jews?

Mark 15:10 For he knew that the chief priests had delivered him for envy.

What a Finish! What a Start! The Month Jesus Met Man's Need

Fred A Kuypers

However the crowd had been stirred up, and they were becoming a mob. They were already shouting to do away with Jesus. Again God points out that Barabbas was a murderer, and he certainly deserved the capital punishment of crucifixion.

Luke 23:18 And they cried out all at once, saying, Away with this man, and release unto us Barabbas:

Luke 23:19 (Who for a certain sedition made in the city, and for murder, was cast into prison.)

Pilate was not sure what to do at this point and would give the crowd a little time to think about their choice. So, Pilate steps back and sits down in his judgment seat to contemplate what to do. Pilate's wife approached him because she had some dreams that were problematic.

Matthew 27:19 When he was set down on the judgment seat, his wife sent unto him, saying, Have thou nothing to do with that just man: for I have suffered many things this day in a dream because of him.

9:30 a.m. on Wednesday, the Fourteenth of Nisan
Passover, Third encounter with Pilate

This certainly bothered Pilate. He is sitting down in his judgment chair, trying to think this through. He decides to question the crowd again. Remember Pilate was before the crowd first and decided to send Jesus to Herod. The second time he makes an offer to release Jesus instead of Barabbas. After hearing from his wife how disturbed she was, Pilate steps before the crowd for a third time and really puts the question to the people.

John 18:29 Pilate then went out unto them, and said, What accusation bring ye against this man?

The chief priests put more pressure on Pilate to carry out his duties of capital punishment.

John 18:30 They answered and said unto him, If he were not a malefactor, we would not have delivered him up unto thee.

Pilate is listening to what his wife told him. He makes an attempt for the first time to back out of the duties his position requires of him.

John 18:31 Then said Pilate unto them, Take ye him, and judge him according to your law. The Jews therefore said unto him, It is not lawful for us to put any man to death:

The Gospel of John moves to a narrative away from quotes to describe a prophecy made by Jesus Christ some three years earlier.

John 18:32 That the saying of Jesus might be fulfilled, which he spake, signifying what death he should die.

Back in John 3, Jesus Himself predicted that in death, He would be raised up.

John 3:14 And as Moses lifted up the serpent in the wilderness, even so must the Son of man be lifted up:

Christ's death could not take place by the Jews. Crucifixion was not a Jewish method of putting one to death. They would have to stone Jesus:

Leviticus 24:16 And he that blasphemeth the name of the LORD, he shall surely be put to death, and all the congregation shall certainly stone him: as well the stranger, as he that is born in the land, when he blasphemeth the name of the LORD, shall be put to death.

Moses described a curse on anyone who would be killed by hanging on a tree (crucifixion)

Deuteronomy 21:22 And if a man have committed a sin worthy of death, and he be to be put to death, and thou hang him on a tree:

Deuteronomy 21:23 His body shall not remain all night upon the tree, but thou shalt in any wise bury him that day; (for he that is hanged is accursed of God;) that thy land be not defiled, which the LORD thy God giveth thee for an inheritance.

Pilate wants out of this decision. He reenters the judgment hall where his judgment seat is. This is the *third* encounter with Jesus since this morning began. He begins by asking Jesus four questions:

Question one:

John 18:33 Then Pilate entered into the judgment hall again, and called Jesus, and said unto him, Art thou the King of the Jews?

Jesus answered this about an hour ago as recorded in Matthew and Mark. Jesus answers again but this time by putting more pressure on Pilate. Jesus may be referring to what Pilate's wife told him with this reply:

John 18:34 Jesus answered him, Sayest thou this thing of thyself, or did others tell it thee of me?

Question two:

John 18:35 Pilate answered, Am I a Jew? Thine own nation and the chief priests have delivered thee unto me: what hast thou done?

What have you done, Jesus? What crime is so terrible that these men of the Jewish religion want you dead? Jesus replies:

John 18:36 Jesus answered, My kingdom is not of this world: if my kingdom were of this world, then would my servants fight, that I should not be delivered to the Jews: but now is my kingdom not from hence.

Jesus' kingdom is not of this world! Pilate starts to think that Jesus is saying something different than what the crowd is accusing Him of saying. He asks Jesus to confirm His statement about being a king.

Question three:

John 18:37a Pilate therefore said unto him, Art thou a king then?

What a Finish! What a Start! The Month Jesus Met Man's Need

Fred A Kuypers

Jesus immediately puts the ball back into Pilate's court. Pilate is not going to escape his role in destiny. God will not have it!

John 18:37b Jesus answered, Thou sayest that I am a king. To this end was I born, and for this cause came I into the world, that I should bear witness unto the truth. Every one that is of the truth heareth my voice.

Jesus tells the whole purpose He came into the world. Jesus was born into this world to die and to shed his blood for man's sin. If a man believes this he is a witness to the truth. The Bible is very clear about this. If you do not have God dwelling in you, you do not hear the truth. Jesus spoke earlier in John:

John 8:42 Jesus said unto them, If God were your Father, ye would love me: for I proceeded forth and came from God; neither came I of myself, but he sent me.

John 8:43 Why do ye not understand my speech? even because ye cannot hear my word.

Question four:

John 18:38a Pilate saith unto him, What is truth?

Jesus had told His disciples earlier what truth was:

John 14:6 Jesus saith unto him, I am the way, the truth, and the life: no man cometh unto the Father, but by me.

9:40 a.m. on Wednesday, the Fourteenth of Nisan
Passover, Fourth encounter with Pilate

Pilate wants out so badly! He approaches the chief priests for the fourth time. He makes an attempt to back out of his duties again:

Luke 23:20 Pilate therefore, willing to release Jesus, spake again to them.

John 18:38b And when he had said this, he went out again unto the Jews, and saith unto them, I find in him no fault *at all*.

No fault at all! Pilate is really scared. Jesus had just declared Himself to be a king. There should have been no decision at all. How can a Jew threaten the procurator of Rome here and claim he is equal to Caesar? Pilate should have annihilated Jesus for this! No man stands up against Caesar and declares himself to be king! The crowd has been stirred up by the chief priests. Pilate even slants his words to advise all present not to ask for Barabbas to be released but to ask for Jesus because he does not want to make this decision. He wants out!

John 18:39 But ye have a custom, that I should release unto you one at the passover: will ye therefore that I release unto you the King of the Jews?

The chief priests were in a frenzy. They wanted Jesus dead! They continued with their barrage to release the murderer Barabbas:

Matthew 27:20 But the chief priests and elders persuaded the multitude that they should ask Barabbas, and destroy Jesus.

Mark 15:11 But the chief priest moved the people, that he should rather release Barabbas unto them.

Pilate asks again who to release. The comments from his wife must have been ringing in his ears at this moment.

Matthew 27:21 The governor answered and said unto them, Whether of the twain will ye that I release unto you? They said, Barabbas.

The Jews insist and cry out that Barabbas be released.

John 18:40 Then cried they all again, saying, Not this man, but Barabbas. Now Barabbas was a robber.

The chant now begins: crucify Jesus:

Luke 23:21 But they cried, saying, Crucify him, crucify him.

9:50 a.m. on Wednesday, the Fourteenth of Nisan
Passover, Fifth encounter with Pilate

Again, Pilate goes into the judgment hall. He is eaten up with this decision. He does not want to make this choice. Pilate comes out again. Luke said earlier in verse 14 that he "found no fault in this man" and now asks "what evil has he done?" Matthew, Mark, and Luke all say the same "what evil hath he done?" But the chant is intensifying: crucify Him!

Matthew:

Matthew 27:22 Pilate saith unto them, What shall I do then with Jesus which is called Christ? They all say unto him, Let him be crucified.

Matthew 27:23 And the governor said, Why, what evil hath he done? But they cried out the more, saying, Let him be crucified.

Mark:

Mark 15:12 And Pilate answered and said again unto them, What will ye then that I shall do unto him whom ye call the King of the Jews?

Mark 15:13 And they cried out again, Crucify him.

Mark 15:14 Then Pilate said unto them, Why, what evil hath he done? And they cried out the more exceedingly, Crucify him.

Luke:

Luke 23:22 And he said unto them the third time, Why, what evil hath he done? I have found no cause of death in him: I will therefore chastise him, and let him go.

Instantly, the crowd starts to cry.

Luke 23:23 And they were instant with loud voices, requiring that he might be crucified. And the voices of them and of the chief priests prevailed.

Matthew alone gives us this next look into the heart and soul of Pilate. Pilate puts on an act of humility and tries to make himself look innocent of the sentence handed down to Jesus. What his wife said must be so loud in his head. Nevertheless, Pilate alone could have pardoned Jesus at this time. He could have released him.

He will take one more opportunity to do just that after Jesus is scourged. The words of Pilate's wife again ring in his ear. As Pilate calls Jesus by the same name that his wife just a few moments earlier had said of Jesus: that just man!

Matthew 27:24 When Pilate saw that he could prevail nothing, but that rather a tumult was made, he took water, and washed his hands before the multitude, saying, I am innocent of the blood of this just person: see ye to it.

As the third hour of the morning approaches the people give out a cry that has affected the Jews for over 2000 years. The Jews have paid a heavy price for their rejection of the Messiah. And yet every man who dies without Christ in their heart says the exact same thing!

Matthew 27:25 Then answered all the people, and said His blood be on us, and on our children.

Luke 23:24 And Pilate gave sentence that it should be as they required.

The Jews have paid the price for this statement that rings for eternity. They were scattered throughout the world less than one generation after this statement was made. In the year AD 70, the city of Jerusalem was entirely destroyed, and the Jewish people were scattered throughout the countries of the world. They have been tortured and murdered like no other nation with perhaps the final assault coming from Hitler and the Nazis with their "Final Solution."[33]

---

[33] "The Final Solution". https://www.ushmm.org/outreach/en/article.php?ModuleId=10007704. viewed Feb 21, 2019.

10:00 a.m. on Wednesday, the Fourteenth of Nisan
Passover, Jesus is scourged

The fourth hour of the day has arrived. Mark, in verse 25, says that it was the third hour when they crucified Him. This must mean that the whole process of crucifixion from the scourging, to the mocking, to the carrying of the cross, and the hanging on the cross must have begun at 9:00 a.m., the third hour. This is because later in verse 33, Mark again says that the darkness was from the sixth hour until the ninth hour when the actual hanging on the cross took place. The whole process of the crucifixion is about six hours long. All this will start right when Barabbas is being released:

Matthew 27:26a Then released he Barabbas unto them:

Mark 15:15a And so Pilate, willing to content the people, released Barabbas unto them,

Luke 23:25a And he released unto them him that for sedition and murder was cast into prison, whom they had desired;

Now Jesus is led to be scourged. Notice how much time the Gospels spend on this moment. God does not want us to dwell on this moment. It happened. Christ's blood was being shed. The remission of sin has begun. The perfect sacrifice is about to take place. But God only has about five words for this moment. They took Jesus and scourged him. Luke, the physician, is silent about the scourging.

Matthew 27:26b and when he had scourged Jesus, he delivered him to be crucified.

Mark 15:15b and delivered Jesus, when he had scourged him, to be crucified.

Luke 23:25b but he delivered Jesus to their will.

John 19:1 Then Pilate therefore took Jesus, and scourged *him*.

Jesus is scourged by Pilate. Notice that this bloody ritual of scourging only has three entries here. All that is said is they scourged him. God spends very little time dwelling on this topic. It is not something He wanted. Yet in Isaiah it says:

Isaiah 53:10 Yet it pleased the LORD to bruise him; he hath put him to grief: when thou shalt make his soul an offering for sin, he shall see his seed, he shall prolong his days, and the pleasure of the LORD shall prosper in his hand.

It pleased the Lord to bruise him? God the Father is only pleased in knowing that the bruising of our Lord Jesus would meet the requirements of the blood sacrifice needed to pay for your sins and mine as it says so clearly in Hebrews:

Hebrews 9:11 But Christ being come an high priest of good things to come, by a greater and more perfect tabernacle, not made with hands, that is to say, not of this building;

Hebrews 9:12 Neither by the blood of goats and calves, but by his own blood he entered in once into the holy place, having obtained eternal redemption for us.

Hebrews 9:13 For if the blood of bulls and of goats, and the ashes of an heifer sprinkling the unclean, sanctifieth to the purifying of the flesh:

Hebrews 9:14 How much more shall the blood of Christ, who through the eternal Spirit offered himself without spot to God, purge your conscience from dead works to serve the living God?

10:45 a.m. on Wednesday, the Fourteenth of Nisan
Passover

The Praetorium hall was a place where many could view the mockery about to take place. The Praetorium was usually a military place, the headquarters of the Roman military governor, wherever he happened to be.[34] The Roman soldiers would have their way with Jesus for the next few moments. The ridicule that Jesus faced was horrible here. He was stripped naked for the purple (scarlet, blueish red) robe.

Matthew:

Matthew 27:27 Then the soldiers of the governor took Jesus into the common hall, and gathered unto him the whole band of soldiers.

Matthew 27:28 And they stripped him, and put on him a scarlet robe.

Matthew 27:29a And when they had platted a crown of thorns, they put it upon his head, and a reed in his right hand:

Mark:

Mark 15:16 And the soldiers led him away into the hall, called Praetorium; and they call together the whole band.

Mark 15:17 And they clothed him with purple, and platted a crown of thorns, and put it about his head,

John:

John 19:2 And the soldiers platted a crown of thorns, and put it on his head, and they put on him a purple robe,

The Roman soldiers not only punished Jesus physically but now begin to mock him:

Matthew 27:29b and they bowed the knee before him, and mocked him, saying, Hail, King of the Jews!

Mark 15:18 And began to salute him, Hail, King of the Jews

John 19:3 And said, Hail, King of the Jews! and they smote him with their hands.

---

[34] https://www.biblestudytools.com/dictionary/praetorium/

With the crown of thorns on his head, they took the reed and pounded the thorns deeper into his brow as they spit on Him. Matthew and Mark are the only gospels that give this account:

Matthew 27:30 And they spit upon him, and took the reed, and smote him on the head.

Matthew 27:31 And after that they had mocked him, they took the robe off from him, and put his own raiment on him, and led him away to crucify him.

Mark 15:19 And they smote him on the head with a reed, and did spit upon him, and bowing their knees worshipped him.

Mark 15:20 And when they had mocked him, they took off the purple from him, and put his own clothes on him, and led him out to crucify him.

This time of mocking by the Roman soldiers lasted for a short time, and they led Him away from Praetorium hall and back to Pilate.

11:00 a.m. on Wednesday, the Fourteenth of Nisan
Passover, Sixth encounter with Pilate

Pilate must still be bothered by what his wife said. "Have thou nothing to do with that just man"! "Have thou nothing to do with that just man"! "Have thou nothing to do with that just man"! Again, Pilate says to the crowd that he will find no fault in Jesus.

John 19:4 Pilate therefore went forth again, and saith unto them, Behold, I bring him forth to you, that ye may know that I find no fault in him.

Jesus is summoned and Pilate makes his infamous statement:

John 19:5 Then came Jesus forth, wearing the crown of thorns, and the purple robe. And *Pilate* saith unto them, Behold the man!

The chief priests continue the chant, Crucify Him! Crucify Him! Pilate tells the chief priests to crucify Him yourself!

John 19:6 When the chief priests therefore and officers saw him, they cried out, saying, Crucify *him*, crucify *him*. Pilate saith unto them, Take ye him, and crucify *him*: for I find no fault in him.

Pilate hears something that rings of what his wife said earlier. He is a just man, and the crowd is saying He made Himself equal to God by declaring to be the Son of God! This was eating away at Pilate who now was showing signs of fear.

John 19:7 The Jews answered him, We have a law, and by our law he ought to die, because he made himself the Son of God.

John 19:8 When Pilate therefore heard that saying, he was the more afraid;

The eternal moment has arrived. Jesus needs to be condemned to death. The "Virgin of Israel" is on trial and Pilate asks the question recorded in Jeremiah 18 "who hath heard such things: the virgin of Israel hath done a very horrible thing."

At this moment God says the price of my sin and all sins must be paid. And it must be paid right now! There will be no more time like this ever again in eternity. In the Catholic belief, the crucifixion of Jesus Christ at every mass that is offered up is a complete devastation to God. Jesus will go once and once only for everyone to the cross.

Hebrews 10:10 By the which will we are sanctified through the offering of the body of Jesus Christ once for all.

Jesus will give no reply to Pilate.

John 19:9 And went again into the judgment hall, and saith unto Jesus, Whence art thou? But Jesus gave him no answer.

Pilate expressing his power and what he can legally do announces to Jesus his alternatives.

John 19:10 Then saith Pilate unto him, Speakest thou not unto me? knowest thou not that I have power to crucify thee, and have power to release thee?

Jesus' reply is swift and to the point.

John 19:11 Jesus answered, Thou couldest have no power *at all* against me, except it were given thee from above: therefore he that delivered me unto thee hath the greater sin.

As the power of God must be seen here, Pilate will make his own decision. God gives him a final opportunity that by Pilate's own decision he can back out. What he has done is not as great a sin as what Judas has done. Judas committed his sin of betrayal while following Christ, yet never professing to know Christ as Lord. Today, most so-called Christians are doing the exact same thing. They are fans of Jesus Christ as long as the music appeals to their flesh. They are fans as long as no one offends their family members who do not believe the truth of the Bible. They are fans as long as they can meet in a church where you can slip in and slip out with no one knowing you or seeing you. That way, today's Christian can drink or go to worldly movies or shack up and no one asks them about it or questions their loyalty to the Scriptures. Pilate, you have no power to do this except it is ordained by God from above. Pilate, you can back out of this! Pilate, by your fruit God shall know you!

Matthew 7:20 Wherefore by their fruits ye shall know them.

A Christian must take on the command to become a servant of God. That is what Jesus being the Lord of your life means:

Romans 6:21 What fruit had ye then in those things whereof ye are now ashamed? for the end of those things is death.

Romans 6:22 But now being made free from sin, and become servants to God, ye have your fruit unto holiness, and the end everlasting life.

The "greater sin" mentioned in John 19:11 above brings to mind that which will take place right after the pretribulation rapture. Those who followed Christ but never knew Him as their personal Savior will believe the lie of the Antichrist:

2 Thessalonians 2:7 For the mystery of iniquity doth already work: only he who now letteth will let, until he be taken out of the way.

2 Thessalonians 2:8 And then shall that Wicked be revealed, whom the Lord shall consume with the spirit of his mouth, and shall destroy with the brightness of his coming:

2 Thessalonians 2:9 Even him, whose coming is after the working of Satan with all power and signs and lying wonders,

2 Thessalonians 2:10 And with all deceivableness of unrighteousness in them that perish; because they received not the love of the truth, that they might be saved.

2 Thessalonians 2:11 And for this cause God shall send them strong delusion, that they should believe a lie:

11:15 a.m. on Wednesday, the Fourteenth of Nisan
Passover, Pilate seeks to release Jesus

Pilate makes his decision. He will release Jesus. He goes to the crowd and wants to tell them Rome has punished this man enough. But the crowd has other ideas.

John 19:12 And from thenceforth Pilate sought to release him: but the Jews cried out, saying, If thou let this man go, thou art not Caesar's friend: whosoever maketh himself a king speaketh against Caesar.

11:20 a.m. on Wednesday, the Fourteenth of Nisan
Passover, Seventh encounter with Pilate

Imagine how Pilate's head was swimming at this moment. He wants to release Jesus, but what if news of this gets to Caesar? Caesar will have his head! For the seventh time Pilate goes before the crowd and sits in his judgment seat again. He is about to change his decision. The fear of Caesar hearing about this has forced him to change his mind.

John 19:13 When Pilate therefore heard that saying, he brought Jesus forth, and sat down in the judgment seat in a place that is called the Pavement, but in the Hebrew, Gabbatha.

What a Finish! What a Start! The Month Jesus Met Man's Need

Fred A Kuypers

11:30 a.m. on Wednesday, the Fourteenth of Nisan
Passover, Pilate speaks

It is about the sixth hour. That means it was getting close to noon. It could be as early as 11:30 a.m. Jesus is bleeding, and wearing a crown of thorns, He is presented to the crowd and given one more chance to be released.

John 19:14 And it was the preparation of the passover, and about the sixth hour: and he saith unto the Jews, Behold your King!

The crowd would have none of it. The Jews turned their back on God and said they have no king but Caesar.

John 19:15 But they cried out, Away with *him*, away with *him*, crucify him. Pilate saith unto them, Shall I crucify your King? The chief priests answered, We have no king but Caesar.

John 19:16 Then delivered he him therefore unto them to be crucified. And they took Jesus, and led *him* away.

The prophecy of Jeremiah says that God will turn his back on the Jews as a nation.

Jeremiah 18:17 I will scatter them as with an east wind before the enemy; I will shew them the back, and not the face, in the day of their calamity.

Isaiah prophesied:

Isaiah 53:8 He was taken from prison and from judgment: and who shall declare his generation? for he was cut off out of the land of the living: for the transgression of my people was he stricken.

11:35 a.m. on Wednesday, the Fourteenth of Nisan
Passover, The road to Calvary

Simon the Cyrenian is ordered to assist Jesus in carrying the cross. Simon was in Jerusalem for the Passover and had his two young boys with him, Alexander and Rufus. They were there probably to offer a lamb for the Passover sacrifice. When they saw the crowd and heard the commotion, Simon's interest must have peaked, and he wanted to get a closer look at what was going on. He was a little too close if he did not want to have any part of this crucifixion. Matthew, Mark, and Luke again all agree as synoptic gospels. John is different.

Matthew:

Matthew 27:32 And as they came out, they found a man of Cyrene, Simon by name: him they compelled to bear his cross.

Mark:

Mark 15:21 And they compel one Simon a Cyrenian, who passed by, coming out of the country, the father of Alexander and Rufus, to bear his cross.

Luke:

Luke 23:26 And as they led him away, they laid hold upon one Simon, a Cyrenian, coming out of the country, and on him they laid the cross, that he might bear it after Jesus.

Only John's Gospel explains that Jesus carried His own cross.

John 19:17 And he bearing his cross went forth into a place called *the place* of a skull, which is called in the Hebrew Golgotha:

Notice the names of Simon's two small boys, Alexander and Rufus. Jesus must have begun the walk to Golgotha carrying the cross. Having trouble and not moving fast enough, Simon was pressured into service to assist Jesus with the weight of the cross. He obliged and assisted. Because of Simon's faithfulness, even his two sons, Alexander and Rufus, are mentioned in the Gospel of Mark for all eternity.

Simon was from Cyrene, a city in Libya, Africa. Cyrene was a Greek colony where tens of thousands of Jews were forced to settle during the reign of Ptolemy I Soter I (367–283 BC).[35] Ptolemy was one of the four generals who divided Alexander the Great's world empire as described in the prophecies of Daniel 8.

Daniel 8:21 And the rough goat is the king of Grecia: and the great horn that is between his eyes is the first king.

Daniel 8:22 Now that being broken, whereas four stood up for it, four kingdoms shall stand up out of the nation, but not in his power.

The four generals were Antigonus (who ruled over Macedonia to the west), Lysimachus (who ruled over Asia to the east), Seleucus (who ruled over Syria and lands to the north), and Ptolemy (who ruled over Egypt and lands to the south). Ptolemy ruled in the south from Egypt and into Africa and liked the idea of being called Pharaoh. His Hellenistic dynasty ended with the death of Cleopatra in 30 BC. The death of Cleopatra at age thirty-nine marked the end of this dynasty, which was the last ruling Hellenistic dynasty to be taken over by the Romans. This is very important as the long rule of the legs of iron, Rome, will now take place. According to Daniel's vision of Nebuchadnezzar's dream, Rome will be the last empire that controls Jerusalem. This will end in 1967 with the Six-Day War when the time known as "the times of the Gentiles" ends as Luke explains:

Luke 21:24 And they shall fall by the edge of the sword, and shall be led away captive into all nations: and Jerusalem shall be trodden down of the Gentiles, until the times of the Gentiles be fulfilled.

---

[35]   https://en.wikipedia.org/wiki/Ptolemaic_Kingdom

What a Finish! What a Start! The Month Jesus Met Man's Need

Fred A Kuypers

11:40 a.m. on Wednesday, the Fourteenth of Nisan
Passover, Jesus speaks

The only words recorded from Jesus during this excruciating march are in Luke:

Luke 23:27 And there followed him a great company of people, and of women, which also bewailed and lamented him.

Luke 23:28 But Jesus turning unto them said, Daughters of Jerusalem, weep not for me, but weep for yourselves, and for your children.

Jesus is talking to the Jewish nation. He is unveiling all the problems that will befall the Jews. He is especially talking about the last week of Daniel's seventy weeks that were determined on the Jews in Daniel 9. Jesus points out that if the Jewish people will reject the Messiah when He is there in person, then how will the Jews speak of Jesus when He is no longer on earth?

Luke 23:29 For, behold, the days are coming, in the which they shall say, Blessed are the barren, and the wombs that never bare, and the paps which never gave suck.

Luke 23:30 Then shall they begin to say to the mountains, Fall on us; and to the hills, Cover us.

Luke 23:31 For if they do these things in a green tree, what shall be done in the dry?

The book of Acts has this history when Jesus is gone and the Jews are dried up on account of denying Him. Just read what happened to Stephen who was a spokesman for Christ in Acts 7.

11:50 a.m. on Wednesday, the Fourteenth of Nisan
Passover, arrival at Calvary, Golgotha

The place where the crucifixion took place had several names. Three of the four gospels call the place Galgotha:

Matthew 27:33 And when they were come unto a place called Golgotha, that is to say, a place of a skull,

Mark 15:22 And they bring him unto the place Golgotha, which is, being interpreted, The place of a skull.

John 19:17 And he bearing his cross went forth into a place called the place of a skull, which is called in the Hebrew Golgotha:

These names include:

1. It was the place of the skull. That is the face of the mountain resembled a skull with small caves for the eye sockets and stone for the mouth.

2. It was also named Golgotha. Outside Jerusalem to the north on the main road coming into Jerusalem from Damascus going through the Damascus gate.

3. It was also called Calvary in Luke:

Luke 23:33 And when they were come to the place, which is called Calvary, there they crucified him, and the malefactors, one on the right hand, and the other on the left.

In Psalm 22 God has given a look at this eventful day. Psalms explains that Jesus would be surrounded by men wanting to tear Him up, to tear Him to pieces like bulls in a bullfight would tear a man up who is helpless with his hands tied.

Psalm 22:12 Many bulls have compassed me: strong bulls of Bashan have beset me round.

As Jesus was being prepared to be nailed to the cross, there were many onlookers. It is interesting to note that the nailing to the cross was unique. Only in the Gospel of John, later in chapter 20 after His resurrection does the mention of nails take place. Because of this torment to Jesus the people would stare and gasp with blood in their eyes and hearts:

Psalm 22:13 They gaped upon me with their mouths, as a ravening and a roaring lion.

Jesus spoke of this time when He was hailed as the King and true Messiah. On that eventful day as He presented Himself on the triumphant entry into Jerusalem back on the eighth of Nisan through the Eastern Gate, Jesus said these words.

John 12:30 Jesus answered and said, This voice came not because of me, but for your sakes.

John 12:31 Now is the judgment of this world: now shall the prince of this world be cast out.

John 12:32 And I, if I be lifted up from the earth, will draw all men unto me.

Jesus said I "will draw all men unto me"! This is so very important to remember. Paul explained that as one witnesses to the lost, some sow, some water, but it is God who gives the increase.

1 Corinthians 3:6 I have planted, Apollos watered; but God gave the increase.

Remember that a Christian is a laborer in the field that is white with harvest. It does not add anything to his merit with God that he win souls for Christ.

1 Corinthians 3:7 So then neither is he that planteth any thing, neither he that watereth; but God that giveth the increase.

What God really looks for in a Christian is that they are faithful in all that is done for Christ. This can only take place through faith. Hebrews 11:6 says that without faith, it is impossible to please God. All day long and everyday stewards of Christ are to be faithful:

1 Corinthians 4:1 Let a man so account of us, as of the ministers of Christ, and stewards of the mysteries of God.

1 Corinthians 4:2 Moreover it is required in stewards, that a man be found faithful.

11:55 a.m. on Wednesday, the Fourteenth of Nisan
Passover

The soldiers offered Jesus a poisonous anesthetic of vinegar and gall (gall is a poison—either a type of snake venom or it could have been made from poppy seed poison known today as opium that morphine and heroin and codeine are derived from) and Jesus rejected it after tasting.

Matthew 27:34 They gave him vinegar to drink mingled with gall: and when he had tasted thereof, he would not drink.

The soldiers then offered Jesus a mild sedative of alcohol and myrrh (oily type of narcotic), and Jesus rejected it even in His pain and anguish.

Mark 15:23 And they gave him to drink wine mingled with myrrh: but he received it not.

He would not break the command of the Old Testament about wine.

Proverbs 23:29 Who hath woe? who hath sorrow? who hath contentions? who hath babbling? who hath wounds without cause? who hath redness of eyes?

Proverbs 23:30 They that tarry long at the wine; they that go to seek mixed wine.

Proverbs 23:31 Look not thou upon the wine when it is red, when it giveth his colour in the cup, when it moveth itself aright.

12:00 noon on Wednesday, the Fourteenth of Nisan
Passover

Many prophecies from the Old Testament will be fulfilled at this moment. Taken from Psalms in particular:

Psalm 22:10 I was cast upon thee from the womb: thou art my God from my mother's belly.

Psalm 22:11 Be not far from me; for trouble is near; for there is none to help.

Psalm 22:12 Many bulls have compassed me: strong bulls of Bashan have beset me round.

Psalm 22:13 They gaped upon me with their mouths, as a ravening and a roaring lion.

Psalm 22:14 I am poured out like water, and all my bones are out of joint: my heart is like wax; it is melted in the midst of my bowels.

Psalm 22:15 My strength is dried up like a potsherd; and my tongue cleaveth to my jaws; and thou hast brought me into the dust of death.

Psalm 22:16 For dogs have compassed me: the assembly of the wicked have inclosed me: they pierced my hands and my feet.

Psalm 22:17 I may tell all my bones: they look and stare upon me.

Psalm 22:18 They part my garments among them, and cast lots upon my vesture.

Psalm 22:19 But be not thou far from me, O LORD: O my strength, haste thee to help me

Matthew:

Matthew 27:35 And they crucified him, and parted his garments, casting lots: that it might be fulfilled which was spoken by the prophet, They parted my garments among them, and upon my vesture did they cast lots.

Mark:

Mark 15:24 And when they had crucified him, they parted his garments, casting lots upon them, what every man should take.

Luke:

Luke 23:32 And there were also two other, malefactors, led with him to be put to death.

Luke 23:33 And when they were come to the place, which is called Calvary, there they crucified him, and the malefactors, one on the right hand, and the other on the left.

John:

John 19:18 Where they crucified him, and two other with him, on either side one, and Jesus in the midst.

The very first prophecy of Christ in the Bible was that He would receive a blow to his heel. Not a death blow which is what Christ would deliver to the head of the serpent. In Genesis 3:15 The "Proto Evangelism" (first mention of Christ) appeared and is now fulfilled. The bruise or blow to the heel of the seed of the woman has taken place.

Genesis 3:15 And I will put enmity between thee and the woman, and between thy seed and her seed; it shall bruise thy head, and thou shalt bruise his heel.

The downfall of the serpent with this death blow to his head is finally accomplished. The price for my sin has been paid! Satan is going down for the count. It will be fulfilled when Satan is finally cast into the lake of fire at the great White Throne Judgement of Revelation 20.

Revelation 20:10 And the devil that deceived them was cast into the lake of fire and brimstone, where the beast and the false prophet are, and shall be tormented day and night for ever and ever.

Revelation 20:11 And I saw a great white throne, and him that sat on it, from whose face the earth and the heaven fled away; and there was found no place for them.

What did Jesus experience on the cross? Remember that He prayed "O my Father, if it be possible, let this cup pass from me: nevertheless not as I will, but as thou wilt." Remember His feelings were so intense at the thought of being the perfect sacrifice that He sweat as it were great drops of blood! This was not for the torture

What a Finish! What a Start! The Month Jesus Met Man's Need

Fred A Kuypers

He was about to endure but for the time that God would die, that is, be separated from God the Father for the next three hours as Jesus, who knew no sin, became sin. The prophecy from Psalm 22 given above is exactly what Jesus experienced, yet presented a thousand years earlier by David.

2Corinthians 5:21 For he hath made him *to be* sin for us, who knew no sin; that we might be made the righteousness of God in him.

Mark writes:

Mark 15:25 And it was the third hour, and they crucified him.

The third hour, 9:00 a.m. marked the beginning of this day when Jesus actually began to be on trial by Pilate. Shifting between Pilate and Harod, and being scourged, Jesus was three hours in torture. Mark notes later in verse 33 that the sky was dark from the sixth hour to the ninth hour, noting the time that Jesus hung on the cross. The sixth hour of the day is 12:00 noon. Jesus hung on the cross for three hours. Being crucified for three hours from 12:00 noon to 3:00 p.m. is a long time. The agony He suffered was given in Psalm 22 above. What else took place at this time? The events of this three-hour ordeal are as follows and will be discussed in detail:

1. Jesus is stripped of His garments:

   Matthew 27:35 And they crucified him, and parted his garments, casting lots: that it might be fulfilled which was spoken by the prophet, They parted my garments among them, and upon my vesture did they cast lots.

   The soldiers who had administered this terrible beating and crucifixion were tired from the punishment they had inflicted.

   Matthew 27:36 And sitting down they watched him there;

   John gives a more detailed account of the soldiers dividing up the clothes of Jesus:

   John 19:23 Then the soldiers, when they had crucified Jesus, took his garments, and made four parts, to every soldier a part; and also his coat: now the coat was without seam, woven from the top throughout.

   John 19:24 They said therefore among themselves, Let us not rend it, but cast lots for it, whose it shall be: that the scripture might be fulfilled, which saith, They parted my raiment among them, and for my vesture they did cast lots. These things therefore the soldiers did.

2. Prophesied a thousand years earlier by David in Psalm 22:18, the soldiers cast lots:

   Psalm 22:18 They part my garments among them, and cast lots upon my vesture.

3. Jesus speaks for the first of seven times from the cross:

   Luke 23:34 Then said Jesus, Father, forgive them; for they know not what they do. And they parted his raiment, and cast lots.

4. The sky became black. But surely the "Light of the world," Jesus, was still in view so that everyone present could still see the Savior on the tree!

5. Two thieves were crucified with Jesus:

Matthew:

Matthew 27:38 Then were there two thieves crucified with him, one on the right hand, and another on the left.

Mark:

Mark 15:27 And with him they crucify two thieves; the one on his right hand, and the other on his left.

Mark 15:28 And the scripture was fulfilled, which saith, And he was numbered with the transgressors.

The scriptures spoken of in Mark 15:28 that were fulfilled are located in Isaiah:

Isaiah 53:12 Therefore will I divide him a portion with the great, and he shall divide the spoil with the strong; because he hath poured out his soul unto death: and he was numbered with the transgressors; and he bare the sin of many, and made intercession for the transgressors.

Also Jesus predicted this the night before just after the Passover meal. In Luke 22:37, Jesus said, "And he was reckoned among the transgressors: for the things concerning me have an end." This is when He was instructing the apostles to sell their garments and purchase a sword:

6. The soldiers again offer Jesus another drink, this time vinegar only:

   Luke 23:35 And the people stood beholding. And the rulers also with them derided him, saying, He saved others; let him save himself, if he be Christ, the chosen of God.

   Luke 23:36 And the soldiers also mocked him, coming to him, and offering him vinegar,

7. Many say the title nailed to the cross above Jesus' head is a contradiction. They say it is not the same in all gospels. But I believe it to be correct and will declare it as so.

   Matthew 27:37 And set up over his head his accusation written,
   THIS IS JESUS THE KING OF THE JEWS.

   Mark 15:26 And the superscription of his accusation was written over,
   THE KING OF THE JEWS.

   Luke 23:38 And a superscription also was written over him in letters of Greek, and Latin, and Hebrew,
   THIS IS THE KING OF THE JEWS.

John 19:19 And Pilate wrote a title, and put it on the cross. And the writing was,
JESUS OF NAZARETH THE KING OF THE JEWS.

There could have been a variation in the three different languages: Greek, and Latin, and Hebrew. Or, there could have been one phrase with each gospel selecting what stood out to each writer. No writer quotes it completely, but surely each of these words appeared in one of the three languages.

John 19:20 This title then read many of the Jews: for the place where Jesus was crucified was nigh to the city: and it was written in Hebrew, *and* Greek, *and* Latin.

THIS IS JESUS OF NAZARETH
THE KING OF THE JEWS.

Pilate has one last thing to say:

John 19:21 Then said the chief priests of the Jews to Pilate, Write not, The King of the Jews; but that he said, I am King of the Jews.

John 19:22 Pilate answered, What I have written I have written.

1:00 p.m. on Wednesday, the Fourteenth of Nisan
Passover, Jesus first statement

Jesus made seven statements as He hung on the cross. Matthew and Mark record the same statement, Luke records three and John records three quotes (speaking to Mary his mother and John the Apostle, the statement is recorded as one). Each gospel explains what was said.

1. Jesus speaks with His first statement from the cross: This comes as He is being nailed and raised up on the beam of the cross or as He is in position for the first few moments.

Luke 23:34 Then said Jesus, Father, forgive them; for they know not what they do. And they parted his raiment and cast lots.

The crowd that had gathered around the cross was relentless in their blasphemy against Jesus. As Jesus was crucified, His clothing was divided up among the soldiers as previously stated:

John 19:23 Then the soldiers, when they had crucified Jesus, took his garments, and made four parts, to every soldier a part; and also *his* coat: now the coat was without seam, woven from the top throughout.

Fred A Kuypers

John 19:24 They said therefore among themselves, Let us not rend it, but cast lots for it, whose it shall be: that the scripture might be fulfilled, which saith, They parted my raiment among them, and for my vesture they did cast lots. These things therefore the soldiers did.

Matthew states that all that passed by mocked Jesus, especially the chief priests:

Matthew 27:39 And they that passed by reviled him, wagging their heads,

Matthew 27:40 And saying, Thou that destroyest the temple, and buildest *it* in three days, save thyself. If thou be the Son of God, come down from the cross.

Matthew 27:41 Likewise also the chief priests mocking him, with the scribes and elders, said,

Matthew 27:42 He saved others; himself he cannot save. If he be the King of Israel, let him now come down from the cross, and we will believe him.

Matthew 27:43 He trusted in God; let him deliver him now, if he will have him: for he said, I am the Son of God.

Mark states:

Mark 15:29 And they that passed by railed on him, wagging their heads, and saying, Ah, thou that destroyest the temple, and buildest it in three days,

Mark 15:30 Save thyself, and come down from the cross.

Mark 15:31 Likewise also the chief priests mocking said among themselves with the scribes, He saved others; himself he cannot save.

Luke states:

Luke 23:35 And the people stood beholding. And the rulers also with them derided him, saying, He saved others; let him save himself, if he be Christ, the chosen of God.

Luke 23:36 And the soldiers also mocked him, coming to him, and offering him vinegar,

Luke 23:37 And saying, If thou be the king of the Jews, save thyself.

Both the thieves mocked Jesus at the beginning of the crucifixion. Matthew and Mark each have their own view of this:

Matthew 27:44 The thieves also, which were crucified with him, cast the same in his teeth.

Mark 15:32 Let Christ the King of Israel descend now from the cross, that we may see and believe. And they that were crucified with him reviled him.

However, Luke is the only gospel that will give an account of the conversation among the two thieves. Luke gives this most detailed account of what happened next with the two thieves.

Luke 23:39 And one of the malefactors which were hanged railed on him, saying, If thou be Christ, save thyself and us.

All of a sudden Luke speaks of an entirely different viewpoint of one of the thieves:

Luke 23:40 But the other answering rebuked him, saying, Dost not thou fear God, seeing thou art in the same condemnation?

Luke 23:41 And we indeed justly; for we receive the due reward of our deeds: but this man hath done nothing amiss.

What a Finish! What a Start! The Month Jesus Met Man's Need

Fred A Kuypers

Luke 23:42 And he said unto Jesus, Lord, remember me when thou comest into thy kingdom.

Notice what happened with the two thieves. One of the thieves repented of his previous blasphemy against Christ. Matthew and Mark stated that both thieves cast the same reviling accusations at Jesus as they all hung on their individual crosses. When the one thief said, "Save thyself and us," conviction came upon the other thief. Repentance is the changing of one's mind. Turning from sin (repent) and turning to God (faith) would have to take place. Only you and God know when this is truly from the heart. No baptism or any other work of man is required so that Jesus Christ will receive all the glory for salvation. And then with the mouth confession is made unto salvation as the thief calls Jesus "Lord" in verse 42.

Romans 10:12 For there is no difference between the Jew and the Greek: for the same Lord over all is rich unto all that call upon him.

Romans 10:13 For whosoever shall call upon the name of the Lord shall be saved.

2 Timothy 2:22 Flee also youthful lusts: but follow righteousness, faith, charity, peace, with them that call on the Lord out of a pure heart.

1:30 p.m. on Wednesday, the Fourteenth of Nisan Passover, Jesus second statement

2. Jesus' second statement from the cross:

Luke 23:43 And Jesus said unto him, Verily I say unto thee, To day shalt thou be with me in paradise.

Paradise is a transliterated word from the Greek. It can be literally interpreted as a place of future happiness. It is used three times in the New Testament, and all three times it speaks of a look into what God has in store for us, His promised place of happiness. The one thief repented of his sin, and with a contrite heart, humbly asked Jesus, "Lord," to remember him. Notice the singular personal pronoun as used exclusively in the King James Version. The words *thee* and *thou* represent a form of speech unavailable in today's modern versions. Jesus deals with the repentant thief as an individual; separate from the unrepentant thief. Jesus saves each of His believers on their own expression of faith and believing that Jesus is the Christ the Son of the living God.

By repentance and faith, the one thief was saved, and the other was not. We are not all going to go to heaven as some believe! God says if you turn to Him in humility and with a contrite heart, asking Him for forgiveness of sins and desiring not to commit them anymore, that is repentance. God, who dwells in the high and holy place which is heaven, will see our repentance, our humility, and our faith in Him.

Isaiah 57:15 For thus saith the high and lofty One that inhabiteth eternity, whose name is Holy; I dwell in the high and holy place, with him also that is of a contrite and humble spirit, to revive the spirit of the humble, and to revive the heart of the contrite ones.

It is God's requirement to come to Him by faith. Repentance alone will not save a person. However, God requires a person to repent (turn from) our sinful thinking of saving ourselves and have faith (turn to) in Him for our salvation. This belief, which can only come through faith in an unseen God:

Ephesians 2:8 For by grace are ye saved through faith; and that not of yourselves: it is the gift of God:

Ephesians 2:9 Not of works, lest any man should boast.

Ephesians 2:10 For we are his workmanship, created in Christ Jesus unto good works, which God hath before ordained that we should walk in them.

Paradise mentioned here by Jesus was not on the cross. The cross is the opposite of paradise. Paradise is a spiritual place of future happiness with the presence of Jesus, a kind of spiritual Garden of Eden.

Revelation 2:7 He that hath an ear, let him hear what the Spirit saith unto the churches; To him that overcometh will I give to eat of the tree of life, which is in the midst of the paradise of God.

Where is paradise then? It must be where Jesus is. Jesus would go immediately after his death on the cross to the heart of the earth. Jesus alluded to this when He told the thief; today (this day of crucifixion) thou shall (future) be with me (future from this moment but before this day is over) in paradise. Paradise would be the mental picture used by Jesus Christ to describe what being with him would be like. Paradise later is described as the third heaven. Jesus already being there makes it paradise. Listen to the one who was caught up:

2Corinthians 12:2 I knew a man in Christ above fourteen years ago, (whether in the body, I cannot tell; or whether out of the body, I cannot tell: God knoweth;) such an one caught up to the third heaven.

2Corinthians 12:3 And I knew such a man, (whether in the body, or out of the body, I cannot tell: God knoweth;)

2Corinthians 12:4 How that he was caught up into paradise, and heard unspeakable words, which it is not lawful for a man to utter.

Being caught up to the third heaven and into paradise where the tree of life is can only mean that paradise is now in heaven. Because that is where Jesus is. Those who had the faith of Abraham before this moment on the cross went to a place called Abraham's bosom:

Romans 4:1 What shall we say then that Abraham our father, as pertaining to the flesh, hath found?

Romans 4:2 For if Abraham were justified by works, he hath whereof to glory; but not before God.

Romans 4:3 For what saith the scripture? Abraham believed God, and it was counted unto him for righteousness.

Abraham's bosom was adjacent to hell. This is where the souls of those who followed Abraham's faithfulness of believing God would go. However, the God Man, Jesus, was not there. David said:

Acts 2:25 For David speaketh concerning him, I foresaw the Lord always before my face, for he is on my right hand, that I should not be moved:

Acts 2:26 Therefore did my heart rejoice, and my tongue was glad; moreover also my flesh shall rest in hope:

Acts 2:27 Because thou wilt not leave my soul in hell, neither wilt thou suffer thine Holy One to see corruption.

David did not want to stay in Abraham's bosom separated from hell only by a great gulf. He asked God not to leave him in hell. Notice David said his flesh shall rest in hope; that is in hope of the first resurrection which has not taken place even as this book is being written (Even so, come, Lord Jesus!) Before Christ's sacrifice, believers could not go to heaven and be with God because their sin had not been paid for; the blood of Christ had not been applied. Jesus was still on the cross, pouring out His precious blood for the perfect sacrifice to meet the requirements of a Holy God, when talking to the thief.

Hebrews 9:20 Saying, This is the blood of the testament which God hath enjoined unto you.

Hebrews 9:21 Moreover he sprinkled with blood both the tabernacle, and all the vessels of the ministry.

Hebrews 9:22 And almost all things are by the law purged with blood; and without shedding of blood is no remission.

Hebrews 9:23 It was therefore necessary that the patterns of things in the heavens should be purified with these; but the heavenly things themselves with better sacrifices than these.

As Hebrews says, heaven was about to get a "better" sacrifice than just animal blood. But now, Jesus had to redeem those positioned in Abraham's bosom. Adam was there. Noah was there, with Abraham and Joshua and David and even Rahab the Harlot among many others. They were positioned in Abraham's bosom, because they believed like Abraham did.

Matthew 8:11 And I say unto you, That many shall come from the east and west, and shall sit down with Abraham, and Isaac, and Jacob, in the kingdom of heaven.

They were separated by a great gulf from a place called hell! The picture is drawn of the two places in this true story from Luke:

Luke 16:19 There was a certain rich man, which was clothed in purple and fine linen, and fared sumptuously every day:

Luke 16:20 And there was a certain beggar named Lazarus, which was where laid at his gate, full of sores,

Luke 16:21 And desiring to be fed with the crumbs which fell from the rich man's table: moreover the dogs came and licked his sores.

Luke 16:22 And it came to pass, that the beggar died, and was carried by the angels into Abraham's bosom: the rich man also died, and was buried;

Luke 16:23 And in hell he lift up his eyes, being in torments, and seeth Abraham afar off, and Lazarus in his bosom.

Luke 16:24 And he cried and said, Father Abraham, have mercy on me, and send Lazarus, that he may dip the tip of his finger in water, and cool my tongue; for I am tormented in this flame.

Luke 16:25 But Abraham said, Son, remember that thou in thy lifetime receivedst thy good things, and likewise Lazarus evil things: but now he is comforted, and thou art tormented.

Luke 16:26 And beside all this, between us and you there is a great gulf fixed: so that they which would pass from hence to you cannot; neither can they pass to us, that *would come* from thence.

A gulf is a deep ravine or a chasm; it can be a real abyss. This great gulf fixed between Abraham's bosom, a position of saved souls, and hell is the distance between saved and lost. In this spiritual setting, souls cannot pass from one side to another. Jesus would deliver the souls from Abraham's bosom for two reasons.

First, the believers of the Old Testament whose souls were gathered into Abraham's bosom would finally receive the gift of entering into the presence of God the Father in heaven for eternity. Prior to this moment sin was unpaid for and still separating man from God. Jesus would bring the captive believers home to heaven and complete the plan of eternal life that God had promised.

Ephesians 4:8 Wherefore he saith, When he ascended up on high, he led captivity captive, and gave gifts unto men.

Ephesians 4:9 (Now that he ascended, what is it but that he also descended first into the lower parts of the earth?

Ephesians 4:10 He that descended is the same also that ascended up far above all heavens, that he might fill all things.)

He came down to this earth, born to endure the suffering of the cross:

Hebrews 2:9 But we see Jesus, who was made a little lower than the angels for the suffering of death, crowned with glory and honour; that he by the grace of God should taste death for every man.

He is the same body, which is His resurrected body. He is the same part of the Godhead, the second part of the Trinity. And He is alive for evermore!

Secondly, all those who died and went to hell were able to see Abraham's bosom but were not a part of it. This was so because they did not believe God. God was revealed to them during their lives in many ways but primarily in their hearts.

Romans 1:18 For the wrath of God is revealed from heaven against all ungodliness and unrighteousness of men, who hold the truth in unrighteousness;

Romans 1:19 Because that which may be known of God is manifest in them; for God hath shewed it unto them.

Jesus went to those in hell to show them that they had as much a chance to believe God as did those who were in Abraham's bosom. Because hell is below and heaven is above, it appears that Jesus would have to be in two places at the same time. Is that possible? Here it is declared that Jesus is in heaven but He also came down from heaven:

John 3:13 And no man hath ascended up to heaven, but he that came down from heaven, even the Son of man which is in heaven.

Jesus proves to them that they are without excuse and will be spending eternity separated from God:

Isaiah 59:1 Behold, the LORD'S hand is not shortened, that it cannot save; neither his ear heavy, that it cannot hear:

Isaiah 59:2 But your iniquities have separated between you and your God, and your sins have hid his face from you, that he will not hear.

Hell will be a place of isolation and loneliness and despair. You will not want to go there! My friend, accept God's plan of salvation to know for sure that you will not spend eternity in hell!

John 3:16 For God so loved the world, that he gave his only begotten Son, that whosoever believeth in him should not perish, but have everlasting life.

2:00 p.m. on Wednesday, the Fourteenth of Nisan Passover, Jesus third statement

3.   Jesus makes His third statement from the cross:

John 19:25 Now there stood by the cross of Jesus his mother, and his mother's sister, Mary the *wife* of Cleophas, and Mary Magdalene.

John 19:26 When Jesus therefore saw his mother, and the disciple standing by, whom he loved, he saith unto his mother, Woman, behold thy son!

John 19:27 Then saith he to the disciple, Behold thy mother! And from that hour that disciple took her unto his own home.

Jesus in His pain and suffering honors His mother. But where was Joseph His earthly stepfather? Should not Joseph have been put in position to care for Mary? Perhaps Joseph was dead at this time. After all, there is no mention of Joseph after Jesus' twelfth year. Jesus tells John, the son of Zebedee, from this moment on to care for His earthly mother. For the past two hours, darkness had fallen across the land since the sixth hour (12:00 noon) until the ninth hour (3:00 p.m.).

Matthew:

Matthew 27:45 Now from the sixth hour there was darkness over all the land unto the ninth hour.

Mark:

Mark 15:33 And when the sixth hour was come, there was darkness over the whole land until the ninth hour.

Luke:

Luke 23:44 And it was about the sixth hour, and there was a darkness over all the earth until the ninth hour.

2:45 p.m. on Wednesday, the Fourteenth of Nisan Passover Jesus fourth statement

It is nearing 3:00 p.m., that is, the ninth hour as Matthew and Mark have stated. Jesus has been on the cross for almost three hours at this time. Matthew and Mark record the same statement that Jesus now makes.

4.   Jesus makes His fourth statement from the cross:

Matthew 27:46 And about the ninth hour Jesus cried with a loud voice, saying, Eli, Eli, lama sabachthani? that is to say, My God, my God, why hast thou forsaken me?

Mark 15:34 And at the ninth hour Jesus cried with a loud voice, saying, Eloi, Eloi, lama sabachthani? which is, being interpreted, My God, my God, why hast thou forsaken me?

Some onlookers knew scripture of Elijah's appearing to herald the coming king as Malachi says:

Malachi 4:5 Behold, I will send you Elijah the prophet before the coming of the great and dreadful day of the LORD:

Malachi 4:6 And he shall turn the heart of the fathers to the children, and the heart of the children to their fathers, lest I come and smite the earth with a curse.

These onlookers thought that Christ was now calling for Elijah, but instead Jesus was saying one of God's names in the Hebrew tongue as *Eloi*, speaking to God the Father, or as in Genesis 1:1 says, "In the beginning Elohim," which is plural.

Matthew 27:47 Some of them that stood there, when they heard that, said, This man calleth for Elias.

Mark 15:35 And some of them that stood by, when they heard it, said, Behold, he calleth Elias.

2:50 p.m. on Wednesday, the Fourteenth of Nisan Passover, Jesus fifth statement

5.   Jesus makes His fifth statement from the cross:

John 19:28 After this, Jesus knowing that all things were now accomplished, that the scripture might be fulfilled, saith, I thirst.

It is amazing that, with His body ripped and torn, Jesus shows that He is still coherent by wanting something for His thirst. Most men would have passed out by now from the pain.

Matthew 27:48 And straightway one of them ran, and took a spunge, and filled it with vinegar, and put it on a reed, and gave him to drink.

Matthew 27:49 The rest said, Let be, let us see whether Elias will come to save him.

Notice that the numbing content of gall is no longer in what is offered Him to drink, just plain vinegar.

Mark 15:36 And one ran and filled a spunge full of vinegar, and put it on a reed, and gave him to drink, saying, Let alone; let us see whether Elias will come to take him down.

John 19:29 Now there was set a vessel full of vinegar: and they filled a spunge with vinegar, and put it upon hyssop, and put it to his mouth.

2:59 p.m. on Wednesday, the Fourteenth of Nisan Passover, Jesus sixth statement

6. Jesus makes His sixth statement from the cross:

John 19:30 When Jesus therefore had received the vinegar, he said, It is finished: and he bowed his head, and gave up the ghost.

This statement stands alone. The awfulness of the cross will never have to happen again!

2:59:50 p.m. on Wednesday, the Fourteenth of Nisan Passover, Jesus seventh statement

7. Jesus makes His seventh and final statement from the cross:

Luke 23:46 And when Jesus had cried with a loud voice, he said, Father, into thy hands I commend my spirit: and having said thus, he gave up the ghost.

He must have said this with a loud voice for Matthew and Mark declares that He cried with a loud voice first and then said the final statements from the cross:

Matthew 27:50 Jesus, when he had cried again with a loud voice, yielded up the ghost.

Mark 15:37 And Jesus cried with a loud voice, and gave up the ghost.

The moment of death has come. Death means separation. He is now separated from His Father as He takes on the sin of the whole world. Matthew and Mark have already recorded this, but all four gospels are in agreement that His spirit was separated from His body at this moment. This is physical death, which all of mankind must face when the body dies and the soul and spirit are separated from the body.

Hebrews 9:27 And as it is appointed unto men once to die, but after this the judgment:

Now God has a plan for all of mankind. Jesus declared the plan earlier through John that all have to be born again:

John 3:3 Jesus answered and said unto him, Verily, verily, I say unto thee, Except a man be born again, he cannot see the kingdom of God.

If you are not born again a second death which is a spiritual death, occurs. Our spirit is eternally separated from God forever in a place He had to enlarge called hell and eventually called the lake of fire!

Isaiah 5:14 Therefore hell hath enlarged herself, and opened her mouth without measure: and their glory, and their multitude, and their pomp, and he that rejoiceth, shall descend into it.

Hell is made larger and larger and eventually is cast into the lake of fire as so many reject God's gift:

Revelation 20:13 And the sea gave up the dead which were in it; and death and hell delivered up the dead which were in them: and they were judged every man according to their works.

Revelation 20:14 And death and hell were cast into the lake of fire. This is the second death.

Revelation 20:15 And whosoever was not found written in the book of life was cast into the lake of fire.

Jesus told Nicodemus he had to be born twice! Physical birth (of water) and spiritual birth (of calling upon the name of the Lord, and accepting God's plan of salvation) must take place.

John 3:4 Nicodemus saith unto him, How can a man be born when he is old? can he enter the second time into his mother's womb, and be born?

John 3:5 Jesus answered, Verily, verily, I say unto thee, Except a man be born of water and of the Spirit, he cannot enter into the kingdom of God.

If you are born twice (physical and spiritual), you die once (physical), but if you are only born once (physically), you die twice (physically and spiritually).

John 3:6 That which is born of the flesh is flesh; and that which is born of the Spirit is spirit.

John 3:7 Marvel not that I said unto thee, Ye must be born again.

3:00 p.m. on Wednesday, the Fourteenth of Nisan Passover Jesus dies

Jesus dies (His body and spirit separate), and all eternity is marked with the strange things that happen at His death. Now, at the moment of Christ's death, is a third set of seven things, which take place.

1. The veil would be torn from top to bottom. The veil to the temple was thirty cubits tall, that is, about forty-five feet—that is over four stories. How could it be torn from the top to the bottom? The God of Heaven did it!

What a Finish! What a Start! The Month Jesus Met Man's Need

Fred A Kuypers

Matthew:

Matthew 27:51 And, behold, the veil of the temple was rent in twain from the top to the bottom; and the earth did quake, and the rocks rent;

Mark:

Mark 15:38 And the veil of the temple was rent in twain from the top to the bottom.

Luke:

Luke 23:45 And the sun was darkened, and the veil of the temple was rent in the midst.

What is this veil all about? Hebrews explains:

Hebrews 10:16 This is the covenant that I will make with them after those days, saith the Lord, I will put my laws into their hearts, and in their minds will I write them;

Hebrews 10:17 And their sins and iniquities will I remember no more.

Hebrews 10:18 Now where remission of these is, there is no more offering for sin.

Hebrews 10:19 Having therefore, brethren, boldness to enter into the holiest by the blood of Jesus,

Hebrews 10:20 By a new and living way, which he hath consecrated for us, through the veil, that is to say, his flesh;

Man could now, because of Jesus' perfect sacrifice, boldly approach God!

Hebrews 4:16 Let us therefore come boldly unto the throne of grace, that we may obtain mercy, and find grace to help in time of need.

2. As Luke has commented, the veil was torn while it was yet dark. The darkness is now lifted as it is the ninth hour.

3. Matthew gave an account of the earthquake that takes place at this time. This earthquake is so strong that the rocks broke into pieces. But what happens next is a sure sign to those who look for a sign.

4. The fourth sign is that graves opened, and many bodies of saints, who were already dead and buried, came back to life. These saints arose here, but they did not come out of the grave and go into Jerusalem until after His resurrection, where they appeared unto many.

Matthew 27:52 And the graves were opened; and many bodies of the saints which slept arose,

Many graves opened, but notice these did not come out of the graves until after Jesus Christ's resurrection:

Matthew 27:53 And came out of the graves after his resurrection, and went into the holy city, and appeared unto many.

The difference here is that those who were resurrected at this time died again and went back to the grave.

But, as it is written, Jesus is alive for evermore:

Revelation 1:18 I am he that liveth, and was dead; and, behold, I am alive for evermore, Amen; and have the keys of hell and of death.

5. The centurion saw the earthquake and feared greatly as Matthew and Mark state. They each gave a verbal testimony of his belief that Jesus truly was the Son of God. Luke is a little different:

Matthew's view of the centurion:

Matthew 27:54 Now when the centurion, and they that were with him, watching Jesus, saw the earthquake, and those things that were done, they feared greatly, saying, Truly this was the Son of God.

Mark's view of the centurion:

Mark 15:39 And when the centurion, which stood over against him, saw that he so cried out, and gave up the ghost, he said, Truly this man was the Son of God.

Luke's view of the centurion:

Luke 23:47 Now when the centurion saw what was done, he glorified God, saying, Certainly this was a righteous man.

John does not give an immediate view of the death of Christ. Perhaps he is off with the mother of Jesus because of Jesus' comment to him to take care of his mother. Also the women and others that were close to Jesus are seen in a distance and probably were kept back by the soldiers or perhaps they are returning home as Luke explains:

Luke 23:48 And all the people that came together to that sight, beholding the things which were done, smote their breasts, and returned.

6. The scene when the darkness was lifted is of Jesus being totally alone. Those who had been still standing by the dead, bloodless, crucified body of our Lord were afar off. His blood had been poured out for our sins:

Hebrews 9:11 But Christ being come an high priest of good things to come, by a greater and more perfect tabernacle, not made with hands, that is to say, not of this building;

Hebrews 9:12 Neither by the blood of goats and calves, but by his own blood he entered in once into the holy place, having obtained eternal redemption for us.

7. Mary the mother of Jesus is not mentioned:

Matthew names three women and does not name Mary the mother of Jesus.

What a Finish! What a Start! The Month Jesus Met Man's Need

Fred A Kuypers

Matthew 27:55 And many women were there beholding afar off, which followed Jesus from Galilee, ministering unto him:

Matthew 27:56 Among which was Mary Magdalene, and Mary the mother of James and Joses, and the mother of Zebedee's children.

Mark names three women and does not name Mary the mother of Jesus but says there are many other women.

Mark 15:40 There were also women looking on afar off: among whom was Mary Magdalene, and Mary the mother of James the less and of Joses, and Salome;

Mark 15:41 (Who also, when he was in Galilee, followed him, and ministered unto him;) and many other women which came up with him unto Jerusalem.

Luke does not name any women. He says only those that followed Him from Galilee stood there. The list of women is in Luke 8:2-3 and, thus, does not name Mary the mother of Jesus.

Luke 23:49 And all his acquaintance, and the women that followed him from Galilee, stood afar off, beholding these things.

John names no one at all.

It is important that Mary is not named here. Mary was the one chosen by God to bring Jesus into the world. But she would not take any of the redeeming virtue from His Son. In fact, Mary is mentioned only once more in scripture. She is listed separate from the other women, in prayer, in the upper room with the twelve as mentioned in Acts:

Acts 1:14 These all continued with one accord in prayer and supplication, with the women, and Mary the mother of Jesus, and with his brethren.

Mary should be the model figure for every young teenage girl to aspire to. But to lift Mary up to a point of worship is a grievous mistake. Every time in Scripture that a man bows down to worship anyone else but Jesus Christ, they are admonished and told not to do so.

3:30 p.m. on Wednesday, the Fourteenth of Nisan Passover

Here are two critical passages to understanding the day on which Jesus must have been crucified.

Mark 15:42 And now when the even was come, because it was the preparation, that is, the day before the sabbath,

John 19:31 The Jews therefore, because it was the preparation, that the bodies should not remain upon the cross on the sabbath day, (for that sabbath day was an high day,) besought Pilate that their legs might be broken, and that they might be taken away.

Fred A Kuypers

"For that Sabbath day was a high day." This was not a regular Saturday Sabbath that would begin on Friday night at 6:00 p.m. This was the Sabbath of the first day of unleavened bread. This day was a holy convocation when no servile work was to be performed, a high Sabbath. It is always the day after the Passover, and it is why the Passover day is called the day of preparation. On Nisan 14, called Passover, preparation needs to be made for the fifteenth of Nisan, which is the first day of unleavened bread, a high Sabbath. The seven days of unleavened bread begin, and then they end with another high Sabbath seven days later. Jesus was on the cross as the high Sabbath was approaching.

Now on a high Sabbath, the Jews can do no servile work. So they had to get the body down before 6:00 p.m. when the high Sabbath would begin. They had to get the body into the tomb. They had to dress the body, and they had to be home by 6:00 p.m. to begin the high Sabbath. Remember, the chief priests and scribes were all watching and would mark anyone who would travel any more than a Sabbath day's journey beginning at 6:00 p.m.

There was not much time for the women to go home and purchase, prepare, and come back to anoint the body. There was not enough time unless you were a high priest, like Nicodemus, who may have had some burial spices in his possession. The women did not have enough time to buy the spices to anoint the body. And now they could not buy the spices because the high Sabbath was upon them.

Jesus will hang on the cross for a period of time. The reason that time goes by is that the guards have to see that the body of Jesus is lifeless. Rigor mortis will set in. A sure sign of death as the body muscles stiffen. This happens before decomposition begins in the body. Jesus faced no decomposition at all. Psalms tells us: Psalm 16:10 For thou wilt not leave my soul in hell; neither wilt thou suffer thine Holy One to see corruption.

His flesh never saw corruption or decay. This is true as decomposition only begins to soften the tissue after rigor mortis. The New Testament declared no corruption also:

Acts 2:27 Because thou wilt not leave my soul in hell, neither wilt thou suffer thine Holy One to see corruption.

Corruption here is the turning of the body into decay. Christ's body had no decay. It did not matter how long He lay in the grave, there was no decay or decomposition of His body. The Bible is very clear on this subject. Just a few verses later in the Acts of the Apostles, it says that His soul is what went to hell, located in the heart of the earth.

Acts 2:31 He seeing this before spake of the resurrection of Christ, that his soul was not left in hell, neither his flesh did see corruption.

A description of what took place with Christ's body and why blood and water came out of Jesus when the soldiers drove a spear into his side is given here.

> Prior to his death, the sustained rapid heartbeat caused by hypovolemic shock also causes fluid to gather in the sacks around the heart (pericardial effusion) and the lungs (pleural effusion). This explains why, after Jesus died and a Roman soldier thrust a spear through Jesus' side(probably His right side, piercing both the lungs and the heart), blood and water came forth (John 19:34).[36]

The passage as explained by John which is the only account of the spear piercing the side of Jesus:

John 19:32 Then came the soldiers, and brake the legs of the first, and of the other which was crucified with him.

John 19:33 But when they came to Jesus, and saw that he was dead already, they brake not his legs:

John 19:34 But one of the soldiers with a spear pierced his side, and forthwith came there out blood and water.

John 19:35 And he that saw it bare record, and his record is true: and he knoweth that he saith true, that ye might believe.

The Jews should have been reminded of Old Testament scripture from Exodus 12:46 and Numbers 9:12 where not a bone of the Passover lamb was to be broken and from Psalm 34:20, also.

John 19:36 For these things were done, that the scripture should be fulfilled, A bone of him shall not be broken.

And the Jews definitely should have known a prophecy from Zechariah:

Zechariah 12:10 And I will pour upon the house of David, and upon the inhabitants of Jerusalem, the spirit of grace and of supplications: and they shall look upon me whom they have pierced, and they shall mourn for him, as one mourneth for his only son, and shall be in bitterness for him, as one that is in bitterness for his firstborn.

That the future King of kings, who comes to defend Jerusalem against the nations, shall be looked upon whom they pierced. And as Zechariah says, soon the house of Israel will mourn as they realize who this one is, the Lord Jesus Christ!

John 19:37 And again another scripture saith, They shall look on him whom they pierced.

Joseph of Arimathea who sees the proof of death asks Pilate for the body of Jesus:

John 19:38 And after this Joseph of Arimathaea, being a disciple of Jesus, but secretly for fear of the Jews, besought Pilate that he might take away the body of Jesus: and Pilate gave him leave. He came therefore, and took the body of Jesus.

---

[36] S. Michael Houdmann. *Questions about Jesus Christ.* WestBow press. 2013 P. 144

4:00 p.m. on Wednesday, the Fourteenth of Nisan
Passover

Joseph of Arimathea was a great man. Without him much scripture would not be fulfilled. This was a man who was seeking God. Business men should pattern their business careers after him. He was always looking out for others.

Matthew records:

Matthew 27:57 When the even was come, there came a rich man of Arimathaea, named Joseph, who also himself was Jesus' disciple:

Matthew 27:58 He went to Pilate, and begged the body of Jesus. Then Pilate commanded the body to be delivered.

Luke records:

Luke 23:50 And, behold, there was a man named Joseph, a counsellor; and he was a good man, and a just:

Luke 23:51 (The same had not consented to the counsel and deed of them;) he was of Arimathaea, a city of the Jews: who also himself waited for the kingdom of God.

Luke 23:52 This man went unto Pilate, and begged the body of Jesus.

During these last hours before the high Sabbath begins at 6:00 p.m. seven things must be accomplished with the body of Jesus:

4:30 p.m. on Wednesday, the Fourteenth of Nisan
Passover

1. The body of Jesus must be taken down off of the cross. This was accomplished by Joseph of Arimathaea. Mark gives the best account of what Joseph did behind the scenes with Pontus Pilate:

Mark 15:43 Joseph of Arimathaea, an honourable counsellor, which also waited for the kingdom of God, came, and went in boldly unto Pilate, and craved the body of Jesus.

Mark 15:44 And Pilate marvelled if he were already dead: and calling unto him the centurion, he asked him whether he had been any while dead.

Mark 15:45 And when he knew it of the centurion, he gave the body to Joseph.

4:45 p.m. on Wednesday, the Fourteenth of Nisan Passover

2. The body of Jesus would need to be anointed, also accomplished by Nicodemus.

John 19:39 And there came also Nicodemus, which at the first came to Jesus by night, and brought a mixture of myrrh and aloes, about an hundred pound weight.

5:00 p.m. on Wednesday, the Fourteenth of Nisan Passover

3. Jesus' body would need to be put into burial clothes. Notice the word *wound*. This literally means "to bind," "to tie," or "to wrap." This is the only time that the Greek word *deo*[37] is translated wound.

John 19:40 Then took they the body of Jesus, and wound it in linen clothes with the spices, as the manner of the Jews is to bury.

Also notice that the burial cloth of Jesus was put on as the manner of the Jews is to bury Him. The other time that this burial scene is familiar is when Lazarus was buried and was dead already for four days. As seen in chapter 6 of this book, Scripture gives a glimpse of proper Jewish custom and manner for burial. He was bound hand and foot. Bound is the exact same word in Greek as wound in the passage above. It is the Greek word *deo*. However, when the head of Lazarus was bound with a napkin as spoken of in chapter 6 at noon; it is a different Greek word, *perideo*,[38][39] meaning this time to "enwrap" or wrap around. This refutes a shroud that would cover Jesus from head to foot draped over His body front and back.

Matthew 27:59 And when Joseph had taken the body, he wrapped it in a clean linen cloth,

5:15 p.m. on Wednesday, the Fourteenth of Nisan Passover

4. The body of Jesus would have to be brought to the tomb. This could have presented a real problem. Most of the gravesites were on the southeast side of the temple in Kidron valley. That is where Zechariah is buried and others. The tombs are still marked even today. But Joseph of Arimathea was an honorable counselor. He had made preparation already for Jesus' body by buying linen and purchasing a gravesite nearby in a garden. Joseph of Arimathea had purchased the garden tomb for himself as Matthew says in verse 60. It was a

---

[37] Dr. James Strong, *Strongs Exhaustive Concordance of the Bible*. Dugan Publishers Inc. Gordonsville, TN. P. 1192
[38] Dr. James Strong, *Strongs Exhaustive Concordance of the Bible*. Dugan Publishers Inc. Gordonsville, TN. P. 139

new tomb where no one had ever been buried before. No doubt, others had been buried near Golgotha—wicked ones that had also been crucified.

Luke says all this was done on the day called the preparation. As previously discussed, this is another term for the Passover day, Nisan 14, which is the preparation for the high Sabbath, the first day of unleavened bread, Nisan 15.

Luke 23:53 And he took it down, and wrapped it in linen, and laid it in a sepulchre that was hewn in stone, wherein never man before was laid.

Luke 23:54a And that day was the preparation,

The Sabbath was about to begin. There could be no work of this burial done after 6:00 p.m. In fact, no one could do any servile work at all this high Sabbath, as John called it in John 19:31.

John 19:41 Now in the place where he was crucified there was a garden; and in the garden a new sepulchre, wherein was never man yet laid.

John 19:42 There laid they Jesus therefore because of the Jews' preparation day; for the sepulchre was nigh at hand.

That the scriptures might be fulfilled according to Isaiah:

Isaiah 53:9 And he made his grave with the wicked, and with the rich in his death; because he had done no violence, neither *was any* deceit in his mouth.

5:30 p.m. on Wednesday, the Fourteenth of Nisan
Passover

5.   The tomb would also have to be sealed.

Matthew 27:60 And laid it in his own new tomb, which he had hewn out in the rock: and he rolled a great stone to the door of the sepulchre, and departed.

5:40 p.m. on Wednesday, the Fourteenth of Nisan
Passover

6.   Also the women, who would be heading home because of the Sabbath, would take notice of the body of Jesus, and how it was laid in the tomb and what would be required when the time would come to return and anoint the body.

Matthew 27:61 And there was Mary Magdalene, and the other Mary, sitting over against the sepulchre.

Mark 15:47 And Mary Magdalene and Mary the mother of Joses beheld where he was laid.

Luke 23:55 And the women also, which came with him from Galilee, followed after, and beheld the sepulchre, and how his body was laid.

What a Finish! What a Start! The Month Jesus Met Man's Need

Fred A Kuypers

5:55 p.m. on Wednesday, the Fourteenth of Nisan Passover

7. All leave the body of Jesus and departed for home at this time as the high Sabbath began.

Chapter 15

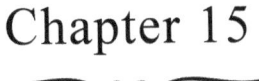

Nisan 15

Month of Nisan

1st day Yom Rishon Sunday	2nd day Yom Sheini Monday	3rd day Yom Shlishi Tuesday	4th day Yom R'vi'i Wednesday	5th day Yom Chamishi Thursday	6th day Yom Shishi Friday	Shabbat Yom Shabbat Saturday
			Nisan 15th 6:00pm Thursday begins	15th Nisan 16th 6:00am to 6:00pm Pesach, first day of unleavened bread, holy convocation, high Sabbath 1st day in tomb		

This chapter includes:

Matthew	Mark	Luke	John
	16:1–16:2	23:54–23:55	

What a Finish! What a Start! The Month Jesus Met Man's Need

Fred A Kuypers

At the Garden Tomb outside of Jerusalem

At the Sepulcher: it is the first day of unleavened bread, a holy convocation, when no servile work is done. It is a high Sabbath.

6:00 p.m. on Wednesday, the Fifteenth of Nisan

High Sabbath, First Day of unleavened bread

Beginning at 6:00 p.m., the Jews must follow the law and could do nothing on this high Sabbath. As far as travel is concerned, they could only do a Sabbath day's journey:

Acts 1:12 Then returned they unto Jerusalem from the mount called Olivet, which is from Jerusalem a sabbath day's journey.

As far as work is concerned:

Exodus 12:16 And in the first day there shall be an holy convocation, and in the seventh day there shall be an holy convocation to you; no manner of work shall be done in them, save that which every man must eat, that only may be done of you.

The scribes and the Pharisees continually looked for things being done on the Sabbath, activities that would break their laws of:

Healing:

Luke 6:7 And the scribes and Pharisees watched him, whether he would heal on the sabbath day; that they might find an accusation against him.

Mark 3:2 And they watched him, whether he would heal him on the sabbath day; that they might accuse him.

Gleaning:

Mark 2:23 And it came to pass, that he went through the corn fields on the sabbath day; and his disciples began, as they went, to pluck the ears of corn.

Mark 2:24 And the Pharisees said unto him, Behold, why do they on the sabbath day that which is not lawful?

Just making clay with spit:

John 9:14 And it was the sabbath day when Jesus made the clay, and opened his eyes.

This is the day following the day of preparation which is Passover. It is the high Sabbath of the first day of unleavened bread, and they could do no servile work at all. What can any Hebrew do on a Sabbath? *Nothing*! They would have to wait until this high Sabbath was over. The Scriptures declare they did no work.

The chief priests and Pharisees wanted to make the sepulcher secure. But if the Sabbath drew on, when could they have done so? Not Thursday, a high Sabbath, and not Saturday, the regular weekly Sabbath. It would have to be done the next day after the high Sabbath. This could only mean that it would be Friday, the second day of unleavened bread, that was a day when work could be performed.

The women wanted to do their work to anoint the body of Jesus. They wanted to prepare to anoint the body as soon as possible. And they had a problem. Perhaps they had no spices. If they had no spices, they could not buy the spices today because the markets were closed. It was a high Sabbath. No store was open. And even if they had purchased the spices earlier, they had to prepare them to anoint the body. This could not be done on this Sabbath day, either.

So they had to wait. They had to wait until the high Sabbath was past. Now, in those days, there would be no Walgreens open twenty-four hours or any of the convenience stores, which are available today. There is a good probability that Mary Magdalene and Mary and Salome had to wait until Friday morning to buy the spices when the stores were open. What scripture has written is that they waited until the Sabbath was over.

6:00 a.m. on Thursday, the Fifteenth of Nisan High Sabbath, First Day of unleavened Bread

Luke has an interesting observation at this point. He establishes the day of preparation. Then he speaks of the Sabbath and establishes that day as a day that would begin to come to light. The words *drew on* mean to "begin to grow light" or "begin to dawn."[39]

Luke 23:54 And that day was the preparation, and the sabbath drew on.

Luke establishes the time during this day following the day of the preparation. It would begin to dawn at daylight and then continue all day until 6:00 p.m. Thursday night. Luke also confirms what Matthew and Mark said that the woman had beheld

---

[39]   Dr. James Strong, Strongs Exhaustive Concordance of the Bible. Dugan Publishers Inc. Gordonsville, TN. P.283

the sepulcher earlier that night. This would be before the stone was rolled into place, but more importantly how the body was laid in the tomb:

Luke 23:55 And the women also, which came with him from Galilee, followed after, and beheld the sepulchre, and how his body was laid.

When did Mary Magdalene and Mary and Salome buy the spices? Perhaps when the high Sabbath had past and the day of no servile work was over or perhaps earlier this week. But prior to the crucifixion why would they need these spices? They had no need until the body was dead and in the tomb. It is only at this point that they had need of the spices to go and buy them. This is very important as another day of rest will soon have to take place on Saturday. What is perhaps hard to follow is that when the two Mary's see where Jesus was laid men have put a chapter break in Mark, however reading this should continue right on into the next chapter. And when chapter 16 begins in Mark, it says "when the Sabbath was passed."

Mark 16:1 And when the sabbath was past, Mary Magdalene, and Mary the mother of James, and Salome, had bought sweet spices, that they might come and anoint him.

The very next verse in Mark is extremely important. Which Sabbath was Mark referring to in verse one? Is it the high Sabbath of the first day of unleavened bread or is it the Saturday Sabbath? The next passage is specific in saying the first day of the week. It could have said the next day or the following day but it does not. It clearly moves to a future date, probably more than one day in the future, by not saying the next day but calling that day a specific day, "the first day of the week":

Mark 16:2 And very early in the morning the first day of the week, they came unto the sepulchre at the rising of the sun.

Mark's use of the term the first day of the week allows for more than one day to occur from the time of buying sweet spices to anoint the body.

12:00 noon on Thursday, the Fifteenth of Nisan
High Sabbath, First Day of unleavened Bread

Now to continue with the woman who had purchased the spices. It is still Thursday, the high Sabbath of the first day of unleavened bread. No market will be open to buy or sell. Even if they had purchased the spices at an earlier date, they could not prepare them until Friday and the regular weekly Sabbath will not begin until Friday night at 6 p.m.

3:00 p.m. on Thursday, the Fifteenth of Nisan High Sabbath, First Day of unleavened Bread

Remember that the women had noticed on Wednesday, Nisan 14, at the end of the day, how the body of Jesus was laid in the grave. First came the eyewitnesses of how the body was laid in the grave. Then the stone rolled to block the view or entry into the tomb. All this must have occurred right before 6:00p.m. on Wednesday. This statement is declared as the high Sabbath drew on. The next day, Friday, would be the only day work could be done. The women return home and did nothing this day, Thursday. Friday they would prepare the spices and rest again the Saturday Sabbath as Luke revealed earlier. Matthew will say that the chief priests wanted to make the grave more sure by sealing the stone. This also would take a lot of work. Not today! This will be discussed on Friday, a day of work.

The high Sabbath continues. Nothing can be done—no work and very little travel. This must have been very frustrating for all those who wanted to do what they could for their Master. But Jesus made it clear that the Sabbath should be used very differently:

Mark 2:27 And he said unto them, The sabbath was made for man, and not man for the sabbath: Mark 2:28 Therefore the Son of man is Lord also of the sabbath.

Chapter 16

Nisan 16

Month of Nisan

1st day Yom Rishon Sunday	2nd day Yom Sheini Monday	3rd day Yom Shlishi Tuesday	4th day Yom R'vi'i Wednesday	5th day Yom Chamishi Thursday	6th day Yom Shishi Friday	Shabbat Yom Shabbat Saturday
				Nisan 16th 6:00pm Friday begins	16th Nisan 17th 6:00am to 6:00pm 2nd day of unleavened bread This is the only day spices could be prepared, and religious leaders could set a watch. Second day in tomb	

This chapter includes:

Matthew	Mark	Luke	John
27:62–27:66	16:1	23:56	

What a Finish! What a Start! The Month Jesus Met Man's Need

Fred A Kuypers

Garden Tomb and in Jerusalem; Chief Priests meet with Pilate

Second Day of Unleavened Bread
The high Sabbath ends

6:00 pm on Thursday, the Sixteenth of Nisan

This day all manner of work and travel can be performed. Many things need to be done on this day as labor can now be performed. Not only do the women have some work to do since the high Sabbath has passed, but the chief priests and the Pharisees have some work to do also.

8:00 a.m. on Friday, the Sixteenth of Nisan
Second Day of Unleavened Bread
At Pilates Hall

The chief priests and Pharisees were concerned about Jesus. They thought that the followers of Jesus would come in the next few days and steal the body of Jesus to make it look like He had risen. Notice in the next verse the awkward way of stating the following day. Instead of Matthew just saying at this point, the next day after the day of preparation; Matthew inserts the words "that followed". This would allow for the next day to be the day that came after the day that followed the day of the preparation which as discussed earlier was Wednesday, the Passover.

Matthew 27:62 Now the next day, that followed the day of the preparation, the chief priests and Pharisees came together unto Pilate,

The chief priests and Pharisees would not come together to see Pilate on the high Sabbath. It would have to be on a non-Sabbatical day, the next day, Friday.

Matthew 27:63 Saying, Sir, we remember that that deceiver said, while he was yet alive, After three days I will rise again.

The chief priests and Pharisees could not make the sepulcher secure until after Thursday, the high Sabbath. Little did they know that the Scriptures they claimed to follow so closely all pointed to a Messiah being cut off but not for Himself:

Daniel 9:26 And after threescore and two weeks shall Messiah be cut off, but not for himself: and the people of the prince that shall come shall destroy the city and the sanctuary; and the end thereof shall be with a flood, and unto the end of the war desolations are determined.

The chief priests and Pharisees are bold with their demands to Pilate:

Matthew 27:64 Command therefore that the sepulchre be made sure until the third day, lest his disciples come by night, and steal him away, and say unto the people, He is risen from the dead: so the last error shall be worse than the first.

"The third day" as quoted here by Matthew literally means after three full days and three full nights. First of all they quoted Jesus by saying "after three days I will rise again" In verse 63. Second, it is Hebrew custom to say "the third day" and mean three full days and three full nights need to be accomplished as quoted in Esther: Esther 4:15 Then Esther bade them return Mordecai this answer,

Esther 4:16 Go, gather together all the Jews that are present in Shushan, and fast ye for me, and neither eat nor drink three days, night or day: I also and my maidens will fast likewise; and so will I go in unto the king, which is not according to the law: and if I perish, I perish.

Esther 4:17 So Mordecai went his way, and did according to all that Esther had commanded him.

Esther 5:1 uses the words "the third day" and means "three days, night and day"!

Esther 5:1 Now it came to pass on the third day, that Esther put on her royal apparel, and stood in the inner court of the king's house, over against the king's house: and the king sat upon his royal throne in the royal house, over against the gate of the house.

The religious leaders should have known the scriptures talking about this Son of God always ruling, and they should have put their trust in Him.

Psalm 2:6 Yet have I set my king upon my holy hill of Zion.

Psalm 2:7 I will declare the decree: the LORD hath said unto me, Thou art my Son; this day have I begotten thee.

Psalm 2:8 Ask of me, and I shall give thee the heathen for thine inheritance, and the uttermost parts of the earth for thy possession.

Psalm 2:9 Thou shalt break them with a rod of iron; thou shalt dash them in pieces like a potter's vessel.

Psalm 2:10 Be wise now therefore, O ye kings: be instructed, ye judges of the earth.

Psalm 2:11 Serve the LORD with fear, and rejoice with trembling.

Psalm 2:12 Kiss the Son, lest he be angry, and ye perish from the way, when his wrath is kindled but a little. Blessed are all they that put their trust in him.

The scribes should have known that this Jesus of the house and lineage of David would be righteous in protecting and loving them and their country and their land:

Zechariah 12:8 In that day shall the LORD defend the inhabitants of Jerusalem; and he that is feeble among them at that day shall be as David; and the house of David shall be as God, as the angel of the LORD before them.

Zechariah 12:9 And it shall come to pass in that day, that I will seek to destroy all the nations that come against Jerusalem.

What a Finish! What a Start! The Month Jesus Met Man's Need

Fred A Kuypers

Zechariah 12:10 And I will pour upon the house of David, and upon the inhabitants of Jerusalem, the spirit of grace and of supplications: and they shall look upon me whom they have pierced, and they shall mourn for him, as one mourneth for his only son, and shall be in bitterness for him, as one that is in bitterness for his firstborn.

So the chief priests and Pharisees consult with Pilate to secure the tomb, and Pilate drops this bombshell on them.

Matthew 27:65 Pilate said unto them, Ye have a watch: go your way, make it as sure as ye can.

Friday can be the only day when work can be done before the events that will transpire on Sunday, the first day of the week. The priests are told that they have to make it as sure as "ye can," speaking to all the religious leaders that were present. If this was a Sabbath day, the leaders would have objected to this work that needed to be done. Imagine how strange it must have looked to see the religious leaders securing the stone! On Resurrection Sunday Peter and Cleopas will comment on this.

My life's work was as a cement mason. I know that to secure a stone as heavy as one that perhaps weighs as much as a ton will take several men. Those who did this type of work would realize how hard the work would be. At the securing of the stone, it will take two or three men with trowels and other tools. But a lot more men would be needed to find the sand, the cement, and the water and then to mix it to secure the stone and make it as sure as they can.

9:00 a.m. on Friday, the Sixteenth of Nisan
Second Day of Unleavened Bread
A day to work

The Scriptures declare they did this exact work.

Matthew 27:66 So they went, and made the sepulchre sure, sealing the stone, and setting a watch.

This work was not done in a couple of minutes but was probably an all-day affair; and with some very tired priests at the end of the day. In order to make the sepulcher sure, they needed to work at this. The Pharisee's would have no part of this on a Sabbath day. To "seal the stone" would take a lot of work. Perhaps they dug it into the dirt to recess it so it would be hard to remove, or perhaps they mixed some type of mortar to seal up any gaps in the openings. Any way you look at this, it would be a lot of work. Finally they could set a watch. I do not know if they hired Roman guards or would consider this servile work or not, but soon it will be seen how the watch would perform over the next couple of days.

What they did not realize was they could never hold the King of kings and Lord of lords with a rock that was made by Jesus himself. He is the Creator of all! The religious leaders who should have known their Holy Scriptures missed the quote of who was promised to come as a lowly servant to all mankind:

Zechariah 9:9 Rejoice greatly, O daughter of Zion; shout, O daughter of Jerusalem: behold, thy King cometh unto thee: he is just, and having salvation; lowly, and riding upon an ass, and upon a colt the foal of an ass.

10:00 a.m. on Friday, the Sixteenth of Nisan
Second Day of Unleavened Bread
A day to work

The women, Mary Magdalene and Mary and Salome, can go purchase and prepare the spices. I do not know how much work this was, but it was work. They would not be able to do this tomorrow on the Saturday Sabbath, either. Scripture says that the women rested on the Sabbath before they had bought the spices.

Mark 16:1 And when the sabbath was past, Mary Magdalene, and Mary the mother of James, and Salome, had bought sweet spices, that they might come and anoint him.

They also needed to prepare all other things prior to the Saturday Sabbath, which will begin at 6:00 p.m. this night.

Luke 23:56 And they returned, and prepared spices and ointments; and rested the sabbath day according to the commandment.

12:00 noon on Friday, the Sixteenth of Nisan
Second Day of Unleavened Bread
A day to work

The women prepared all their spices before the Saturday Sabbath which began at 6:00 p.m. this night. A lot of work by the chief priests needed to be accomplished also. Tomorrow would be a day that nothing else could be done.

Today the light of the world is revealed in Jesus Christ. Have you trusted in the work of the Savior, the Lord Jesus Christ? He worked the work of salvation so that you would have to do no work. Only trust Him!

John 9:4 I must work the works of him that sent me, while it is day: the night cometh, when no man can work.

John 9:5 As long as I am in the world, I am the light of the world.

Chapter 17

Nisan 17

Month of Nisan

1st day Yom Rishon Sunday	2nd day Yom Sheini Monday	3rd day Yom Shlishi Tuesday	4th day Yom R'vi'i Wednesday	5th day Yom Chamishi Thursday	6th day Yom Shishi Friday	Shabbat Yom Shabbat Saturday
					Nisan 17th 6:00pm Saturday begins	17th Nisan 18th 6:00am to 6:00pm Third day of unleavened bread Sabbath day of rest. Jesus could have risen at any time after 6:00 p.m Third and final day in tomb

This chapter includes:

Matthew	Mark	Luke	John

What a Finish! What a Start! The Month Jesus Met Man's Need

Fred A Kuypers

Garden Tomb outside of Jerusalem, Third Night and Day a Saturday Sabbath

Third Day of Unleavened Bread Saturday Sabbath begins.

6:00 p.m. on Friday, the Seventeenth of Nisan

The regular Saturday Sabbath officially begins.

6:00 a.m. on Saturday, the Seventeenth of Nisan Third Day of Unleavened Bread Nothing is written in the scriptures about this day. This is the Saturday Sabbath.

The Bible contains the truth of God. It is God's letter of instruction, direction, and love to anyone who will accept it. In the Bible, it can be discerned God's plan for the redemption of a condemned race (John 3:18). In the Bible, one can draw facts that the tradition of men have distorted. One principle fact that has been followed for centuries is the crucifixion being on a Friday. However the Bible spells out the truth of a Wednesday crucifixion. Here is a list of seven facts that I believe proves Jesus died on a Wednesday:

1. The Witness of Jesus and His Own Testimony

He was very clear. It would have to be after three twenty-four-hour days. Jesus said no other sign of His resurrection would be given:

Matthew 12:39 But he answered and said unto them, An evil and adulterous generation seeketh after a sign; and there shall no sign be given to it, but the sign of the prophet Jonas:

Matthew 12:40 For as Jonas was three days and three nights in the whale's belly; so shall the Son of man be three days and three nights in the heart of the earth.

Three days and three nights require three twelve hour days and three twelve hour nights or Jesus was wrong when He said:

John 11:9 Jesus answered, Are there not twelve hours in the day? If any man walk in the day, he stumbleth not, because he seeth the light of this world.

Jonah would understand this exactly. Jesus said He would be in the heart of the earth for at least this length of time. The nay-sayers can one day in heaven ask Jonah if he was in the belly of the whale for just 36 hours or for seventy-two hours. Be careful asking Jonah; he may be insulted! A total of seventy-two hours minimum are required. He would be killed, and then after three days and three nights rise again!

Mark 8:31 And he began to teach them, that the Son of man must suffer many things, and be rejected of the elders, and of the chief priests, and scribes, and be killed, and after three days rise again.

This passage makes it clear that Jesus began to teach the disciples the only sign that He would give, that the Son of man must suffer many things from the religious leaders of His day, and be rejected of them, and He would then be killed and "after three days rise again." From just before 6:00PM on Wednesday to just after 6:00PM on Saturday is after 72 hours. The only scenario that can qualify for three days and three nights and after that He would rise again.

Working backward in time from the empty tomb discovered by Mary Magdalene, who was at the grave during darkness Sunday morning, will prove point one of a Wednesday crucifixion. The first day of the week (Resurrection Sunday) begins at 6:00 p.m. Saturday night. To be in the "heart of the earth," Jesus needs to be in the grave at least that long, seventy-two hours, and perhaps longer. Any time after three days and three nights, a full seventy-two hours, Jesus can appear as the risen Lord. The sign would be the empty grave. The exact hour of the resurrection is not known; however, the empty grave was discovered while it was still dark on Sunday morning, perhaps 4:30 to 5:30 a.m., before any light of the sunrise appeared.

John 20:1 says that the first day of the week, Mary Magdalene came early, while it was yet dark. This means before 6:00 a.m. or before any indication of sunrise, Mary Magdalene was at the tomb. She came unto the sepulcher and witnessed the stone had been rolled away from the grave and that the tomb was empty.

His resurrection would have to take place after 6:00 p.m. Saturday and prior to Mary Magdalene coming to the tomb at around 4:30 a.m. or so on the first day of the week, Sunday morning while it was dark. He could have risen at any time Sunday morning. This includes Saturday night after 6:00 p.m., which begins the first day of the week according to the Jews.

The timeframe to be in the heart of the earth leading up to a Sunday morning resurrection:

Twelve hours Wednesday 6:00 p.m. to Thursday 6:00 a.m. first night
Twelve hours Thursday 6:00 a.m. to 6:00 p.m. first day

Twelve hours Thursday 6:00 p.m. to Friday 6:00 a.m. second night
Twelve hours Friday 6:00 a.m. to 6:00 p.m. second day
Twelve hours Friday6:00 p.m. to Saturday 6:00 a.m. third night
Twelve hours Saturday 6:00 a.m. to 6:00 p.m. third day

This is a total of seventy-two hours or three days and three nights.
He would have to be buried before 6:00 p.m. on Wednesday to be in "the heart of the earth" three days and three nights after which He could rise again. The Bible verses quoted in this first proof are the words of Jesus.

2. The Witness of the Gospels

It has been said that Jesus would be resurrected "on the third day." However this is incorrect. Not all but most modern versions of the Bible have added the word "on" to this phrase. Nowhere in the King James Bible does it say "on the third day" speaking about Jesus. It just says "the third day." This type of sloppy handling of the Words of God has led to a much more sound belief in a Friday crucifixion. But without the word "on" in this phrase the two words third day can now be correctly understood. Greek Definitions follow:

"Third" is the Greek word "tritos" pronounced tree'-tos From G5140; third; neuter (as noun) a third part, or (as adverb) a (or the) third time, thirdly:—third (-ly). Meaning a third of something or needing three parts.[40]

"Day" is the Greek word "ishēmera" pronounced hay-mer'-ah Feminine (with G5610 implied) of a derivative of ἧμαι hēmai (to sit; akin to the base of G1476) meaning tame, that is, gentle; day, that is, (literally) the time space between dawn and dark, or the whole 24 hours (but several days were usually reckoned by the Jews as inclusive of the parts of both extremes);[41]

Meaning three parts of twenty-four hours.

Together they say three parts of the whole twenty-four hours. Jesus says in Matthew:
Matthew 16:21 From that time forth began Jesus to shew unto his disciples, how that he must go unto Jerusalem, and suffer many things of the elders and chief priests and scribes, and be killed, and be raised again the third day.

---

[40]   Dr. James Strong, *Strongs Exhaustive Concordance of the Bible*. Dugan Publishers Inc. Gordonsville, TN.
[41]   Dr. James Strong, *Strongs Exhaustive Concordance of the Bible*. Dugan Publishers Inc. Gordonsville, TN.

Jesus began to show His disciples that He would be raised again "the third day." Notice that He does not say "on" the third day but says three parts of twenty-four-hour days.

A review of the verses where the third day is mentioned:

Matthew 17:23 And they shall kill him, and the third day he shall be raised again. And they were exceeding sorry.

Matthew 20:19 And shall deliver him to the Gentiles to mock, and to scourge, and to crucify him: and the third day he shall rise again.

Matthew 27:64 Command therefore that the sepulchre be made sure until the third day, lest his disciples come by night, and steal him away, and say unto the people, He is risen from the dead: so the last error shall be worse than the first.

Mark 9:31 For he taught his disciples, and said unto them, The Son of man is delivered into the hands of men, and they shall kill him; and after that he is killed, he shall rise the third day.

Mark 10:34 And they shall mock him, and shall scourge him, and shall spit upon him, and shall kill him: and the third day he shall rise again.

Luke 9:22 Saying, The Son of man must suffer many things, and be rejected of the elders and chief priests and scribes, and be slain, and be raised the third day.

Luke 13:32 And he said unto them, Go ye, and tell that fox, Behold, I cast out devils, and I do cures to day and to morrow, and the third day I shall be perfected.

Luke 24:39 Behold my hands and my feet, that it is I myself: handle me, and see; for a spirit hath not flesh and bones, as ye see me have.

Luke 18:33 And they shall scourge him, and put him to death: and the third day he shall rise again.

Luke 24:7 Saying, The Son of man must be delivered into the hands of sinful men, and be crucified, and the third day rise again.

Luke 24:21 But we trusted that it had been he which should have redeemed Israel: and beside all this, to day is the third day since these things were done.

Luke 24:46 And said unto them, Thus it is written, and thus it behoved Christ to suffer, and to rise from the dead the third day:

In the book of Esther there is another indication of what "on the third day" means:

Esther 4:16 Go, gather together all the Jews that are present in Shushan, and fast ye for me, and neither eat nor drink three days, night or day: I also and my maidens will fast likewise; and so will I go in unto the king, which is not according to the law: and if I perish, I perish.

Esther 4:17 So Mordecai went his way, and did according to all that Esther had commanded him.

This is Esther's request for fasting. All the Jews were not to eat nor drink three days, night or day: Notice it is for both night and day these three days. This would be three twenty-four-hour periods, or seventy-two hours total. Esther would also fast, along with her maidens, before she goes into the king. Mordecai did all Esther had commanded him. Mordecai and all the Jews fasted and prayed for three twenty-four hour periods. Then in chapter 5, Esther dressed up and "on the third day," she went to the king.

What a Finish! What a Start! The Month Jesus Met Man's Need

Fred A Kuypers

Esther 5:1 Now it came to pass on the third day, that Esther put on her royal apparel, and stood in the inner court of the king's house, over against the king's house: and the king sat upon his royal throne in the royal house, over against the gate of the house.

If "on the third day" means any part of three days as people have been taught by church leaders for centuries, then all the Jews could not have fasted for three twenty-four-hour days as was originally stated in chapter 4. Here in chapter 5 of Esther, I contend that "on the third day" means after fasting for three full twenty- four-hour days and not three parts of any day.

3. The Witness of the Women with the Spices.

Jesus dies on a Wednesday (Passover). Nicodemus brings his spices to anoint the body of Jesus as declared by John in his Gospel. John 19:39 describes how Nicodemus arrived on the scene, who back in chapter 3 of the Gospel of John first came to Jesus by night to question Jesus about how to get to heaven. This Nicodemus brought a mixture of myrrh and aloes, about a hundred pounds in weight. This is a lot of myrrh and aloes. A lot of burial spices were applied to Jesus' body before it was laid in the tomb.

John 19:40 then says they took the body of Jesus, and wound it in linen clothes with the spices, as the manner of the Jews is for burial. This passage refutes the burial cloth known as the Shroud of Turin. That shroud would not have been a wrap. It would have covered Jesus from head to toe, draped, not wrapped as the scriptures say. The word *wound* appearing here is the Greek word *deh'o*, meaning to bind or to knit or to tie or to wind.[42] To dispel another false teaching of the Roman church, the Shroud of Turin shows no such winding and is a fake.

The body is laid in the tomb just before 6:00 p.m. on Wednesday. John 19:31 explains that the Jews would ask, because it was the preparation, that the Romans would break the legs of those on the cross. The preparation is always the day before a Sabbath, which in this case is a high Sabbath or the first day of unleavened bread. This of course means that the preparation day happens to be also the Passover day. Also it is noted that the bodies should not remain upon the cross on the Sabbath day, (for that Sabbath day was a high day,). At the end of the process of crucifixion, it was customary that their legs would be broken. However, Jesus' legs were not broken; a sword pierced His side instead. Joseph of Arimathea asked Pilate to have the body of Jesus and take it away.

---

[42]   Dr. James Strong, *Strongs Exhaustive Concordance of the Bible*. Dugan Publishers Inc. Gordonsville, TN. P 1192

From Wednesday at 6:00 p.m. to Thursday at 6:00 p.m. is a high Sabbath for the first day of unleavened bread. This Sabbath had to end, so the women could prepare other spices to anoint the body.

After 6: 00 p.m. on Thursday night, Friday began; a day when work could be done. On this Friday the women could buy and prepare the spices to anoint the body of Jesus.

Mark explains that when the Sabbath was past:

Mark 16:1 And when the sabbath was past, Mary Magdalene, and Mary the mother of James, and Salome, had bought sweet spices, that they might come and anoint him.

The women wait for the high Sabbath (Thursday, the first day of unleavened bread) to end so they can buy the spices. Some say that the women had bought the spices much earlier. But there was no need of these spices to be purchased earlier because no one knew of this upcoming death. "Had bought" here means "to hold" or *agorazō* and means to go to market, to purchase[43]; then they went home to prepare the spices. They rested again for the Saturday Sabbath. Simply this high Sabbath could not be the Saturday Sabbath because Luke says they still had to prepare the spices and then rest again for the Saturday Sabbath:

Luke 23:56 And they returned, and prepared spices and ointments; and rested the sabbath day according to the commandment.

Luke reveals the fact that the Sabbath would take place after the spices were prepared. First they bought the spices, then they returned and prepared the spices and ointments on Friday. Luke then says they rested the Sabbath day according to the commandment. Why would the women have to rest again? This is after the spices which they had bought were prepared!

After 6:00 p.m. Saturday, the Sabbath ends, and they can go at first light or daybreak or very early Sunday in the morning to anoint the body. Luke declares that the woman brought the spices on the first day of the week, very early in the morning.

Luke 24:1 Now upon the first day of the week, very early in the morning, they came unto the sepulchre, bringing the spices which they had prepared, and certain others with them.

However John states:

John 20:1 The first day of the week cometh Mary Magdalene early, when it was yet dark, unto the sepulchre, and seeth the stone taken away from the sepulchre.

---

[43]   Dr. James Strong, *Strongs Exhaustive Concordance of the Bible*. Dugan Publishers Inc. Gordonsville, TN. P 138

John says while it was yet dark, Mary Magdalene came to the sepulcher. There is no record of her bringing the spices at this time, but she was involved in purchasing the spices with Mary the mother of James and Salome on the only day that work of this nature could be performed—Friday, the sixth day of the week.

The order is:

1. Jesus dies and is anointed by Nicodemus with spices. Nicodemus, being a priest, would be prepared for such occasions. He is buried on Wednesday just before 6:00 p.m. before the high Sabbath of the first day of unleavened bread begins.

2. Thursday—the high Sabbath begins, and it is a day of no servile work (the first day of unleavened bread)

3. Friday—this is the day to buy and prepare spices. It is the only day work can be performed.

4. Saturday—this is the regular weekly Sabbath rest, and no work can be performed.

5. Early Sunday—Jesus rises some time before daybreak, and the empty tomb is discovered in the dark of the morning.

4. The Witness of the Pharisees

In Matthew, there is a statement: "the next day, that followed the day of the preparation," the chief priests and Pharisees came to Pilate. It is contended that "the next day" which is the day after "that followed the day of preparation written today would be:

"the next day that comes after the day that followed the day of preparation."

The words here are rather awkward. However it is definitely a different way of describing this time frame. If the day of preparation is the Passover, which was a Wednesday, the phrase should read:

"the next day after the day of the preparation."

Stating it this way would point to Thursday which is the first day of unleavened bread. The chief priests broke many laws by having the trial of Jesus illegally. These were not Sabbatical laws and they did this behind closed doors. But in front of the people they would not do anything that might be construed as breaking the laws of the Sabbath. Of course, the religious Pharisees would not be able to work on this day. But because the translators stated the time frame as they did:

Matthew 27:62 Now the next day, that followed the day of the preparation, the chief priests and Pharisees came together unto Pilate,

Three literal days can be surmised from this statement. If "the next day" is Friday, The term "that followed" can refer to the day that followed "the day of the preparation." The day that follows the day of the preparation is Thursday. That would make "the day of preparation" fall on a Wednesday, the day that followed the day of the preparation would be Thursday and the next day after that would be Friday.

Matthew 27:63 Saying, Sir, we remember that that deceiver said, while he was yet alive, After three days I will rise again.

The Pharisees are addressing Pilate, and they say, we remember that deceiver (Jesus) said, while He (Jesus) was yet alive, *after* three days I will rise again. Notice that the Pharisees knew the meaning of "the third day" meant *after* three full days. The Pharisees knew that Jesus would rise after three days. So they plotted how to stop Jesus from this resurrection. The Pharisees would break no commands in public as they proved with the Passover meal:

John 18:28 Then led they Jesus from Caiaphas unto the hall of judgment: and it was early; and they themselves went not into the judgment hall, lest they should be defiled; but that they might eat the passover.

The Pharisees could do no work Thursday but were able to come together to Pilate the following day, Friday. Pilate said:

Matthew 27:65 Pilate said unto them, Ye have a watch: go your way, make it as sure as ye can.

In order to make the sepulcher sure, they needed to work at this and that work would be where everyone could see. The Pharisees would never have had a part of this on a Sabbath day. They could not work at making the stone secure on Thursday (high Sabbath) or Saturday (regular Sabbath) to "seal the stone." This would take a lot of work and not behind closed doors. Perhaps they dug it into the dirt to recess it, so it would be harder to remove. Or, perhaps they mixed some type of mortar to seal up any gaps in the openings. Any way you look at this, it would be a lot of work; work that would take all day! Friday, which was not a Sabbath, would be the only day this work could be performed. And then they could set a watch.

Matthew 27:66 So they went, and made the sepulchre sure, sealing the stone, and setting a watch.

What a Finish! What a Start! The Month Jesus Met Man's Need

Fred A Kuypers

Notice the scripture says they went and made the sepulchre sure. Make no mistake it was the chief priests and Pharisees who did the work. The watch, of course, was just some paid soldiers, because the religious leaders would do no work on the following day, the Saturday Sabbath, just before Resurrection Sunday.

5. The Witness of the So-Called Early Church Fathers

To be perfectly clear the early church fathers should be the eight men who God used to write the New Testament. All other men designated by church tradition as "early church fathers" are mere men and not any smarter or better or more intelligent than the rest. However, turning to them for insight as to that era, or teaching of the scriptures, information can still be ascertained from their writings. Be sure to know that the scriptures themselves are the standard of our truth. The following was written around the late second/early third century. Though not inspired scripture, there is still much that can be gleaned from this:

> For when we had eaten the passover on the third day of the week at even (This would be Tuesday night), we went forth to the Mount of Olives; and in the night they seized our Lord Jesus. And the next day, which was the fourth of the week (This would be Wednesday morning), He remained in ward in the house of Caiaphas the high priest. And on the same day the chiefs of the people were assembled and took counsel against Him.[44]

In the third century, the bishop named Saint Victorinus of Pettau or of Poetovio (died AD 303 or 304) who was martyred by Diocletian wrote:

> Now is manifested the reason of the truth why the fourth day (This would be what today is called Wednesday) is called the Tetras, why we fast even to the ninth hour, or even to the evening, or why there should be a passing over even to the next day… The man Christ Jesus, the originator of these things whereof we have above spoken, was taken prisoner by wicked hands, by a quaternion of soldiers. Therefore on account of His captivity by a quaternion, on account of the majesty of His works,—that the seasons also, wholesome to humanity, joyful for the harvests, tranquil for the

---

[44]   R. Hugh Connolly. *Didascalia Apostolorum*. version Oxford: Clarendon Press, 1929. chapter 21, verse 14.

tempests, may roll on,– therefore we make the fourth day a station or a supernumerary fast.[45]

The fourth day in the above account would be modern-day Wednesday. The Hebrew language did not have names for the days of the week. Sunday was the first day; Monday was the second day; Tuesday the third day, and so on until Saturday the seventh day, which was the only day with a name, the Sabbath.

6. The Witness of the rising of Lazarus, proving that after three days Jesus still saw no decomposition.

In the Gospel of John, speaking of Lazarus, it says:

John 11:38 Jesus therefore again groaning in himself cometh to the grave. It was a cave, and a stone lay upon it.

John 11:39 Jesus said, Take ye away the stone. Martha, the sister of him that was dead, saith unto him, Lord, by this time he stinketh: for he hath been dead four days.

Jesus groaned when He came to the grave which was a cave with a stone on its opening. Jesus said to take away the stone and Martha, the sister of Lazarus, said to the Lord, "by this time he stinketh: for he hath been dead four days."

Jesus allowed Lazarus to be dead for longer than three days to prove that he was truly dead and that Jesus has the power to truly raise one from the dead. After rigor mortis has set in, the body becomes limp again; it moves quickly from this stage to decomposition. This is an unmistakable sign of death. Jesus lay in His grave for a minimum of three full days while He was in the heart of the earth. But the scriptures speak in Psalms that God will not allow His "Holy One," that is the Lord Jesus Christ, to see corruption:

Psalm 16:10 For thou wilt not leave my soul in hell; neither wilt thou suffer thine Holy One to see corruption.

The unmistakable sign of death is rigor mortis. Soon after rigor mortis has set in, which is the stiffening of the muscles in a dead corpse, decomposition begins. However the Holy One, Jesus Christ, did not see any of this corruption set in. Perhaps one reason that the women were going to the grave with the spices was to control the smell of decomposition. With three full days and three full nights in the heart of the earth, Jesus should have started to decompose, but there is no testimony of that. There is no sign that decomposition ever set in. To be dead for more than that period of three full days should have resulted in the stench of decomposition! But Jesus'

---

45   Victorinus. *On the Creation of the World*. Excerpted from Ante-Nicene Fathers, Volume 7. Edited by Alexander Roberts & James Donaldson. American Edition, 1886. Online Edition Copyright © 2004 by K. Knight.

What a Finish! What a Start! The Month Jesus Met Man's Need

Fred A Kuypers

body never began the process, and if His body did, Psalm 16:10 would be a lie and the Bible would not be infallible.

It is not known for sure the total amount of time Jesus' body laid in the grave. But to follow His words, He would need to be seventy-two hours minimum in the tomb, which would allow Him to go to the heart of the earth. This is where hell is located, according to Luke chapter sixteen. He dies on the cross at 3:00 p.m. on Wednesday. He is taken down, and before 6:00 p.m., He is laid in the tomb. From Wednesday night at 6:00 p.m. to Saturday night at 6:00 p.m. is a total of seventy-two hours. If He rose from the dead at 1:00 a.m. on Sunday, He would have been dead for eighty-two hours and actually in the tomb for seventy-nine hours, which would fulfill the requirement of after seventy-two hours. This is surmised for it is not known when He rose from the dead. It is only known that His tomb was found empty while it was still dark on the first day of the week.

Matthew describes that in the end of the Sabbath, as it began to dawn toward the first day of the week, Mary Magdalene and the other Mary came to see the tomb. John even says that it was still dark on that first day of the week.

7. The Witness of the Calendar as Being Honed by the Computer.

Most computer programs have now established the year of crucifixion at AD 30 or 31. That Passover, Nisan 14, starting at 6:00 p.m. Tuesday (or the third day on the Jewish weekly calendar), and that Nisan 15 (the first day of unleavened bread, a high Sabbath) began at 6:00 p.m. Wednesday has become the favored scenario, based on Pilate's reign and Herod's reign and Caiaphas as high priest and other worldly events to construct the time of Christ's crucifixion.[46] Also, that Passover can only occur on four days of the week has been established because Rosh Hashanah and Yom Kippur cannot occur on consecutive days with the Sabbath[47]. Therefore Nisan 15, or Pesach, cannot occur on Monday, Wednesday, or Friday, which begins at 6:00 p.m. the night before! Check out any year since the Julian calendar went into effect in 45 BC, that is, before the birth of Christ, and then the Gregorian calendar, which took effect in AD 1582. This means Nisan 14, Passover has never been on a Sunday, Tuesday, or Thursday.

---

[46] http://www.cgsf.org/dbeattie/calendar/?roman=30 viewed February 28, 2018

[47] Rabbi Nathan Bushwick. Understanding the Jewish Calendar. Moznaim Publishing Corporation. New York/Jerusalem. 1989. P84

Also the fact that the Jewish calendar which is based on the creation of God since the universe began has established what days of the week special Sabbaths can take place.

I considered this calendar proof to be a secular proof because it is not a part of scripture. But, now it has become more accurate and trustworthy with history and the information of the world coming together in the computer age.

Chapter 18

Nisan 18

Month of Nisan

1st day Yom Rishon Sunday	2nd day Yom Sheini Monday	3rd day Yom Shlishi Tuesday	4th day Yom R'vi'i Wednesday	5th day Yom Chamishi Thursday	6th day Yom Shishi Friday	Shabbat Yom Shabbat Saturday
.						Nisan 18th 6:00pm Sunday begins
18th Nisan 19th 6:00am to 6:00pm 4th day of unleavened bread Resurrection Sunday Grave already empty at daylight.						

This chapter includes:

Matthew	Mark	Luke	John
28:1–28:20	16:2–16:18	24:1–24:53	20:1–20:25

What a Finish! What a Start! The Month Jesus Met Man's Need

Fred A Kuypers

Resurrection Sunday, Fourth Day of Unleavened Bread

Saturday Sabbath Ends First Day of Week

6:00 p.m. on Saturday, the Eighteenth of Nisan

At this precise time begins the promise of Jesus Christ that after three days He will rise again. It is now after seventy-two hours since Christ was laid in the tomb He could have risen at any time, starting now.

8:00 p.m. on Saturday, the Eighteenth of Nisan First Day of Week, Fourth Day of Unleavened Bread

He could have arisen any time by now.

12:00 Midnight on Sunday, the Eighteenth of Nisan First Day of Week, Fourth Day of Unleavened Bread

He could have arisen any time by now.

3:00 a.m. on Sunday, the Eighteenth of Nisan First Day of Week, Fourth Day of Unleavened Bread

He could have arisen any time by now.

4:45 a.m. on Sunday, the Eighteenth of Nisan First Day of Week, Fourth Day of Unleavened Bread

The Gospel of John tells about Mary Magdalene. It is still dark outside. Morning daylight, dawn, has not happened, but it is close. Mary Magdalene makes her way to the gravesite. She notices quickly the stone removed from the grave.

John 20:1 The first day of the week cometh Mary Magdalene early, when it was yet dark, unto the sepulchre, and seeth the stone taken away from the sepulchre.

Mary Magdalene runs to Peter. She came to the grave in the dark at first; but now it is just beginning to be daylight. This is hard enough to do on a well-paved and lit street. So it must have been early dawn when you can just start to make out certain things, and Mary could see where she was running. She must be a very fast runner. She meets with Peter and John:

John 20:2 Then she runneth, and cometh to Simon Peter, and to the other disciple, whom Jesus loved, and saith unto them, They have taken away the Lord out of the sepulchre, and we know not where they have laid him.

5:00 a.m. on Sunday, the Eighteenth of Nisan First Day of Week, Fourth Day of Unleavened Bread

The gospel of Matthew in addition to John's gospel says another Mary also comes to the grave. Mary Magdalene, who came first as seen above, is joined by Mary, the mother of James, who now comes to the grave of Jesus. Perhaps they have the proper spices already prepared to anoint the body of Jesus prepared on Friday.

Matthew 28:1 In the end of the sabbath, as it began to dawn toward the first day of the week, came Mary Magdalene and the other Mary to see the sepulchre.

However, Jesus is gone. He is already resurrected. He did not have to have the stone rolled away to be resurrected. He could pass through solid objects with His glorified body. The stone was rolled away by the angel of the Lord so that the women could see the empty tomb.

Matthew 28:2 And, behold, there was a great earthquake: for the angel of the Lord descended from heaven, and came and rolled back the stone from the door, and sat upon it.

Matthew 28:3 His countenance was like lightning, and his raiment white as snow:

With Mary Magdalene and Mary the mother of James came certain others.

Luke 24:1 Now upon the first day of the week, very early in the morning, they came unto the sepulchre, bringing the spices which they had prepared, and certain others with them.

One of the certain others was Joanna from Luke 24:10. Another may have been Salome. Salome was with them when they went to purchase the spices on Friday, according to Mark 16:1. All of these women did not have to come together. But they had the same thing on their mind. They wanted to care for and anoint the body of Jesus that they expected to see in the tomb. These other women come to the grave very early in the morning. They were a little behind Mary Magdalene who has seen the miracle of the stone rolled away:

Mark 16:2 And very early in the morning the first day of the week, they came unto the sepulchre at the rising of the sun.

The women ask an obvious question that all of us would ask in the flesh. They are unaware of the miracle:

Mark 16:3 And they said among themselves, Who shall roll us away the stone from the door of the sepulchre?

Mark records that the result of the first miracle is viewed. This does not contradict what Matthew said. Mark just does not describe in detail the miracle. He simply states they (the other women) "saw that the stone was rolled away":

Mark 16:4 And when they looked, they saw that the stone was rolled away: for it was very great.

Luke confirms this:

Luke 24:2 And they found the stone rolled away from the sepulchre.

The guards or keepers in front of the tomb see this happen also. They are scared and shake from fear. They are described as dead men.

Matthew 28:4 And for fear of him the keepers did shake, and became as dead men.

Luke says they entered the tomb:

Luke 24:3 And they entered in, and found not the body of the Lord Jesus.

The women who entered the grave, see another man, who was an angel clothed in white, sitting on the right side in a white garment:

Mark 16:5 And entering into the sepulchre, they saw a young man sitting on the right side, clothed in a long white garment; and they were affrighted.

Luke, who has not mentioned any of the men in white, or angels, now mentions that there are two of them.

Luke 24:4 And it came to pass, as they were much perplexed thereabout, behold, two men stood by them in shining garments:

These are angels, and both angels have something to say. The angel that rolled away the stone that Matthew recorded said this:

Matthew:

Matthew 28:5 And the angel answered and said unto the women, Fear not ye: for I know that ye seek Jesus, which was crucified.

Matthew 28:6 He is not here: for he is risen, as he said. Come, see the place where the Lord lay.

Mark:

Mark 16:6 And he saith unto them, Be not affrighted: Ye seek Jesus of Nazareth, which was crucified: he is risen; he is not here: behold the place where they laid him.

Mark adds:

Mark 16:7 But go your way, tell his disciples and Peter that he goeth before you into Galilee: there shall ye see him, as he said unto you.

The two angels together, in their white and shining garments, say this:

Luke 24:5 And as they were afraid, and bowed down their faces to the earth, they said unto them, Why seek ye the living among the dead?

Luke 24:6 He is not here, but is risen: remember how he spake unto you when he was yet in Galilee,

Luke 24:7 Saying, The Son of man must be delivered into the hands of sinful men, and be crucified, and the third day rise again.

It would bring back to memory what Jesus had said earlier:

John 2:21 But he spake of the temple of his body.

John 2:22 When therefore he was risen from the dead, his disciples remembered that he had said this unto them; and they believed the scripture, and the word which Jesus had said.

And the women remembered these words of Jesus:

Luke 24:8 And they remembered his words,

The women are told by one of the angels to run and tell the disciples that He is risen!

Matthew 28:7 And go quickly, and tell his disciples that he is risen from the dead; and, behold, he goeth before you into Galilee; there shall ye see him: lo, I have told you.

Matthew and Mark say that they went out quickly. Their emotions were high. Trembling, in joy, fear, and amazement, they wanted to tell the disciples.

Matthew:

Matthew 28:8 And they departed quickly from the sepulchre with fear and great joy; and did run to bring his disciples word.

Mark:

Mark 16:8 And they went out quickly, and fled from the sepulchre; for they trembled and were amazed: neither said they any thing to any man; for they were afraid.

5:30 a.m. on Sunday, the Eighteenth of Nisan First Day of Week, Fourth Day of Unleavened Bread

The order of appearance is given in Scripture. Notice in Mark that the first event is that Jesus was risen already:

Mark 16:9 Now when Jesus was risen early the first day of the week, he appeared first to Mary Magdalene, out of whom he had cast seven devils.

What a Finish! What a Start! The Month Jesus Met Man's Need

Fred A Kuypers

Mark 16:10 And she went and told them that had been with him, as they mourned and wept.

Mary Magdalene runs to Peter. She came to the grave in the dark at first; but now it is just beginning to be daylight. This is hard enough to do on a well-paved and lit street. So it must have been early dawn when you can just start to make out certain things, and Mary could see where she was running. She must be a very fast runner. She meets with Peter and John:

John 20:2 Then she runneth, and cometh to Simon Peter, and to the other disciple, whom Jesus loved, and saith unto them, They have taken away the Lord out of the sepulchre, and we know not where they have laid him.

Luke adds that the other women had also left the tomb. There was a lot of skepticism from the apostles themselves:

Luke 24:9 And returned from the sepulchre, and told all these things unto the eleven, and to all the rest.

Luke 24:10 It was Mary Magdalene, and Joanna, and Mary the mother of James, and other women that were with them, which told these things unto the apostles.

None of the disciples believed that Jesus could have been taken.

Luke 24:11 And their words seemed to them as idle tales, and they believed them not.

Peter and John take action and run to the grave:

Luke 24:12 Then arose Peter, and ran unto the sepulchre; and stooping down, he beheld the linen clothes laid by themselves, and departed, wondering in himself at that which was come to pass.

John explains also that Peter and John run as fast as they can to the grave.

John 20:3 Peter therefore went forth, and that other disciple, and came to the sepulchre.

John usually called himself in his own gospel by the name "other disciple" or "one who Jesus loveth."

John 20:4 So they ran both together: and the other disciple did outrun Peter, and came first to the sepulchre.

John looks in the grave, and then Peter arrives:

John 20:5 And he stooping down, and looking in, saw the linen clothes lying; yet went he not in.

John 20:6 Then cometh Simon Peter following him, and went into the sepulchre, and seeth the linen clothes lie,

They see the linens from the burial of Jesus folded in a certain way:

John 20:7 And the napkin, that was about his head, not lying with the linen clothes, but wrapped together in a place by itself.

Many believe that the folding of these burial clothes represent the fact that Jesus will return. By faith, it is believed that He is returning again just as He said in John 14:3, and no sign is needed from Christ for this.

What the burial clothes prove is that Jesus was not overlaid with a shroud but with at least two pieces of cloth, one wrapped about His head and not lying with the other linen clothes but separate. It is Peter who first sees this, and then John enters the tomb. It is evident that a shroud did not cover Jesus from head to foot, but as the scriptures declare, His body was wrapped with two separate and distinct pieces of cloth. This refutes the worship as many today do of the Shroud of Turin and proves it to be a fake.

John 20:8 Then went in also that other disciple, which came first to the sepulchre, and he saw, and believed.

He is risen! He is risen! But it still has not sunk into them. The Holy Spirit has to do a great work to take away unbelief and convince man that God's plan is for real:

John 20:9 For as yet they knew not the scripture, that he must rise again from the dead.

Peter and John leave the grave and head back to the other disciples.-

John 20:10 Then the disciples went away again unto their own home.

6:00 a.m. on Sunday, the Eighteenth of Nisan First Day of Week, Fourth Day of Unleavened Bread

Once Peter and John leave, Jesus makes His first appearance to Mary Magdalene. Mary is heartbroken and is weeping as neither Peter nor John have shed any light on what has happened. Mary thinks Jesus was kidnapped.

John 20:11 But Mary stood without at the sepulchre weeping: and as she wept, she stooped down, and looked into the sepulchre,

John 20:12 And seeth two angels in white sitting, the one at the head, and the other at the feet, where the body of Jesus had lain.

John 20:13 And they say unto her, Woman, why weepest thou? She saith unto them, Because they have taken away my Lord, and I know not where they have laid him.

It is now more than seventy-two hours since the death of our Lord. He has been in the heart of the earth and preparing to gather those held captive in Abraham's bosom which is now paradise because Jesus is there with His precious gift of His blood sacrifice.

Ephesians 4:8 Wherefore he saith, When he ascended up on high, he led captivity captive, and gave gifts unto men.

Ephesians 4:9 (Now that he ascended, what is it but that he also descended first into the lower parts of the earth?

Ephesians 4:10 He that descended is the same also that ascended up far above all heavens, that he might fill all things.)

Mary is not sure of what Jesus looks like now in His glorified body. She hears the angels say, "Why weepest thou?" and turns to see Jesus:

John 20:14 And when she had thus said, she turned herself back, and saw Jesus standing, and knew not that it was Jesus.

Mary hears Jesus say, "Woman, why weepest thou?" and still does not recognize Jesus. She thinks He is the gardener. She even thinks that the gardener has removed the body of Jesus.

John 20:15 Jesus saith unto her, Woman, why weepest thou? whom seekest thou? She, supposing him to be the gardener, saith unto him, Sir, if thou have borne him hence, tell me where thou hast laid him, and I will take him away.

Then Jesus says her name and she immediately recognizes Him at this point.

John 20:16 Jesus saith unto her, Mary. She turned herself, and saith unto him, Rabboni; which is to say, Master.

John 20:17 Jesus saith unto her, Touch me not; for I am not yet ascended to my Father: but go to my brethren, and say unto them, I ascend unto my Father, and your Father; and to my God, and your God.

This is a very interesting statement that Jesus made. He tells Mary not to touch Him. Jesus is in His glorified body. Also, it is now after three twelve hour days and three twelve hour nights. So the one and only sign as explained in verse 40 of Matthew chapter 12 is about Jesus being in the heart of the earth for three twenty-four hour days has been fulfilled.

Matthew 12:38 Then certain of the scribes and of the Pharisees answered, saying, Master, we would see a sign from thee.

Matthew 12:39 But he answered and said unto them, An evil and adulterous generation seeketh after a sign; and there shall no sign be given to it, but the sign of the prophet Jonas:

Matthew 12:40 For as Jonas was three days and three nights in the whale's belly; so shall the Son of man be three days and three nights in the heart of the earth.

Jesus died, and for three days and three nights, He was in the heart of the earth. What He did in the tomb is not exactly spelled out in scripture. But surely He used this time to prove to all in hell and in heaven and on earth that He truly was God's plan for a perfect sacrifice. Jesus proved that the law could not make anyone perfect!

Hebrews 10:1 For the law having a shadow of good things to come, and not the very image of the things, can never with those sacrifices which they offered year by year continually make the comers thereunto perfect.

Showing that once purged of sins, man should have not sinned again, but that did not happen.

Hebrews 10:2 For then would they not have ceased to be offered? because that the worshippers once purged should have had no more conscience of sins.

Hebrews 10:3 But in those sacrifices there is a remembrance again made of sins every year.

God established the requirement for sin and the blood of animals would not meet that requirement.

Fred A Kuypers

Hebrews 10:4 For it is not possible that the blood of bulls and of goats should take away sins.

And it was determined by the Godhead of God the Father, God the Son, and God the Holy Spirit, that Jesus would be delivered to be crucified and become the perfect sacrifice.

Acts 2:22 Ye men of Israel, hear these words; Jesus of Nazareth, a man approved of God among you by miracles and wonders and signs, which God did by him in the midst of you, as ye yourselves also know:

Acts 2:23 Him, being delivered by the determinate counsel and foreknowledge of God, ye have taken, and by wicked hands have crucified and slain:

Acts 2:24 Whom God hath raised up, having loosed the pains of death: because it was not possible that he should be holden of it.

His was the body prepared for the perfect sacrifice.

Hebrews 10:5 Wherefore when he cometh into the world, he saith, Sacrifice and offering thou wouldest not, but a body hast thou prepared me:

God never intended for the sacrifice of animals to be the final offering;

Hebrews 10:6 In burnt offerings and sacrifices for sin thou hast had no pleasure.

Hebrews 10:7 Then said I, Lo, I come (in the volume of the book it is written of me,) to do thy will, O God.

Hebrews 10:8 Above when he said, Sacrifice and offering and burnt offerings and offering for sin thou wouldest not, neither hadst pleasure therein; which are offered by the law;

Hebrews 10:9 Then said he, Lo, I come to do thy will, O God. He taketh away the first, that he may establish the second.

Hebrews 10:10 By the which will we are sanctified through the offering of the body of Jesus Christ once for all.

Hebrews 10:11 And every priest standeth daily ministering and offering oftentimes the same sacrifices, which can never take away sins:

Hebrews 10:12 But this man, after he had offered one sacrifice for sins for ever, sat down on the right hand of God;

Hebrews 10:13 From henceforth expecting till his enemies be made his footstool.

Hebrews 10:14 For by one offering he hath perfected for ever them that are sanctified.

Mary tells the disciples that she has seen the Lord:

John 20:18 Mary Magdalene came and told the disciples that she had seen the Lord, and that he had spoken these things unto her.

But the disciples did not believe her:

Mark 16:11 And they, when they had heard that he was alive, and had been seen of her, believed not.

What a Finish! What a Start! The Month Jesus Met Man's Need

Fred A Kuypers

6:30 a.m. on Sunday, the Eighteenth of Nisan First
Day of Week, Fourth Day of Unleavened Bread

As the women went along to get back to where the disciples were, Jesus appears to the rest of the woman.

Matthew 28:9 And as they went to tell his disciples, behold, Jesus met them, saying, All hail. And they came and held him by the feet, and worshipped him.

This must be after He ascended up to heaven with the precious blood sacrifice. They are allowed to touch Him, and they held Him by the feet. This also shows that the mercy seat could be in heaven, waiting for the blood sacrifice of Jesus, at this time just as Revelation 11:19 declares:

Revelation 11:19 And the temple of God was opened in heaven, and there was seen in his temple the ark of his testament: and there were lightnings, and voices, and thunderings, and an earthquake, and great hail.

Jesus tells the women He wants to meet the disciples in Galilee, a four-day journey from Jerusalem.

Matthew 28:10 Then said Jesus unto them, Be not afraid: go tell my brethren that they go into Galilee, and there shall they see me.

8:00 a.m. on Sunday, the Eighteenth of Nisan First
Day of Week, Fourth Day of Unleavened Bread

The Roman soldiers or guards, who may have been assigned to guard the tomb of Jesus, decide to tell the chief priests what has just happened:

Matthew 28:11 Now when they were going, behold, some of the watch came into the city, and shewed unto the chief priests all the things that were done.

9:00 a.m. on Sunday, the Eighteenth of Nisan First
Day of Week, Fourth Day of Unleavened Bread

It takes about an hour to call a counsel together. The chief priests call a counsel and figure out a scheme:

Matthew 28:12 And when they were assembled with the elders, and had taken counsel, they gave large money unto the soldiers,

Matthew 28:13 Saying, Say ye, His disciples came by night, and stole him away while we slept.

Matthew 28:14 And if this come to the governor's ears, we will persuade him, and secure you.

The chief priests were so afraid of Jesus that they figured out a bribe for the Roman soldiers who may have been assigned to guard the tomb of Jesus:

Matthew 28:15 So they took the money, and did as they were taught: and this saying is commonly reported among the Jews until this day.

10:00 a.m. on Sunday, the Eighteenth of Nisan First Day of Week, Fourth Day of Unleavened Bread

The disciples have received word that Peter and John have seen the empty tomb. The women with Mary Magdalene have actually seen Jesus. The disciples return, and apparently Peter, because he is mentioned in Luke 24:34 as having seen the Lord, and another disciple named Cleopas head to Emmaus. Emmaus is a town about seven or eight miles from Jerusalem.

Luke 24:13 And, behold, two of them went that same day to a village called Emmaus, which was from Jerusalem about threescore furlongs.

Luke 24:14 And they talked together of all these things which had happened.

12:00 noon on Sunday, the Eighteenth of Nisan First Day of Week, Fourth Day of Unleavened Bread

The two disciples are discussing the events of the past few days. They are trying to figure out exactly what has happened this morning. Jesus approaches them:

Luke 24:15 And it came to pass, that, while they communed together and reasoned, Jesus himself drew near, and went with them.

Luke 24:16 But their eyes were holden that they should not know him.

Once again the disciples do not recognize Him. Earlier, Mary Magdalene did not recognize Jesus, either. Their eyes, being "holden" means they were restrained by God from recognizing Jesus. They are inquisitive in this discussion but are also sad as Jesus says, thinking perhaps that the body of Jesus has been taken, when suddenly Jesus appears to them and they knew Him not. Jesus, still unrecognized, speaks to them:

Luke 24:17 And he said unto them, What manner of communications are these that ye have one to another, as ye walk, and are sad?

One of the two, Cleopas speaks:

Luke 24:18 And the one of them, whose name was Cleopas, answering said unto him, Art thou only a stranger in Jerusalem, and hast not known the things which are come to pass there in these days?

Jesus shows His sense of humor and His caring and concern for His disciples by wanting them to spell out what was really on their hearts. This is always good witnessing to answer a question with a question.

Luke 24:19 And he said unto them, What things? And they said unto him, Concerning Jesus of Nazareth, which was a prophet mighty in deed and word before God and all the people:

Luke 24:20 And how the chief priests and our rulers delivered him to be condemned to death, and have crucified him.

These two disciples give what was really on their hearts, that concerning Jesus of Nazareth who truly was the Redeemer. Many strange things have been going on with the chief priests and rulers. They have been doing manual labor on Friday and this was extremely strange to them. Friday the chief priests and rulers worked all day to seal the stone that the crucified body was laid in. Crucifixion was not that unknown to these two.

After all two other thieves were crucified with Jesus. What was strange were the chief priests acting in a way that was not part of their custom. These strange events along with the crucifixion and death of Jesus led to the statement saying three days ago that is this past Friday all these strange things were done.

Luke 24:21 But we trusted that it had been he which should have redeemed Israel: and beside all this, to day is the third day since these things were done.

To day as it appears in the verse above is a unique Greek word for Day. It means currently or at present.[48] *To day* can describe the current events of this day, and how crazy people have acted for the last three days going back to Friday when the chief priests worked hard and literally sealed the stone covering the tomb of Jesus. Sunday also represents that three twelve hour days and three twelve hour nights have passed since the crucifixion was done. Remember that "the third day" will refer to three parts of twenty-four hours as stated in the last chapter; point two of the seven points proving a Wednesday crucifixion.

Witnessing will produce results when you let someone talk and say what they know or do not know. It is a good thing to let a lost person speak enough to condemn himself and realize that they need Jesus to save them. The two of them start to expound:

Luke 24:22 Yea, and certain women also of our company made us astonished, which were early at the sepulchre;

Luke 24:23 And when they found not his body, they came, saying, that they had also seen a vision of angels, which said that he was alive.

The two disciples confirm that John and Peter did not see Jesus at the tomb.

---

48   Dr. James Strong, Strongs Exhaustive Concordance of the Bible. Dugan Publishers Inc. Gordonsville, TN. P.243

Luke 24:24 And certain of them which were with us went to the sepulchre, and found it even so as the women had said: but him they saw not.

The word for *fool* used here is a unique use of the Greek word *anoētos* (an-o'-ay-tos); and means unintelligent; by implication sensual:—fool (-ish), unwise.[49] It is not fool or foolish as Jesus used in other situations meaning stupid, or mindless, or simpleton.

Luke 24:25 Then he said unto them, O fools, and slow of heart to believe all that the prophets have spoken:

Jesus was with them for three years, explaining to them continually that He was the Messiah and that He came to die. Left to our own strength, no one will ever turn to Jesus Christ and understand the scriptures. The Holy Spirit is needed to open our eyes from being "holden." We are not to be unwise (fools) but rather to ask for the Spirit of truth. Jesus goes through the entire Old Testament concerning Him:

Luke 24:26 Ought not Christ to have suffered these things, and to enter into his glory?

Luke 24:27 And beginning at Moses and all the prophets, he expounded unto them in all the scriptures the things concerning himself.

Luke 24:28 And they drew nigh unto the village, whither they went: and he made as though he would have gone further.

Mark confirms that this walk in the country took place:

Mark 16:12 After that he appeared in another form unto two of them, as they walked, and went into the country.

3:00 p.m. on Sunday, the Eighteenth of Nisan First Day of Week, Fourth Day of Unleavened Bread

Jesus was strongly compelled to stay with the two as they sat to eat:

Luke 24:29 But they constrained him, saying, Abide with us: for it is toward evening, and the day is far spent. And he went in to tarry with them.

Luke 24:30 And it came to pass, as he sat at meat with them, he took bread, and blessed it, and brake, and gave to them.

Jesus must have prayed or in some way said the things that made Him recognizable, perhaps repeating what took place at the Passover meal. Their eyes are opened, and suddenly Jesus vanishes:

Luke 24:31 And their eyes were opened, and they knew him; and he vanished out of their sight.

---

49   Dr. James Strong, Strongs Exhaustive Concordance of the Bible. Dugan Publishers Inc. Gordonsville, TN. P. 361

4:00 p.m. on Sunday, the Eighteenth of Nisan First Day of Week, Fourth Day of Unleavened Bread

Mark describes how they left Emmaus and went back to the disciples.

Mark 16:13 And they went and told it unto the residue: neither believed they them.

Emmaus is about seven or eight miles from Jerusalem, sixty furlongs. You can run that in an hour if you are trained. In these days all were trained to go on foot faster if needed.

Luke 24:32 And they said one to another, Did not our heart burn within us, while he talked with us by the way, and while he opened to us the scriptures?

Luke 24:33 And they rose up the same hour, and returned to Jerusalem, and found the eleven gathered together, and them that were with them,

5:00 p.m. on Sunday, the Eighteenth of Nisan First Day of Week, Fourth Day of Unleavened Bread

Now it says that the Lord appeared to Simon. He must be the other disciple on the road to Emmaus. The disciples are being told what happened to Simon and Cleopas in Emmaus:

Luke 24:34 Saying, The Lord is risen indeed, and hath appeared to Simon.

Luke 24:35 And they told what things were done in the way, and how he was known of them in breaking of bread.

Suddenly, the Lord Jesus appears to all the disciples who are still gathered:

Luke 24:36 And as they thus spake, Jesus himself stood in the midst of them, and saith unto them, Peace be unto you.

Luke 24:37 But they were terrified and affrighted, and supposed that they had seen a spirit.

Luke 24:38 And he said unto them, Why are ye troubled? and why do thoughts arise in your hearts?

The identifying marks on the body of Jesus that all are to look for, are those that were from the cross. The price that was paid on the cross is the reason why Jesus came to this world.

Luke 24:39 Behold my hands and my feet, that it is I myself: handle me, and see; for a spirit hath not flesh and bones, as ye see me have.

Luke 24:40 And when he had thus spoken, he shewed them his hands and his feet.

The disciples are stunned and are still unbelieving.

Luke 24:41 And while they yet believed not for joy, and wondered, he said unto them, Have ye here any meat?

Jesus shows that when a Christian is in their glorified body, they will be able to eat and enjoy food:

Luke 24:42 And they gave him a piece of a broiled fish, and of an honeycomb.

Luke 24:43 And he took it, and did eat before them.

This is what a believer can expect his glorified body to be like. Whatever the Lord did after His resurrection so will we in our glorified bodies:

1 John 3:2 Beloved, now are we the sons of God, and it doth not yet appear what we shall be: but we know that, when he shall appear, we shall be like him; for we shall see him as he is.

Mark also gives an account of what takes place this evening:

Mark 16:14 Afterward he appeared unto the eleven as they sat at meat, and upbraided them with their unbelief and hardness of heart, because they believed not them which had seen him after he was risen.

Mark reveals what the sign of Jesus' return should accomplish in all who believe. To go and tell everyone the Gospel or "Good News" that Jesus Christ is risen!

Mark 16:15 And he said unto them, Go ye into all the world, and preach the gospel to every creature.

Mark 16:16 He that believeth and is baptized shall be saved; but he that believeth not shall be damned.

Notice above that "believing not" is what will damn a person to hell. Here Jesus explains what it takes to be saved. Believing in the death, burial, and resurrection of Christ, that is, the Gospel will save a man. That is what we are to preach. Baptism is added here only to explain to us what the appropriate outward display of showing that inwardly one believes in Christ. A great analogy of this is someone saying "Get on the bus and take a seat". What is the important event here? Not missing the bus! If you miss the bus "sitting" or "baptism' means nothing.

Mark 16:17 And these signs shall follow them that believe; In my name shall they cast out devils; they shall speak with new tongues;

Mark 16:18 They shall take up serpents; and if they drink any deadly thing, it shall not hurt them; they shall lay hands on the sick, and they shall recover.

Some special miracles are described above. They are to be signs to all that the apostles had the authority to deliver the Gospel to the entire world. Second Corinthians describes what the apostles had.

2Corinthians 12:12 Truly the signs of an apostle were wrought among you in all patience, in signs, and wonders, and mighty deeds.

John also writes of a sign as Jesus appears even after the doors are shut:

John 20:19 Then the same day at evening, being the first day of the week, when the doors were shut where the disciples were assembled for fear of the Jews, came Jesus and stood in the midst, and saith unto them, Peace be unto you.

John 20:20 And when he had so said, he shewed unto them his hands and his side. Then were the disciples glad, when they saw the Lord.

John here gives an interesting statement. Jesus gives a command to go to the whole world and preach the Gospel.

John 20:21 Then said Jesus to them again, Peace be unto you: as my Father hath sent me, even so send I you.

But John writes something strange. Jesus makes a sound by blowing. It is the sound of wind as He blows on the disciples. Could this be a sign of what was to come on the day of Pentecost when the Holy Ghost was given with a mighty rushing wind?

John 20:22 And when he had said this, he breathed on them, and saith unto them, Receive ye the Holy Ghost:

The sound of wind was one sign of the gift of the Holy Ghost:

Acts 2:2 And suddenly there came a sound from heaven as of a rushing mighty wind, and it filled all the house where they were sitting.

Jesus speaks of the importance of telling others of this Gospel message. If you do not tell others the Gospel of Jesus Christ, their sins cannot be dealt with. They will not be remitted. If you give someone the Gospel, you have the power to remit their sins by telling them the Gospel as Jesus has just explained to them.

John 20:23 Whose soever sins ye remit, they are remitted unto them; and whose soever sins ye retain, they are retained.

Luke gives his account of the Gospel—Jesus truly was the Messiah as the prophets had predicted.

Luke 24:44 And he said unto them, These are the words which I spake unto you, while I was yet with you, that all things must be fulfilled, which were written in the law of Moses, and in the prophets, and in the psalms, concerning me.

Luke 24:45 Then opened he their understanding, that they might understand the scriptures,

Luke 24:46 And said unto them, Thus it is written, and thus it behoved Christ to suffer, and to rise from the dead the third day:

Luke makes it clear that it is the preaching of Jesus Christ that will remit sins. First as always, repentance is needed. Repentance means to turn from sin, and then one turns to Christ in faith. Many say repentance is a work, and works cannot save you. However, if repentance is a work that you turn from your sin or false belief, then faith is also a work as you turn to Christ. Neither repentance nor faith are works of the flesh as both are a frame of mind.

Luke 24:47 And that repentance and remission of sins should be preached in his name among all nations, beginning at Jerusalem.

Luke 24:48 And ye are witnesses of these things.

Notice repentance must be preached. Luke says power from on high, known as the Holy Ghost, is promised:

Luke 24:49 And, behold, I send the promise of my Father upon you: but tarry ye in the city of Jerusalem, until ye be endued with power from on high.

5:30 p.m. on Sunday, the Eighteenth of Nisan First Day of Week, Fourth Day of Unleavened Bread

The disciples go for a short walk to Bethany as the day ends.

Luke 24:50 And he led them out as far as to Bethany, and he lifted up his hands, and blessed them.

Luke finishes his gospel with the account of the ascension of Jesus Christ

Luke 24:51 And it came to pass, while he blessed them, he was parted from them, and carried up into heaven.

Luke 24:52 And they worshipped him, and returned to Jerusalem with great joy:

Luke 24:53 And were continually in the temple, praising and blessing God. Amen.

Which took place forty days later according to Luke's account in the book of Acts of the Apostles:

Acts 1:3 To whom also he shewed himself alive after his passion by many infallible proofs, being seen of them forty days, and speaking of the things pertaining to the kingdom of God:

This had to be a great moment. The disciples had all heard that Jesus had risen from the dead, but imagine the skepticism. Did He really rise from the dead? Or was He taken away with some evil plot? But the moment the disciples saw Jesus, there was no doubt in their minds. But what about Thomas who was not there?

John 20:24 But Thomas, one of the twelve, called Didymus, was not with them when Jesus came.

John 20:25 The other disciples therefore said unto him, We have seen the Lord. But he said unto them, Except I shall see in his hands the print of the nails, and put my finger into the print of the nails, and thrust my hand into his side, I will not believe.

Today there are still many "doubting Thomas" individuals. Jesus told the one who was sick of the palsy that his sins would be forgiven. Can someone today remit the sins of an unbeliever? Only by giving them what Jesus said to give them. "Go ye into all the world, and preach the gospel to every creature." That is our command. It is the power of the Gospel that will remit the sins of the world! Are you following Christ's command? This is the fruit that God is looking for. Is this what you are all about? This is what the book of James is all about! This is what the Bible is all about! This is what the Great Commission is all about!

Chapter 19

Nisan 19

Month of Nisan

1st day Yom Rishon Sunday	2nd day Yom Sheini Monday	3rd day Yom Shlishi Tuesday	4th day Yom R'vi'i Wednesday	5th day Yom Chamishi Thursday	6th day Yom Shishi Friday	Shabbat Yom Shabbat Saturday
Nisan 19th 6:00pm Monday begins	19th Nisan 20th 6:00am to 6:00pm Fifth day of unleavened bread Travel begins to Galilee					

This chapter includes:

Matthew	Mark	Luke	John
28:16			

What a Finish! What a Start! The Month Jesus Met Man's Need

Fred A Kuypers

From Jerusalem to Galilee; the First Kilometers

Monday, Fifth Day of Unleavened Bread

6:00 p.m. on Sunday, the Nineteenth of Nisan Fifth Day of Unleavened Bread

The disciples take their meal and rest now as a journey ordered by the Master is about to take place,

6:00 a.m. on Monday, the Nineteenth of Nisan Fifth Day of Unleavened Bread

The disciples decide to go to Galilee. Jesus tells them where to go, and He will meet them in a mountain.

Matthew 28:16 Then the eleven disciples went away into Galilee, into a mountain where Jesus had appointed them.

This is a long journey and would take about three or four days. The journey from Jerusalem to Capernaum in Galilee is about 190 kilometers. A marathon is 42.195 kilometers. A marathon is a long hard day journey by foot, especially over hills and rocky terrain. If there is any problem, this distance could not be accomplished. During this week, there are only four days they can travel this far. If they can average forty-five kilometers a day, they can make it in four days. Yesterday, Jesus was seen for the first time after the Resurrection. On this day, they can travel as much as they like; it is not a Sabbath. On Tuesday, they can also travel, but at 6:00 p.m. on Tuesday, the last high Sabbath to end the days of Unleavened Bread will take place. No one can travel on Wednesday. On Thursday, they can travel, and on Friday they can also travel; however, Friday night and into Saturday marks the regular weekly Sabbath, another day of rest.

Perhaps along the route to the Sea of Galilee, the apostles are talking about the amazing events that occurred during the time that the Master was with them. They begin to discuss the prophecies of the Old Testament, which they had read in the past and perhaps discussed if these prophecies were fulfilled by Jesus. They knew Micah said that the Messiah was to be born in Bethlehem.

Micah 5:2 But thou, Bethlehem Ephratah, though thou be little among the thousands of Judah, yet out of thee shall he come forth unto me that is to be ruler in Israel; whose goings forth have been from of old, from everlasting.

The apostles knew the books of the Old Testament. Since no scripture or new writings had been added since the time of Malachi, over four hundred years earlier, the discussion could go for several days. There is a prophecy in Malachi about Elias and when He would return.

Malachi 4:4 Remember ye the law of Moses my servant, which I commanded unto him in Horeb for all Israel, with the statutes and judgments.

Malachi 4:5 Behold, I will send you Elijah the prophet before the coming of the great and dreadful day of the LORD:

Malachi 4:6 And he shall turn the heart of the fathers to the children, and the heart of the children to their fathers, lest I come and smite the earth with a curse.

All of their life, the disciples have been following the customs of their Jewish heritage. They have sat to dine at many Passover meals and have seen an empty plate set for Elijah as the verse above describes. They knew that John the Baptist had come in the spirit and power of Elijah as Luke would attest to in his Gospel:

Luke 1:15 For he shall be great in the sight of the Lord, and shall drink neither wine nor strong drink; and he shall be filled with the Holy Ghost, even from his mother's womb.

Luke 1:16 And many of the children of Israel shall he turn to the Lord their God.

Luke 1:17 And he shall go before him in the spirit and power of Elias, to turn the hearts of the fathers to the children, and the disobedient to the wisdom of the just; to make ready a people prepared for the Lord.

This surely may have been one of the topics as they walked and continued north to Galilee on this first day after the resurrection. It says the eleven went on this four-day walk to Galilee since Judas Iscariot, one of the twelve, had killed himself.

12:00 noon on Monday, the Nineteenth of Nisan Fifth Day of Unleavened Bread

Bread

Skeptics continue to say that the two passages about the death of Judas are proof that the Bible cannot be infallible. It states two different ways of Judas dying. But if the scriptures are studied as written, without changing any of the words, this is what is said:

Matthew 27:3 Then Judas, which had betrayed him, when he saw that he was condemned, repented himself, and brought again the thirty pieces of silver to the chief priests and elders,

Matthew 27:4 Saying, I have sinned in that I have betrayed the innocent blood. And they said, What is that to us? see thou to that.

Matthew 27:5 And he cast down the pieces of silver in the temple, and departed, and went and hanged himself.

Matthew here says that Judas went and hanged himself. How is this accomplished? The only way is to put a noose around one's neck and either jump down from a tree, or kick out a chair or animal, or jump over a cliff. Luke explains in the book of the Acts of the Apostles that the method used by Judas to hang himself was one of jumping headlong. As Judas jumped, obviously something happened with the rope around his neck and either he slammed against the rocky cliff and busted his belly open or the rope broke and he fell to the ground with his body bursting open as witnessed below:

Acts 1:16 Men and brethren, this scripture must needs have been fulfilled, which the Holy Ghost by the mouth of David spake before concerning Judas, which was guide to them that took Jesus.

Acts 1:17 For he was numbered with us, and had obtained part of this ministry.

Acts 1:18 Now this man purchased a field with the reward of iniquity; and falling headlong, he burst asunder in the midst, and all his bowels gushed out.

Acts 1:19 And it was known unto all the dwellers at Jerusalem; insomuch as that field is called in their proper tongue, Aceldama, that is to say, The field of blood.

Acts 1:20 For it is written in the book of Psalms, Let his habitation be desolate, and let no man dwell therein: and his bishoprick let another take.

Judas hanged himself but died because his bowels gushed out. The eleven must have been discussing this and, knowing the Psalm that Luke quotes from, are beginning to wonder if they should replace Judas so that another would take his bishopric. Later in Acts, it is understood that the eleven cast lots, and the lot fell on Mattathias as Luke records:

Acts 1:26 And they gave forth their lots; and the lot fell upon Matthias; and he was numbered with the eleven apostles.

5:00 p.m. on Monday, the Nineteenth of Nisan
Fifth Day of Unleavened Bread

The eleven have reached a point in this day's journey, and it is time to prepare for the evening meal and then to rest through the night. This takes place perhaps about forty-five kilometers north of Jerusalem as they travel up to Galilee. This is rugged country, and the night's rest is needed for the continuation of this trip on the twentieth of Nisan.

Chapter 20

Nisan 20

Month of Nisan

1st day Yom Rishon Sunday	2nd day Yom Sheini Monday	3rd day Yom Shlishi Tuesday	4th day Yom R'vi'i Wednesday	5th day Yom Chamishi Thursday	6th day Yom Shishi Friday	Shabbat Yom Shabbat Saturday
	Nisan 20th 6:00pm Tuesday begins	20th Nisan 21st 6:00am to 6:00pm 6th day of unleavened bread Travel to Galilee second day.				

This chapter includes:

Matthew	Mark	Luke	John

From Jerusalem to Galilee; the Second leg of Forty Kilometers

Tuesday, the Sixth Day of Unleavened Bread

6:00 p.m. on Monday, the Twentieth of Nisan
Sixth Day of Unleavened Bread

After perhaps forty to forty-five kilometers, or twenty-eight miles, of walking on Monday, it is time for a night of rest.

6:00 a.m. on Tuesday, the Twentieth of Nisan Sixth Day of Unleavened Bread

It is a long journey, and this day would be a full day of walking, perhaps as much as forty-five to fifty kilometers. There are many things to talk about as the apostles walk north to Galilee. There is still some doubt as to whether the Savior was raised or not. In just a short period of time, doubting Thomas will face the Lord and realize He has truly come back. Peter will learn not to give up and go back to being a fisherman. But most of the eleven have seen the Savior back in Jerusalem. The apostles are still comparing their experience to what was revealed in the Tanakh (Torah, Nevi'im, and Kethuvim, or the entire Old Testament) sometimes simply called the Torah[50] (the Law or the books of Moses). The Torah was the scroll of the first five books of the Bible commonly called the Pentateuch, or the Law or the books of Moses. The Tanakh would be all of the books that were part of what every Jew would strive to learn and would include the Torah, the Nevi'im (or what we call the prophets), and the Kethuvim (or what is called today the writings). Here is a breakdown of what books in the Old Testament belong to what category:

Torah

1. Genesis
2. Exodus
3. Leviticus

---

[50]   http://www.jewfaq.org/torah.htm

4. Numbers

5. Deuteronomy

Nevi'im

1. Joshua

2. Judges

3. I and II Samuel

4. I and II Kings

5. Isaiah

6. Jeremiah

7. Ezekiel

8. The twelve Minor Prophets are treated as one book

Kathuvim

1. Psalms

2. Proverbs

3. Job

4. Song of Solomon

5. Ruth

6. Lamentations

7. Ecclesiastes

8. Esther

9. Daniel

10. Ezra and Nehemiah (treated as one book)

11. I and II Chronicles

This totals the thirty-nine books of our Old Testament that agrees with the Jewish faith. Some Bibles have added six books to the Old Testament, but the apostles would not look at them as inspired. The discussion would go all morning as they walked northward. The apostles would rehearse their knowledge of these books and also what the Lord Jesus had spoken to them. Remember that at this time, though they had seen the Lord in His glorified body, they had not yet received the gift of the Holy

Ghost who would guide them into all truth as Jesus had promised at the last supper in chapter 14:

John 16:13 Howbeit when he, the Spirit of truth, is come, he will guide you into all truth: for he shall not speak of himself; but whatsoever he shall hear, that shall he speak: and he will shew you things to come.

The Holy Ghost would not be given to the apostles until Acts 2, when the day of Pentecost would occur, fifty days after the resurrection of Jesus. This would take place in the Jews third month, the month of Sivan.

12:00 noon on Tuesday, the Twentieth of Nisan
Sixth Day of Unleavened Bread

It is time for a lunch break and perhaps the disciples are between Mount Ebal and Mount Gerizim in Shechem. After two days journey they would be close to this vicinity.

2:00 p.m. on Tuesday, the Twentieth of Nisan
Sixth Day of Unleavened Bread

The apostles could be spending the night in Samaria. At this time, they could have been discussing some things that they did not understand earlier. This was recorded by the apostle John that they would know certain things after seeing Jesus glorified. Perhaps it was at this time that the apostles discussed the triumphal entry of Jesus Christ into Jerusalem. As John stated, the disciples did not understand this:

John 12:16 These things understood not his disciples at the first: but when Jesus was glorified, then remembered they that these things were written of him, and that they had done these things unto him.

Since the apostles did not have any of the books of the New Testament, they had to remember what was written in the Old Testament. The time spent walking from Jerusalem to Galilee was an excellent time to review some of the passages. Now that Jesus was seen in His glorified body, the apostles are bringing to remembrance what took place when Jesus presented Himself as the King on the tenth of Nisan. It was a fulfillment of the prophecy from Zechariah:

Zechariah 9:9 Rejoice greatly, O daughter of Zion; shout, O daughter of Jerusalem: behold, thy King cometh unto thee: he is just, and having salvation; lowly, and riding upon an ass, and upon a colt the foal of an ass.

5:00 p.m. on Tuesday, the Twentieth of Nisan
Sixth Day of Unleavened Bread

The apostles could be spending this night in Samaria. They would be about half way to Galilee where Jesus said He would meet them. They needed to find a place to stop and rest as in one hour; it would be another high Sabbath, the last day of unleavened bread, a day of holy convocation in which no one could do any servile work. The high Sabbath day approaching will be a reminder to rest and Christ will bring to mind as He promised that all need to rest in the finished work done at the cross. The apostles start to understand that Christ paid it all and nothing can be done to earn eternal life. It is a free gift from God and can only be obtained by faith in this finished work of Christ.

They had some very good scriptures at this point even though no part of the New Testament had been written. They could turn to passages from Isaiah:

Isaiah 12:2 Behold, God is my salvation; I will trust, and not be afraid: for the LORD JEHOVAH is my strength and my song; he also is become my salvation.

And again Isaiah would write:

Isaiah 26:4 Trust ye in the LORD for ever: for in the LORD JEHOVAH is everlasting strength:

Today the complete Word of God is available to all. How about You? Have you trusted in Christ for your salvation? Are you resting in the completed work of Jesus Christ by His death, burial, and resurrection? If not, why not right now. Simply believe that Jesus Christ, through the finished work on the cross, paid for your sin debt. And follow the scripture that those who call on the name of the Lord will be saved. It is the same New Testament and Old.

Psalms 116:13 I will take the cup of salvation, and call upon the name of the LORD.

Isaiah 45:3 And I will give thee the treasures of darkness, and hidden riches of secret places, that thou mayest know that I, the LORD, which call thee by thy name, am the God of Israel.

Joel 2:32 And it shall come to pass, that whosoever shall call on the name of the LORD shall be delivered: for in mount Zion and in Jerusalem shall be deliverance, as the LORD hath said, and in the remnant whom the LORD shall call.

Acts 2:21 And it shall come to pass, that whosoever shall call on the name of the Lord shall be saved.

Romans 10:13 For whosoever shall call upon the name of the Lord shall be saved.

1 Corinthians 1:2 Unto the church of God which is at Corinth, to them that are sanctified in Christ Jesus, called to be saints, with all that in every place call upon the name of Jesus Christ our Lord, both theirs and ours:

Chapter 21

Nisan 21

Month of Nisan

1st day Yom Rishon Sunday	2nd day Yom Sheini Monday	3rd day Yom Shlishi Tuesday	4th day Yom R'vi'i Wednesday	5th day Yom Chamishi Thursday	6th day Yom Shishi Friday	Shabbat Yom Shabbat Saturday
		Nisan 21st 6:00pm Wednesday begins	21st Nisan 22nd 6:00am to 6:00pm Seventh day of unleavened bread, high Sabbath. End of Feast of Unleavened Bread			

This chapter includes:

Matthew	Mark	Luke	John

What a Finish! What a Start! The Month Jesus Met Man's Need

Fred A Kuypers

From Jerusalem to Galilee Sabbath Rest

Wednesday, Seventh Day of Unleavened Bread

Last day of unleavened Bread, a high Sabbath, Starts Tuesday at 6:00 p.m.

6:00 p.m. on Tuesday, the Twenty-First of Nisan Seventh Day of Unleavened Bread; a High Sabbath

This high Sabbath night could possibly have been spent in Samaria. Remember that the Jews would have no dealings with the Samaritans.

John 4:4 And he must needs go through Samaria.

John 4:5 Then cometh he to a city of Samaria, which is called Sychar, near to the parcel of ground that Jacob gave to his son Joseph.

John 4:6 Now Jacob's well was there. Jesus therefore, being wearied with his journey, sat thus on the well: and it was about the sixth hour.

John 4:7 There cometh a woman of Samaria to draw water: Jesus saith unto her, Give me to drink.

John 4:8 (For his disciples were gone away unto the city to buy meat.)

John 4:9 Then saith the woman of Samaria unto him, How is it that thou, being a Jew, askest drink of me, which am a woman of Samaria? for the Jews have no dealings with the Samaritans.

9:00 a.m. on Wednesday, the Twenty-First of Nisan Seventh Day of Unleavened Bread; a High Sabbath

On this day, the apostles have probably completed half of their journey to the Sea of Galilee. This journey will return them to the place where Jesus first selected most of them, at the Sea of Galilee. Peter is thinking about all that has happened, and it is not sitting well with him. He still has many doubts about what has happened and will make a decision in the next upcoming days to return to his old profession of fisherman. They have a day to stop and pray and think about what all has transpired. Questions begin to arise. Peter is thinking about making a decision to leave the group and return to the fishing business. He has these days of travel to think about what the Lord has told them and what has actually happened.

12:00 noon on Wednesday, the Twenty-First of Nisan
Seventh Day of Unleavened Bread; a High Sabbath

Sychar means that the disciples are about halfway finished with their journey to Capernaum which is on the Sea of Galilee. One of their most revered places is in Sychar: Jacob's well. This could easily have been the stopping point for the disciples on this day. They had stopped here before when Jesus met the woman at the well, recorded by the apostle John in chapter four of his gospel. The disciples are resting now because they prepared for the high Sabbath of this last day of unleavened bread. They will need to go and obtain what they need after 6:00 p.m. this night. So, they will have to go to the local market just as they did when Jesus met the woman at the well as recorded in John chapter four.

3:00 p.m. on Wednesday, the Twenty-First of Nisan
Seventh Day of Unleavened Bread; a High Sabbath

On this high Sabbath day of rest the apostles would learn how God would bring everything to rest upon Him by God's Holy Spirit:

Isaiah 11:1 And there shall come forth a rod out of the stem of Jesse, and a Branch shall grow out of his roots:

Isaiah 11:2 And the spirit of the LORD shall rest upon him, the spirit of wisdom and understanding, the spirit of counsel and might, the spirit of knowledge and of the fear of the LORD;

Chapter 22

Nisan 22

Month of Nisan

1st day Yom Rishon Sunday	2nd day Yom Sheini Monday	3rd day Yom Shlishi Tuesday	4th day Yom R'vi'i Wednesday	5th day Yom Chamishi Thursday	6th day Yom Shishi Friday	Shabbat Yom Shabbat Saturday
			Nisan 22nd 6:00pm Thursday begins	22nd Nisan 23rd 6:00am to 6:00pm Leave Samaria Travel to Galilee third day of travel.		

This chapter includes:

Matthew	Mark	Luke	John

What a Finish! What a Start! The Month Jesus Met Man's Need

Fred A Kuypers

From Jerusalem to Galilee the Third Day of Travel

Thursday, a Day of Travel Arriving at Galilee to Meet Jesus

6:00 p.m. on Wednesday, the Twenty-Second of Nisan

The high Sabbath is over. The disciples sleep this night and prepare to pick up their journey in the morning.

6:00 a.m. on Thursday, the Twenty-Second of Nisan

The disciples leave Samaria and continue their trip toward Galilee. Perhaps they traveled another thirty to forty kilometers or so this day. The disciples realize that they only have today and tomorrow to travel, as in two days will be the regular weekly Sabbath. Again what is coming to mind are all the times that Jesus spoke of His death and that in three days He would rise again. For the past month, the apostles were never able to comprehend this. There were those who still doubted. But Jesus was always very clear, as Luke recorded Jesus saying at the start of this month of Nisan:

Luke 18:31 Then he took unto him the twelve, and said unto them, Behold, we go up to Jerusalem, and all things that are written by the prophets concerning the Son of man shall be accomplished.

Luke 18:32 For he shall be delivered unto the Gentiles, and shall be mocked, and spitefully entreated, and spitted on:

Luke 18:33 And they shall scourge him, and put him to death: and the third day he shall rise again.

Luke 18:34 And they understood none of these things: and this saying was hid from them, neither knew they the things which were spoken.

What were all the things recorded by the prophets? Now that Jesus went through the torture of the cross and all the things that happened to Him before the actual crucifixion, the apostles were slowly starting to put this together. Of course, Isaiah had much to say about the King who would come. Isaiah would describe the scene of Christ's torture better than all the other prophets in chapter 53:

Isaiah 53:3 He is despised and rejected of men; a man of sorrows, and acquainted with grief: and we hid as it were our faces from him; he was despised, and we esteemed him not.

Isaiah 53:4 Surely he hath borne our griefs, and carried our sorrows: yet we did esteem him stricken, smitten of God, and afflicted.

Isaiah 53:5 But he was wounded for our transgressions, he was bruised for our iniquities: the chastisement of our peace was upon him; and with his stripes we are healed.

Isaiah 53:6 All we like sheep have gone astray; we have turned every one to his own way; and the LORD hath laid on him the iniquity of us all.

Isaiah 53:7 He was oppressed, and he was afflicted, yet he opened not his mouth: he is brought as a lamb to the slaughter, and as a sheep before her shearers is dumb, so he openeth not his mouth.

Isaiah 53:8 He was taken from prison and from judgment: and who shall declare his generation? for he was cut off out of the land of the living: for the transgression of my people was he stricken.

Isaiah 53:9 And he made his grave with the wicked, and with the rich in his death; because he had done no violence, neither was any deceit in his mouth.

12:00 noon on Thursday, the Twenty-Second of Nisan

Not only did the apostles have an understanding of the prophets in the Tanakh, the Old Testament, but they knew the Psalms of King David also. David spoke of the brutality of the crucifixion one thousand years earlier. Can you imagine how much of the scriptures the apostles knew and what they must be thinking now that they actually heard Jesus Christ utter these words from the cross:

Psalm 22:1 My God, my God, why hast thou forsaken me? why art thou so far from helping me, and from the words of my roaring?

Psalm 22:2 O my God, I cry in the daytime, but thou hearest not; and in the night season, and am not silent.

When they heard the soldiers and others in the crowd asking Jesus to save Himself from the cross, did their thoughts go back to this part of the Psalms as recorded again by David some one thousand years earlier: Psalm 22:7 All they that see me laugh me to scorn: they shoot out the lip, they shake the head, saying,

Psalm 22:8 He trusted on the LORD that he would deliver him: let him deliver him, seeing he delighted in him.

Everyone today has an opportunity to read the scriptures and learn of Jesus Christ. One day the great question will be asked not about what you did in this life but what you did with Jesus the Son of God!

Matthew 16:13 When Jesus came into the coasts of Caesarea Philippi, he asked his disciples, saying, Whom do men say that I the Son of man am?

Chapter 23

Nisan 23

Month of Nisan

1st day Yom Rishon Sunday	2nd day Yom Sheini Monday	3rd day Yom Shlishi Tuesday	4th day Yom R'vi'i Wednesday	5th day Yom Chamishi Thursday	6th day Yom Shishi Friday	Shabbat Yom Shabbat Saturday
				Nisan 23rd 6:00 pm Friday begins	23rd Nisan 24th 6:00 am to6:00 pm Travel to Galilee. Arrival on the fourth day of travel.	

This chapter includes:

Matthew	Mark	Luke	John

What a Finish! What a Start! The Month Jesus Met Man's Need

Fred A Kuypers

From Jerusalem to Galilee Fourth and Last Day of Travel

Friday, Final Day of Travel and Arrival in Galilee before the Saturday Sabbath.

6:00 p.m. on Thursday, the Twenty-Third of Nisan

The disciples spend another night after hiking approximately forty-five kilometers of hills and rough terrain. This will begin the fourth and final day of travel to the Sea of Galilee where Jesus said He would meet them on a mountain located there.

6:00 a.m. on Friday, the Twenty-Third of Nisan

The disciples leave for their final leg of the trip from Jerusalem to the Sea of Galilee. The journey from Jerusalem to Capernaum, on the Sea of Galilee, is about one hundred and ninety kilometers. A marathon is 42.195 kilometers. A marathon is a good day's journey by foot especially over hills and rocky terrain. This is about a four-day journey. If you have strong men and women it may be a little less. But if there is any problem it will be more.

When given this much time to think and rehearse what has happened in the last week or so, doubt begins to come into place. Thomas, who is one of the apostles on this trip northward, has already expressed his doubt. He is not sure of what is to happen in the next few days. It would be easy for him to abandon the eleven and have nothing to do with the Lord from this day forward. But he does not, and he stays with the eleven. There is not much recorded for this day, but it takes very little to understand what some of the apostles are going through. Certainly there was questions and many of these questions had to go unanswered. But in a few short days, Jesus would keep His word and appear to them at the Sea of Galilee.

12:00 noon on Friday, the Twenty-Third of Nisan

This would be the last stop for the noon break, and they were coming close to their final destination of the Sea of Galilee. This body of water was many different names. In John 6, it is also called the Sea of Tiberias.

John 6:1 After these things Jesus went over the sea of Galilee, which is the sea of Tiberias.

In Luke 5, it is called the lake of Gennesaret:

Luke 5:1 And it came to pass, that, as the people pressed upon him to hear the word of God, he stood by the lake of Gennesaret,

Today it is called by a fourth name, the lake of Kinneret or Kinnereth. This is a modernized name of the sea used in the Old Testament, the sea of Chinnereth.[51]

Numbers 34:11 And the coast shall go down from Shepham to Riblah, on the east side of Ain; and the border shall descend, and shall reach unto the side of the sea of Chinnereth eastward:

Numbers 34:12 And the border shall go down to Jordan, and the goings out of it shall be at the salt sea:

No matter what name was used; the apostles knew what body of water was being discussed. It was their beloved lake that many were yearning to see again.

5:00 p.m. on Friday, the Twenty-Third of Nisan

The Sea of Galilee is in full view as the apostles are about to finish this long journey from Jerusalem in Judea. They are tired. The Sabbath rest coming up looks very inviting to them. They will have to find the place of rest where they will spend tomorrow for the Saturday Sabbath, which will begin at 6:00 p.m. Perhaps they will stay at the house belonging to Peter's family or somewhere near the Synagogue at Capernaum spoken of by Mark:

Mark 1:21 And they went into Capernaum; and straightway on the sabbath day he entered into the synagogue, and taught.

Are you being taught about God?

2Timothy 2:15 Study to shew thyself approved unto God, a workman that needeth not to be ashamed, rightly dividing the word of truth.

---

[51] https://en.wikipedia.org/wiki/Sea_of_Galilee

Chapter 24

Nisan 24

Month of Nisan

1st day Yom Rishon Sunday	2nd day Yom Sheini Monday	3rd day Yom Shlishi Tuesday	4th day Yom R'vi'i Wednesday	5th day Yom Chamishi Thursday	6th day Yom Shishi Friday	Shabbat Yom Shabbat Saturday
					Nisan 24th 6:00 pm Saturday begins	24th Nisan 25th 6:00am to 6:00pm Sabbath rest at Sea of Galilee.

This chapter includes:

Matthew	Mark	Luke	John

What a Finish! What a Start! The Month Jesus Met Man's Need

Fred A Kuypers

Sea of Galilee Sabbath Rest Near Capernaum

Saturday Seventh Day of the Week the Weekly Sabbath

6:00 p.m. on Friday, the Twenty-Fourth of Nisan Saturday Sabbath Begins

By this evening, the disciples would perhaps have arrived in Capernaum on the Sea of Galilee, which is also called the Sea of Kinneret or Lake of Gennesaret or Sea of Tiberias. This starts the Saturday Sabbath. No work or travel is allowed. Many of the disciples are from this area, so they have a chance to stay with family or friends. It will be a happy day of rest, and one can only imagine the discussions and the witnessing being explained as the disciples tell everyone that they have seen the risen Lord Jesus.

10:00 a.m. on Saturday, the Twenty-Fourth of Nisan Saturday Sabbath

On this Sabbath, the disciples can worship at a synagogue. A synagogue is a building that would take the place of the temple in Jerusalem as the place to meet together for worship and scripture study.[52] In Hebrew the word is *beit k'nesset*, which literally means the House of Assembly. The nation of Israel uses this term also for its government meeting, which is called the Knesset.[53] Perhaps at this time, the eleven are gathered together at the synagogue in Capernaum. This is a building that Jesus had visited at the beginning of His earthly ministry:

Mark 1:21 And they went into Capernaum; and straightway on the sabbath day he entered into the synagogue, and taught.

Today the synagogue at Capernaum can still be visited. However, there are not many other places left that can be traced back to Jesus Christ and His time on earth. The synagogue at Capernaum is perhaps the only building site that exists. Remember that all the time Jesus spent at Jerusalem; the entire city was completely destroyed in

---

[52] http://www.jewfaq.org/shul.htm

[53] http://www.mfa.gov.il/mfa/aboutisrael/state/pages/the%20state-%20legislature-%20the%20knesset.aspx

AD 70 by Titus of Rome. The Arch of Titus has been restored in Rome and still stands as a monument to the destruction of Jerusalem and the dispersion of all Jews.[54]

12:00 noon on Saturday, the Twenty-Fourth of Nisan
Saturday Sabbath

This day will be spent in rest and worship as the apostles are still following their Jewish customs and are honoring the Sabbath. They are looking back at the statements their Master, the Lord Jesus Christ, had made.

Still many of them have questions and doubts about Jesus. But in just two more days, Jesus will appear to them again, and many of the doubts and fears will be lifted.

3:00 p.m. on Saturday, the Twenty-Fourth of Nisan
Saturday Sabbath

Tomorrow, Sunday, will be an important day. After spending the Sabbath with family, friends, and other Jews in the synagogue, much discussion will take place about the resurrection of Jesus. He already has appeared to most all of the apostles, and they are trying to convince all others around them that Jesus was truly the Messiah, the Christ they should be looking for. But there was little power in what they could say. Why was this? Because the Holy Spirit had not come down to earth to establish the new age that Jesus had talked about when they ate the last supper. This was on that eventful night of the fourteenth of Nisan when they all had dined with Him at Jerusalem in the upper room.

John 16:7 Nevertheless I tell you the truth; It is expedient for you that I go away: for if I go not away, the Comforter will not come unto you; but if I depart, I will send him unto you.

Also during this last supper, Jesus elaborated on who this Comforter is:

John 14:26 But the Comforter, which is the Holy Ghost, whom the Father will send in my name, he shall teach you all things, and bring all things to your remembrance, whatsoever I have said unto you.

On the last day that the apostles had seen the resurrected Lord, Resurrection Sunday, Jesus did something special. On this day back in chapter eighteen, Jesus described how His followers would receive the Gift of God, the Holy Ghost.

John 20:22 And when he had said this, he breathed on them, and saith unto them, Receive ye the Holy Ghost:

---

54   http://www.encyclopedia.com/people/history/ancient-history-rome-biographies/titus

What a Finish! What a Start! The Month Jesus Met Man's Need

Fred A Kuypers

This had not happened to the apostles as of yet. They were still wondering what Jesus was talking about. But Jesus was showing them of a day soon to come. Fifty days after His resurrection God would send His gift to all of mankind; when with a great rush of air the Holy Spirit would descend upon them:

Act 2:1 And when the day of Pentecost was fully come, they were all with one accord in one place.

Act 2:2 And suddenly there came a sound from heaven as of a rushing mighty wind, and it filled all the house where they were sitting.

Act 2:3 And there appeared unto them cloven tongues like as of fire, and it sat upon each of them.

Act 2:4 And they were all filled with the Holy Ghost, and began to speak with other tongues, as the Spirit gave them utterance.

Has the Holy Spirit come upon you? Have you received this gift of God? Many people look to a miracle as a sign that they can perform like speaking in tongues, or healing, or handling deadly snakes. But that is not the gift that God has promised to the believer in Christ. The gift God has promised is the gift of the Holy Ghost Himself; who comes to dwell in the heart of every believer. That is how you can know for sure that you are saved! Do you have the gift of the Holy Ghost? Does your life reveal that?

Chapter 25

Nisan 25

Month of Nisan

1st day Yom Rishon Sunday	2nd day Yom Sheini Monday	3rd day Yom Shlishi Tuesday	4th day Yom R'vi'i Wednesday	5th day Yom Chamishi Thursday	6th day Yom Shishi Friday	Shabbat Yom Shabbat Saturday
						Nisan 25th 6:00pm Sunday begins
25th Nisan 26th 6:00am to 6:00pm Jesus meets the disciples at Galilee just as he promised not many days hence						

This chapter includes:

Matthew	Mark	Luke	John

What a Finish! What a Start! The Month Jesus Met Man's Need

Fred A Kuypers

At the Sea of Galilee; the Apostles prepare to go Fishing

Sunday, First Day of the Week
Eight Days after the Disciples Had Seen Christ and Received Instruction on Where to Meet Him.

6:00 p.m. on Saturday, the Twenty-Fifth of Nisan Saturday Sabbath Ends

The Sabbath has ended, and the apostles have rested. They are back in the area where several of them had been fisherman. Some of them will be singled out in the next day or two as the gospel of John will declare.

6:00 a.m. on Sunday, the Twenty-Fifth of Nisan

Two of the apostles will now come into focus. Thomas was a fearless follower. He would not be afraid to say how far he would go to follow the Lord Jesus Christ. Remember back on the second of Nisan when Jesus received word of the death of Lazarus from Martha and Mary. Thomas makes a bold statement at that time:

John 11:16 Then said Thomas, which is called Didymus, unto his fellowdisciples, Let us also go, that we may die with him.

Thomas has so many doubts about the resurrection. But he has always had doubts. He is no different than anyone else. Remember when he first questioned the Savior?

John 14:5 Thomas saith unto him, Lord, we know not whither thou goest; and how can we know the way?

The reply that Jesus gives him silences everyone and every question. There is no refuting what Jesus implied or the clarity of what He said:

John 14:6 Jesus saith unto him, I am the way, the truth, and the life: no man cometh unto the Father, but by me.

12:00 noon on Sunday, the Twenty-Fifth of Nisan

Just seven days before, Thomas doubted the existence of the resurrected Lord Jesus. He was very clear back in Judea before they left on this trip up to Galilee that Jesus had come back from the dead. Tomorrow he will not only see the Lord Jesus Christ but also surrender to Him. Thomas, since he missed the lecture by Jesus back on the eighteenth of Nisan when Jesus expounded on all the scriptures that spoke of Him since Moses, was not able to understand what the other disciples had learned. One can only imagine the talk Jesus had with His disciples a week ago—and Thomas missed it!

3:00 p.m. on Sunday, the Twenty-Fifth of Nisan

Thomas is not the only one questioning his master. Peter is full of doubt. He is not ready to surrender to his Lord and Master at this time. Peter must have been looking forward to this trip back to Galilee. In a very short period of time, he will lead others into returning to his old lifestyle. Fishing is not a bad lifestyle. It was and is a commendable way to make a living. There is nothing wrong with that type of work. But Peter is still thinking of his betrayal that he committed during the night of the fourteenth of Nisan. He denied the Savior three times. It must have been devastating to Peter to question whether he would still be allowed to be a servant of the Master. In just a day or two, Jesus will confront Peter face to face with the same question He asks all of mankind. The question is: Do you love me?

Chapter 26

Nisan 26

Month of Nisan

1st day Yom Rishon Sunday	2nd day Yom Sheini Monday	3rd day Yom Shlishi Tuesday	4th day Yom R'vi'i Wednesday	5th day Yom Chamishi Thursday	6th day Yom Shishi Friday	Shabbat Yom Shabbat Saturday
Nisan 26th 6:00pm Monday begins	26th Nisan 27th 6:00am to 6:00pm After eight days Jesus showed Himself again to Thomas and His other disciples					

This chapter includes:

Matthew	Mark	Luke	John
			20:26–20:31

What a Finish! What a Start! The Month Jesus Met Man's Need

Fred A Kuypers

At the Sea of Galilee and Jesus Appears toThomas

Monday, Second Day of the Week

6:00 p.m. on Sunday, the Twenty-Sixth of Nisan

After eight days Jesus showed Himself again to His disciples. This would be to stop the rumors and the unbelief of at least one of the apostles.

John 20:26 And after eight days again his disciples were within, and Thomas with them: then came Jesus, the doors being shut, and stood in the midst, and said, Peace be unto you.

The apostles have arrived at Galilee where Jesus had said He would meet them on a mountain. Everywhere around the Sea of Galilee are mountains that rise up high above the water. The Golan Heights, which is north of the Sea of Galilee, is very mountainous. But remember that by Capernaum, it is also very mountainous as that is where the Sermon on the Mount probably took place. At this time, they are with some family or friends in the area. Obviously indoors as Jesus stood in their midst with the doors all shut. Again proving that walls and objects are no barrier to those in their glorified bodies, Jesus came when the doors were shut and stood in their midst. One day Christians will be able to do just that:

1 John 3:2 Beloved, now are we the sons of God, and it doth not yet appear what we shall be: but we know that, when he shall appear, we shall be like him; for we shall see him as he is.

The apostle Thomas is instructed by Jesus to behold the wounds from the cross. This describes the recognizable features of our Savior when the saved get to meet Jesus in heaven. He will be recognized by the wounds in His body.

John 20:27 Then saith he to Thomas, Reach hither thy finger, and behold my hands; and reach hither thy hand, and thrust it into my side: and be not faithless, but believing.

Today the world wants to display the Lord Jesus Christ as a suave and debonair man, handsome with long flowing hair and with a wonderful physique. But the scriptures have given a different view of our Savior as He came at this time. Isaiah says it very well:

Isaiah 53:2 For he shall grow up before him as a tender plant, and as a root out of a dry ground: he hath no form nor comeliness; and when we shall see him, there is no beauty that we should desire him.

Jesus, our loving Lord, responds to Thomas in a way that blesses all believers. Remember that Zechariah describes how Jesus will be recognized as the Messiah by the Jews nationally:

Zechariah 13:6 And one shall say unto him, What are these wounds in thine hands? Then he shall answer, Those with which I was wounded in the house of my friends.

Thomas recognizes Jesus and shows his surrender to Him by calling Him Lord:

John 20:28 And Thomas answered and said unto him, My Lord and my God.

Jesus declares how blessed one can be if only believing without seeing Him:

John 20:29 Jesus saith unto him, Thomas, because thou hast seen me, thou hast believed: blessed are they that have not seen, and yet have believed.

9:00 a.m. on Monday, the Twenty-Sixth of Nisan

Jesus worked many other signs with His disciples present. This must have been a very revealing time as the apostle John records, but they are not shared with us.

John 20:30 And many other signs truly did Jesus in the presence of his disciples, which are not written in this book:

But John does tell us that Jesus is the one who gives us life!

John 20:31 But these are written, that ye might believe that Jesus is the Christ, the Son of God; and that believing ye might have life through his name.

12:00 noon on Monday, the Twenty-Sixth of Nisan

Peter by now is not sure of anything. Remember on the fourteenth of Nisan when he denied Jesus those three times? He is thinking of this and believes he is not worthy of being a follower of the Christ. On that night before the crucifixion, Peter wept bitterly:

Luke 22:62 And Peter went out, and wept bitterly.

3:00 p.m. on Monday, the Twenty-Sixth of Nisan

By this time, Peter has beaten himself up over and over again. He is not sure what to do with his life. He decides that tomorrow he will go to the Sea of Galilee. There he will search for what he can do. He is making all these decisions on his own, without aid or help from the Holy Spirit as He has not yet been given. Have you received the gift of the Holy Ghost?

Chapter 27

Nisan 27

Month of Nisan

1st day Yom Rishon Sunday	2nd day Yom Sheini Monday	3rd day Yom Shlishi Tuesday	4th day Yom R'vi'i Wednesday	5th day Yom Chamishi Thursday	6th day Yom Shishi Friday	Shabbat Yom Shabbat Saturday
	Nisan 27th 6:00pm **Tuesday begins**	27th Nisan 28th 6:00am to 6:00pm Disciples at Galilee. Peter says he will go fishing.				

This chapter includes:

Matthew	Mark	Luke	John
			21:1–21:3

What a Finish! What a Start! The Month Jesus Met Man's Need

Fred A Kuypers

At the Sea of Galilee and Jesus Appears for the Third Time

Tuesday, Third Day of the Week

6:00 p.m. on Monday, the Twenty-Seventh of Nisan

Some of the apostles were fishermen. Peter and Andrew were fishermen for sure. However Levi or Matthew was not a fisherman. He was a tax collector. John and James, the two sons of Zebedee known as the sons of Thunder, were fishermen also. Thomas and Nathaniel (Bartholomew) are listed here as returning to the sea of Tiberias and may have been fishermen also. That makes six fishermen. The remaining five apostles are not listed as far as their jobs go. Simon the Canaanite was zealous and may have been some type of religious person. Phillip, James (the son of Alphaeus), and Judas (Thaddaeus) have no jobs given in scripture and may have also been fishermen. Judas Iscariot was given the treasury for the group which may mean he had some retail job and was good at accounting.

6:00 a.m. on Tuesday, the Twenty-Seventh of Nisan

There are seven apostles who decide to go to the actual coast of the Sea of Galilee. Jesus appears outside of a house at the Sea of Tiberias (Galilee) to these seven disciples:

John 21:1 After these things Jesus shewed himself again to the disciples at the sea of Tiberias; and on this wise shewed he himself.

John now describes the apostles Jesus appears to. This time at the Sea of Galilee, Peter's home base, Jesus meets with these seven disciples. Peter is still in much confusion and denial. He does not understand what is happening with the Christ appearing again and again. The next verse describes seven of the disciples at the sea. Perhaps these were the only fisherman of the twelve who were called. Or, these could have been the ones with the most doubt about Jesus and all of the appearances of Him that were taking place.

John 21:2 There were together Simon Peter, and Thomas called Didymus, and Nathanael of Cana in Galilee, and the sons of Zebedee, and two other of his disciples.

9:00 a.m. on Tuesday, the Twenty-Seventh of Nisan

Peter had been thinking all along as they walked back to Galilee. He is not willing to surrender to Jesus as of yet. His heart is not yielded to Jesus, and Jesus will soon make him realize his lost state. Without the gift of the Holy Spirit, which will not take place for another forty-two days, a man's heart is easily turned against the things of God.

John 21:3 Simon Peter saith unto them, I go a fishing. They say unto him, We also go with thee. They went forth, and entered into a ship immediately; and that night they caught nothing.

Living for Jesus includes how you act in your occupation. Being a child of God is just like being a child of your earthly mom and dad. You are always His child day and night. Therefore always represent Jesus:

1 Corinthians 10:31 Whether therefore ye eat, or drink, or whatsoever ye do, do all to the glory of God.

Chapter 28

Nisan 28

Month of Nisan

1st day Yom Rishon Sunday	2nd day Yom Sheini Monday	3rd day Yom Shlishi Tuesday	4th day Yom R'vi'i Wednesday	5th day Yom Chamishi Thursday	6th day Yom Shishi Friday	Shabbat Yom Shabbat Saturday
		Nisan 28th 6:00pm Wednesday begins	28th Nisan 29th 6:00am to 6:00pm Disciples are out all night fishing. They catch nothing			

This chapter includes:

Matthew	Mark	Luke	John
			21:4–21:23

What a Finish! What a Start! The Month Jesus Met Man's Need

Fred A Kuypers

At the Sea of Galilee; the Apostles Are Fishing

Wednesday, Fourth Day of the Week

6:00 p.m. on Tuesday, the Twenty-Eighth of Nisan

Peter and the disciples are all out fishing this night. They catch nothing.

6:00 a.m. on Wednesday, the Twenty-Eighth of Nisan

Jesus is standing on the shore of the Sea of Galilee. Peter and the other disciples do not recognize Him.

John 21:4 But when the morning was now come, Jesus stood on the shore: but the disciples knew not that it was Jesus.

8:00 a.m. on Wednesday, the Twenty-Eighth of Nisan

There is more daylight as morning dawns. Peter and the disciples who were from this area thought they were great fishermen. But Jesus knew better. Jesus put these great fishermen on the spot:

John 21:5 Then Jesus saith unto them, Children, have ye any meat? They answered him, No.

Jesus tells them to cast the net to the right side of the ship. Most all fishermen cast to the port (left) side of a ship. Jesus instructs the opposite—starboard (right):

John 21:6 And he said unto them, Cast the net on the right side of the ship, and ye shall find. They cast therefore, and now they were not able to draw it for the multitude of fishes.

9:00 a.m. on Wednesday, the Twenty-Eighth of Nisan

It takes some time to haul this gathering of fish in. John recognizes Jesus at this moment. He knew that this amount of fish could only be by the hand of Jesus. Jesus did this for them when He fed the five thousand. However, Peter is brought to the exact moment as Adam and Eve when they were standing before God naked. He too will try to hide his nakedness by his own works and shame:

John 21:7 Therefore that disciple whom Jesus loved saith unto Peter, It is the Lord. Now when Simon Peter heard that it was the Lord, he girt his fisher's coat unto him, (for he was naked,) and did cast himself into the sea.

11:00 a.m. on Wednesday, the Twenty-Eighth of Nisan

Peter is not with them when the fish net is first being dragged up on shore. He is already on the shore after casting himself into the sea. He was embarrassed and ashamed and not with the other disciples:

John 21:8 And the other disciples came in a little ship; (for they were not far from land, but as it were two hundred cubits,) dragging the net with fishes.

John 21:9 As soon then as they were come to land, they saw a fire of coals there, and fish laid thereon, and bread. John 21:10 Jesus saith unto them, Bring of the fish which ye have now caught.

Peter, after swimming ashore, is back on land to help with the net, and Jesus has a meal ready for the disciples.

John 21:11 Simon Peter went up, and drew the net to land full of great fishes, an hundred and fifty and three: and for all there were so many, yet was not the net broken.

A hundred and fifty-three fish have been questioned for many years. How significant is this number? Some say that it is the total number of countries that will be around when the final day of the Gospel is preached unto all the world. Some say that this number is the central number of the entire numbering system as it is the smallest three-digit number that can be expressed as the sum of cubes of its digits which point to a trinity. Amos said something also:

Amos 9:9 For, lo, I will command, and I will sift the house of Israel among all nations, like as corn is sifted in a sieve, yet shall not the least grain fall upon the earth.

Could Amos be saying that it is the number of countries that Israel will come out of to replenish the land in the last days? Jesus says one of the great Baptist slogans: come and dine!

John 21:12 Jesus saith unto them, Come and dine. And none of the disciples durst ask him, Who art thou? knowing that it was the Lord.

12:00 noon on Wednesday, the Twenty-Eighth of Nisan

Jesus appeared to the disciples for the first time on the night of His resurrection in Jerusalem. Now He appears to them again:

John 21:13 Jesus then cometh, and taketh bread, and giveth them, and fish likewise.

This is the third time Jesus appears to the discples. The second time He appeared to them was at the house on the hilltop here in Galilee after eight days. Today, it is the third time:

John 21:14 This is now the third time that Jesus shewed himself to his disciples, after that he was risen from the dead.

Jesus will begin to concentrate on Peter. However, this is the problem all of us have with our love of Christ:

John 21:15 So when they had dined, Jesus saith to Simon Peter, Simon, son of Jonas, lovest thou me more than these? He saith unto him, Yea, Lord; thou knowest that I love thee. He saith unto him, Feed my lambs.

Many things are happening at this moment. First Jesus uses the name "son of Jonas" to pinpoint Peter. He is not talking to Simon the Canaanite of Matthew chapter 10:4. Jesus uses Peter's old name, indicating a return to Peter's old nature. Remember he had denied Jesus three times. He was skeptical at the grave a week ago, and just moments ago, he was just naked and jumped overboard. He needed to be dealt with by our Lord. Jesus then asked Peter "Lovest thou me?" and uses the word *agape*, which is the deepest love one would have for another such as between a husband and a wife or Christ for His church. It is a love that shows one would lay down his life for another, a love that gives (charity). Peter responds with the word *phileo*, or brotherly love. The city of Philadelphia is the city of "brotherly love." So Peter has responded with "I love you as a brother, Jesus." Jesus then says feed my lambs. Lambs require milk. Peter will have to surrender to the Lord and then follow Jesus with the Great Commission. He will need to be familiar with the doctrines that God will give us in the near future through the apostle Paul. This will not be easy for Peter, who was a Jew. But feeding lambs will require the milk of the Word of God as Peter later describes:

1 Peter 2:1 Wherefore laying aside all malice, and all guile, and hypocrisies, and envies, and all evil speakings,

1 Peter 2:2 As newborn babes, desire the sincere milk of the word, that ye may grow thereby:

1 Peter 2:3 If so be ye have tasted that the Lord is gracious.

Jesus presents the statement for the second time. Jesus by this time has dropped the name *Peter* and just uses the name of Simon. Jesus also uses the term *agape* again and Peter responds with the term *phileo* and says again, "Jesus, I love you like a brother."

John 21:16 He saith to him again the second time, Simon, son of Jonas, lovest thou me? He saith unto him, Yea, Lord; thou knowest that I love thee. He saith unto him, Feed my sheep.

Simon, son of Jonas (Peter) is directed by Jesus to feed his sheep now, not lambs. Jesus expects all of His followers to progress. Christians are not to remain feeding on the milk. Instead, all believers need to advance to the meat of the doctrines of the "Word of God":

Hebrews 5:12 For when for the time ye ought to be teachers, ye have need that one teach you again which be the first principles of the oracles of God; and are become such as have need of milk, and not of strong meat.

Hebrews 5:13 For every one that useth milk is unskilful in the word of righteousness: for he is a babe.

Hebrews 5:14 But strong meat belongeth to them that are of full age, even those who by reason of use have their senses exercised to discern both good and evil.

Peter should have been a leader at this point. He had a brother, Andrew, and good friends that were looking up to him. And what does he do? He undresses, is naked, and and jumps overboard at the sight of Jesus. Well, Jesus decides` to turn the table on Peter, and at this moment Jesus takes and uses the word *phileo* when He says, "Simon, do you just love me as a brother?"

John 21:17 He saith unto him the third time, Simon, son of Jonas, lovest thou me? Peter was grieved because he said unto him the third time, Lovest thou me? And he said unto him, Lord, thou knowest all things; thou knowest that I love thee. Jesus saith unto him, Feed my sheep.

Peter's heart is broken. He confesses to Jesus the fact that Jesus knows his heart. He says Jesus knows all things. Now Christ can use him. He gives the command that all those who have surrendered to the Lord Jesus Christ need to follow; "Go ye into all the world and preach the Gospel" by saying feed my sheep. Jesus reveals some things to Peter about his future life of serving Christ. He will no longer do whatever his flesh desires to do like he did just this morning, naked, or even in his younger years.

John 21:18 Verily, verily, I say unto thee, When thou wast young, thou girdedst thyself, and walkedst whither thou wouldest: but when thou shalt be old, thou shalt stretch forth thy hands, and another shall gird thee, and carry thee whither thou wouldest not.

Peter has been learning the importance of following the Savior. He will soon follow Christ all the way, even to death:

John 21:19 This spake he, signifying by what death he should glorify God. And when he had spoken this, he saith unto him, Follow me.

Peter still has the old nature. When salvation comes, God gives man a new nature and does nothing with the old nature.

2 Corinthians 5:17 Therefore if any man be in Christ, he is a new creature: old things are passed away; behold, all things are become new.

All things are new, but Christians still have their old nature. This old nature needs to be kept down or die daily as 1 Corinthians explains:

1 Corinthians 15:31 I protest by your rejoicing which I have in Christ Jesus our Lord, I die daily.

What a Finish! What a Start! The Month Jesus Met Man's Need

Fred A Kuypers

God says we are to die to our old nature, so that a believer will want to walk in this new nature.

Galatians 6:14 But God forbid that I should glory, save in the cross of our Lord Jesus Christ, by whom the world is crucified unto me, and I unto the world.

Galatians 6:15 For in Christ Jesus neither circumcision availeth any thing, nor uncircumcision, but a new creature.

Galatians 6:16 And as many as walk according to this rule, peace be on them, and mercy, and upon the Israel of God.

What does He do with our old nature? Nothing! It is still a part of the believer. The battle of Romans 7 takes place in everyone who follows Christ.

Romans 7:18 For I know that in me (that is, in my flesh,) dwelleth no good thing: for to will is present with me; but how to perform that which is good I find not.

Romans 7:19 For the good that I would I do not: but the evil which I would not, that I do.

Romans 7:20 Now if I do that I would not, it is no more I that do it, but sin that dwelleth in me.

Romans 7:21 I find then a law, that, when I would do good, evil is present with me.

Romans 7:22 For I delight in the law of God after the inward man:

Romans 7:23 But I see another law in my members, warring against the law of my mind, and bringing me into captivity to the law of sin which is in my members.

Romans 7:24 O wretched man that I am! who shall deliver me from the body of this death?

Romans 7:25 I thank God through Jesus Christ our Lord. So then with the mind I myself serve the law of God; but with the flesh the law of sin.

Peter asks a question about John that Christ admonishes him for:

John 21:20 Then Peter, turning about, seeth the disciple whom Jesus loved following; which also leaned on his breast at supper, and said, Lord, which is he that betrayeth thee?

John 21:21 Peter seeing him saith to Jesus, Lord, and what shall this man do?

John 21:22 Jesus saith unto him, If I will that he tarry till I come, what is that to thee? follow thou me.

Christ tells Peter and all of us to follow Him. Do not follow a TV preacher! Do not follow a false leader! Do not follow anyone but Jesus Christ.

John 21:23 Then went this saying abroad among the brethren, that that disciple should not die: yet Jesus said not unto him, He shall not die; but, If I will that he tarry till I come, what is that to thee?

Chapter 29

Nisan 29

Month of Nisan

1st day Yom Rishon Sunday	2nd day Yom Sheini Monday	3rd day Yom Shlishi Tuesday	4th day Yom R'vi'i Wednesday	5th day Yom Chamishi Thursday	6th day Yom Shishi Friday	Shabbat Yom Shabbat Saturday
			Nisan 29th 6:00pm **Thursday begins**	29th Nisan 30th 6:00am to 6:00pm Last passages of the Gospels. Tomorrow the month of Nisan will end.		

This chapter includes:

Matthew	Mark	Luke	John
28:18–28:20	16:19–16:20	24:50–24:53	21:24–21:25

What a Finish! What a Start! The Month Jesus Met Man's Need

Fred A Kuypers

At the Sea of Galilee

Thursday, Fifth Day of the Week
Last Words of the Gospels

6:00 p.m. on Wednesday, the Twenty-Ninth of Nisan

The apostles are gathered together near the Sea of Galilee. They have been discussing the events of the past month and Jesus is revealing things to them.

Luke 24:27 And beginning at Moses and all the prophets, he expounded unto them in all the scriptures the things concerning himself.

6:00 a.m. on Thursday, the Twenty-Ninth of Nisan

Today is the twenty-ninth of Nisan and in just twenty-eight days, the ascension of our Lord Jesus Christ will occur. Luke explains this as he begins his writing of the Acts of the Apostles.

Acts 1:1 The former treatise have I made, O Theophilus, of all that Jesus began both to do and teach,

Acts 1:2 Until the day in which he was taken up, after that he through the Holy Ghost had given commandments unto the apostles whom he had chosen:

Acts 1:3 To whom also he shewed himself alive after his passion by many infallible proofs, being seen of them forty days, and speaking of the things pertaining to the kingdom of God:

The Acts of the Apostles actually begins forty days after Jesus showed Himself alive, once He was resurrected, as stated in verse three above. Jesus will have some final words to speak in the next verses about the Comforter, who is the Holy Ghost, He promised to send when He spoke to the apostles at the last supper on the evening of the fourteenth of Nisan and will be taken into heaven.

Acts 1:4 And, being assembled together with them, commanded them that they should not depart from Jerusalem, but wait for the promise of the Father, which, saith he, ye have heard of me.

Acts 1:5 For John truly baptized with water; but ye shall be baptized with the Holy Ghost not many days hence.

Acts 1:6 When they therefore were come together, they asked of him, saying, Lord, wilt thou at this time restore again the kingdom to Israel?

Acts 1:7 And he said unto them, It is not for you to know the times or the seasons, which the Father hath put in his own power.

Acts 1:8 But ye shall receive power, after that the Holy Ghost is come upon you: and ye shall be witnesses unto me both in Jerusalem, and in all Judaea, and in Samaria, and unto the uttermost part of the earth.

Acts 1:9 And when he had spoken these things, while they beheld, he was taken up; and a cloud received him out of their sight.

Acts 1:10 And while they looked stedfastly toward heaven as he went up, behold, two men stood by them in white apparel;

Acts 1:11 Which also said, Ye men of Galilee, why stand ye gazing up into heaven? this same Jesus, which is taken up from you into heaven, shall so come in like manner as ye have seen him go into heaven.

Acts 1:12 Then returned they unto Jerusalem from the mount called Olivet, which is from Jerusalem a sabbath day's journey.

12:00 noon on Thursday, the Twenty-Ninth of Nisan

Matthew ends his Gospel with the Great Commission:

Matthew 28:18 And Jesus came and spake unto them, saying, All power is given unto me in heaven and in earth.

Matthew 28:19 Go ye therefore, and teach all nations, baptizing them in the name of the Father, and of the Son, and of the Holy Ghost:

Matthew 28:20 Teaching them to observe all things whatsoever I have commanded you: and, lo, I am with you alway, even unto the end of the world. Amen.

Mark ends his Gospel with the ascension taking place forty days after the resurrection:

Mark 16:19 So then after the Lord had spoken unto them, he was received up into heaven, and sat on the right hand of God.

Mark 16:20 And they went forth, and preached every where, the Lord working with them, and confirming the word with signs following. Amen.

Luke ended his Gospel earlier in Bethany and Jerusalem and picked up with the book of the Acts of the Apostles:

Luke 24:50 And he led them out as far as to Bethany, and he lifted up his hands, and blessed them.

Luke 24:51 And it came to pass, while he blessed them, he was parted from them, and carried up into heaven.

Luke 24:52 And they worshipped him, and returned to Jerusalem with great joy:

Luke 24:53 And were continually in the temple, praising and blessing God. Amen.

John ends his Gospel by again calling himself the "disciple that Jesus loved." John testifies of other things that Jesus did and will write four more books, First, Second, and Third John, and Revelation about Him.

John 21:24 This is the disciple which testifieth of these things, and wrote these things: and we know that his testimony is true.

John 21:25 And there are also many other things which Jesus did, the which, if they should be written every one, I suppose that even the world itself could not contain the books that should be written. Amen.

Chapter 30

Nisan 30

Month of Nisan

1st day Yom Rishon Sunday	2nd day Yom Sheini Monday	3rd day Yom Shlishi Tuesday	4th day Yom R'vi'i Wednesday	5th day Yom Chamishi Thursday	6th day Yom Shishi Friday	Shabbat Yom Shabbat Saturday
				Nisan 30th 6:00pm **Friday begins**	30th Nisan 1st 6:00am to 6:00pm At 6:00 p.m. this evening, the month of Nisan will end.	1st of Iyar

This chapter includes:

Matthew	Mark	Luke	John

What a Finish! What a Start! The Month Jesus Met Man's Need

Fred A Kuypers

End of the Month of Nisan

Friday, Sixth Day of the Week Last Day of the Month of Nisan

All day beginning Thursday, the Thirtieth of Nisan

In conclusion, I would like to state the objectives and goals of writing this book. Systems of traditional duties have permeated the organization that Jesus Christ calls His church. These beliefs were started mostly by the leaders of the church hierarchy that controlled the church back in the fourth century and forward. As stated in point six of my seven points listed in chapter 17 to prove a Wednesday crucifixion, the early church fathers believed that the Lord's death occurred on the fourth day of the week. As history shows, followers of the only organization to have control and understanding of the scriptures for well over a thousand years muddied the truth with many of the inconsistencies there are today. Seeing the need to take down the body of Christ off of the cross before the Sabbath was to lead to a sloppy and lazy misunderstanding that the crucifixion must have taken place on a Friday, the sixth day of the week! This sloppy handling of the Word of God is not hard to understand with just a little knowledge of European history and the dominance of the Roman Catholic Church. It is easy to unveil.

This book is a view of Jesus Christ that is probably new to most of those who read it. It brings many things to question, especially the traditions of men, which most people have been taught from generation to generation without any thought or question of what the actual account of the life of Jesus Christ really says. My prayer is that this book will force the reader into a deeper look and understanding of what Jesus Christ did and what was accomplished for all mankind at the Cross of Calvary. The only way to accomplish this is to be more familiar with the Word of God. Read it! The power of God lies within the Bible.

The apostles, after this month concludes, are going to head back to Judea, in particular to the Mount of Olives. It is here that in just a few short days, Jesus will ascend into heaven. It has been twelve days since the resurrection occurred on the eighteenth of Nisan. The last chapter in Acts of the Apostles says that Jesus would ascend forty days from the resurrection. That would place the date on the twenty-eighth of Iyar, the month following Nisan. Days would be needed for the travel back to Judea, and there would be enough time for this to happen during the following month.

No other evidence of Jesus appearing to the apostles takes place after the ascension until Jesus appears to Paul on the road to Damascus. However the appearance of God is seen just fifty days after the resurrection. It is on this day that the promise of Jesus Christ is fulfilled as the Comforter, the Holy Ghost is gifted to all of mankind that believes.

This account of love that God has given us in the four gospels describes an undeniable love for each and every man. The love that Jesus Christ has for each and every person on earth is what pushed Him to the cross of Calvary. Love is what makes a man want to give. Love will make a man give the truth to another even when it hurts so much to say it. Love is the only thing that will unveil the way through darkness that evil can bring. The only way eternal life can come is through love. Jesus Christ said it must be by Him. The great I AM said, "I AM the only way":

John 14:6 Jesus saith unto him, I am the way, the truth, and the life: no man cometh unto the Father, but by me.

www.ingramcontent.com/pod-product-compliance
Lightning Source LLC
Chambersburg PA
CBHW041508120626
46551CB00018B/2348